THE MAKING OF NEIL KINNOCK

THE MAKING OF
NEIL KINNOCK
ROBERT HARRIS

faber and faber
LONDON · BOSTON

First published in 1984
by Faber and Faber Limited
3 Queen Square London WC1N 3AU

Phototypeset by Wyvern Typesetting Limited, Bristol
Printed in Great Britain by
Redwood Burn Limited, Trowbridge Wiltshire
All rights reserved

British Library Cataloguing in Publication Data

Harris, Robert
The making of Neil Kinnock.
1. Labour Party——Great Britain
I. Title
324.24107   JN1129.L32

ISBN 0-571-13266-9
ISBN 0-571-13267-7 Pbk

CONTENTS

7

Contents

PART FOUR: CANDIDATE

ILLUSTRATIONS

PREFACE

In the year 2000 – assuming he and we survive that long in what he calls 'this dangerous, beautiful world' – Neil Kinnock will be fifty-eight. At an age at which most successful politicians would perhaps be hoping to reach a senior level in the Cabinet, Kinnock, if he has not by then retired, will have been leader of the Labour Party for seventeen years. By virtue of age, if nothing else, he is set to become one of the dominant figures in British political life.

It has been a spectacular rise, incredible even, considering that Kinnock has never held any government job. If he enters 10 Downing Street, his only previous experience of office outside the Labour Party itself will have been running Cardiff Students' Union. Yet he was not so much elected by the Labour Party in October 1983 as crowned, winning over 71 per cent of the votes cast in the electoral college. The aim of this book is to describe how this came about.

Kinnock, as even most of his political opponents concede, has an attractive personality. He has ambition, stamina and courage. He has great skill as a communicator, both on the platform and, perhaps more importantly, on television: 'You don't need to tell me what to do,' he said to his advisers before his first appearance on Brian Walden's television programme *Weekend World*. 'I got to be leader of the Labour Party by being good on television.' He also has enormous charm, a useful talent for a rising politician: few Labour MPs have enjoyed a better press. He has the gift of treating everyone alike, no matter how powerful. Senior colleagues are greeted with a cheerful 'Hiya, kid.' Kinnock begins on first-name terms and is calling you by a nickname within five minutes. On his first official trip abroad, to Greece in 1984, he and his wife Glenys were shown round Athens by a government guide called Pericles. 'Neil,' says Glenys, 'kept calling him Perry.'

But Kinnock's personality is only part of the explanation for his success. To make sense of his achievement, his rise has to be set in a wider context: that of the breakdown of the old structures of power within the Labour Party. It may be that his qualities are such that he would have risen to the top eventually whatever happened to the party. But his propulsion into the leadership while still so young and inexperienced was almost entirely the result of the upheaval on the British left in the 1970s and 1980s. The milestones on Kinnock's road to power include the birth of the Campaign for Labour Party Democracy in 1973, the establishment of Labour's electoral college in 1981 and the general election disaster of 1983; these external events were as important to the making of Neil Kinnock as his election to the National Executive Committee in 1978 or his appointment to the Shadow Cabinet in 1979.

This book ends with Kinnock's election as leader: the point at which the most important phase of his life begins. I have deliberately avoided, therefore, making too many settled judgements. Biographies of still-active politicians are notoriously ephemeral, and the vantage point of 1984 is certainly no place to start reaching firm conclusions about a career which may stretch into the next century. As most of the interviews I conducted were on the record, I have tried to leave participants to tell their own stories through their own words. Neil Kinnock built his career on his talents as a speaker; for that reason, I have aimed to include extracts from his speeches wherever possible.

Although this is not an authorized biography, Mr Kinnock has been extremely helpful towards me, meeting me both before and after he became the Labour Party's leader, and patiently answering my questions. I am very grateful to him, as I am to his wife Glenys, who spent a long time talking to me and gave me access to the family's collection of photographs, from which many of the illustrations in this book are drawn. Other members of the Kinnock family, particularly Dorothy and Bill, Neil Kinnock's aunt and uncle, were generous with their recollections and their hospitality.

Among those outside Neil Kinnock's family who were kind enough to give me interviews I would like to thank: Joe Ashton, Terry Burns, Dick Clements, Robin Cook, Jill Craigie, Ray Davies, Ron Davies, Vladimir Derer, Terry Duffy, Gwyn Evans, Michael Foot, Alan Fox, John Golding, Roy Grantham, Bill Harry, David Hill, Clive Jenkins, Russell Kerr, Alex Kitson, Jon Lansman, Barry Moore, Michael Meacher, Chris Mullin, Tony Page, Allan Rogers and Tony Wilkins. A number of others talked to me but asked me not to name them.

I would also like to acknowledge my gratitude to the Islwyn Constituency Labour Party; to the staff at the Labour Party's headquarters in Walworth Road; to Sheila Noble and other members of the staff of *Tribune*; to Nick Butler, who was kind enough to share with me his encyclopaedic knowledge of the Labour Party; and to Laurence Rees, who read the manuscript in its early stages.

Finally, I would like to thank David Dickinson, the editor of *Newsnight*, who generously allowed me to take the leave from the BBC which enabled me to finish this book.

ROBERT HARRIS
May 1984

Part One
CARD

A little group of councillors were discussing Denry.

'What a card!' said one, laughing joyously. 'He's a rare 'un, no mistake.'

'Of course, this'll make him more popular than ever,' said another. 'We've never had a man to touch him for that.'

'And yet,' demanded Councillor Barlow, 'what's he done? Has he ever done a day's work in his life? What great cause is he identified with?'

'He's identified,' said the speaker, 'with the great cause of cheering us all up.'

Arnold Bennett, The Card

Chapter One

PROLOGUE: BLACKWOOD,
31 JANUARY 1969

Napoleon is said to have judged a man's practical value by the answer to a single question: 'Is he lucky?' In the case of Neil Gordon Kinnock, Member of Parliament at the age of twenty-eight, leader of the Labour Party at forty-one, the question is superfluous. Luck has walked with Kinnock as a friend for the best part of twenty years.

Their journey began on 31 January 1969 in the small town of Blackwood in South Wales. It was a Friday night and the Executive Committee of the Bedwellty Constituency Labour Party had reached item four on its agenda. Neil Kinnock, the young minutes secretary, was busy taking notes when he heard the news which, he later said, almost made his heart stop beating.

> Letter from Mr J. H. Finch MP announcing his intention not to seek nomination at the next General Election. Heartfelt tributes were paid to Mr Finch by members of the executive who had known him throughout his career in the trade union movement and as a devoted, dedicated and able Member of Parliament for the Bedwellty Division.[1]

The news was unexpected. Harold Finch was sixty-nine but looked younger, and few had expected him to retire. 'There was a gasp from the older members,' recalls Barry Moore, one of the delegates to the party's General Management Committee (GMC). 'We younger ones just looked at one another thinking, "What do we do now?" '

Neil Kinnock was then a full-time tutor and organizer with

the Workers' Educational Association. He was twenty-six and had been living with his wife Glenys in the constituency for almost two years. He claims to have been as taken aback by the announcement as the others. 'To tell you the truth,' he says, 'I thought Finchy was in his late fifties or early sixties.' Kinnock believes Finch's decision to relinquish the seat was a result of the Caerphilly by-election the previous July, at which the Welsh Nationalist candidate had come within 2,000 votes of taking a safe, English-speaking Labour seat, similar to Bedwellty. Finch was one of a number of elderly South Wales MPs worried about their majorities who decided to resign around this time.

Although respected and popular in the constituency, Finch was hardly known outside his own small corner of South Wales. It was quite common for members of the GMC to bump into him shopping on Blackwood's main street in the middle of the week, at a time when most MPs are normally at work in Westminster. With these easy-going ways, he had gradually set the political tone for the whole constituency. The 1960s may have been a time of great political upheaval elsewhere in the world, but Bedwellty stood unmoved. 'The local Labour Party was moribund,' recalls one member of that period, 'and dominated by the miners' union. It was fairly right-wing. Most of the people of the GMC were middle-aged or old, and anyway the GMC only met once a year.'

To the young people around Blackwood the Kinnocks, educated at University College, Cardiff, and both committed party activists since their mid-teens, were refreshingly different. According to Moore: 'The two of them livened up the constituency. They had about them some of the atmosphere of student politics – the belief that the struggle was serious but could also be fun. Those were the days when someone would grab a guitar and Neil and Glenys would do a duet together and we'd all end up singing protest songs.' The Kinnocks brought to the area a breath of the outside world: of CND, of sit-ins, of demonstrations against the Vietnam war and apartheid, of the liberating new horizons being opened up by

18

further education. Neil and Glenys quickly became the centre of attention for a circle of young Labour activists in the constituency. It was a group which eventually included Barry Moore, a shop steward at South Wales Switchgear, and his wife, Doreen; Gywn Evans, employed at a local ICI factory; Ron Davies, a 21-year-old trade union activist; and Terry Burns, an apprentice fitter in an engineering works.

A crowd of these young left-wingers stayed behind to talk to Kinnock on the evening that Finch announced his retirement. After the GMC meeting had ended a group of about ten went for a drink at the Llanarth working men's club in the nearby village of Pontllanfraith to discuss what they should do. That Kinnock would be a candidate for the seat was not even debated. 'There was never any question about whether or not Neil would stand,' says Gwyn Evans. 'It was taken for granted that he'd run. The only question we asked was "Can he get it?" '

The answer, most thought, was almost certainly no. Bedwellty had had only two MPs since 1918: Charles Edwards and Harold Finch. Both of them had been on the right of the party and both had been miners. In 1969 the seat was still dominated by the National Union of Mineworkers: local officials saw the constituency as essentially a private fiefdom. Nevertheless, Kinnock and his supporters were determined to try for the nomination. 'I didn't really expect to get it,' Kinnock says today. 'But what we decided at the beginning was that on selection night we'd have nothing to kick ourselves for. So it meant putting in the maximum effort and working hard.' They added an extra year to his age to make him sound more mature, consulted the rulebook to see how a selection conference was organized and began drawing up a list of branches and organizations that were allowed to make nominations.

Neil Kinnock was about to display an ability he was to show again and again over the next fifteen years: a remarkable talent for being in the right place at exactly the right moment.

Chapter Two

THE KINNOCK INHERITANCE

The future leader of the Labour Party was born on 28 March 1942, delivered into the world by Nurse Stanley in a bed-sitting room in No. 1 Vale View, a small terraced house in the South Wales mining town of Tredegar. His mother, Mary Howells, was Nurse Stanley's predecessor as Tredegar's district nurse. His father, Gordon Kinnock, was a miner, as were both of baby Neil's grandfathers, three of his uncles on his father's side of the family and his two uncles on his mother's side.

To be born into a mining family is a rich inheritance in the Labour Party. But to be born into a mining family in South Wales, in Aneurin Bevan's constituency when Bevan was at the height of his powers, is, for a British socialist, to be born one of Labour's aristocrats. Socialism in Tredegar was not a matter of intellectual conversion: it was a reflex action, and Neil Kinnock can lay claim to one of the purest working-class pedigrees a Labour leader has ever had.

His grandfather, Archibald James Kinnock, was born in Bristol of Scottish parents in 1882. When he was aged about nineteen, in the early years of this century, he crossed the border into Wales in search of work. At first he tried his hand as baker. That did not last long, and soon he was hired as a faceworker in one of the collieries around Tredegar. He met a local girl, then working 'in service', called Margaret Herbert. They married, and over the next twenty years she bore him eight children. One, a baby girl, died in infancy. The others, six sons and one daughter, all survived. Gordon, Neil's father, was the second eldest, born in 1907.

Archie was a formidable character. 'He was only five foot three inches tall,' recalls Kinnock, 'but he was five foot three inches broad and as strong as an ox. He used to get drunk once a week, on a Saturday night.' According to family legend, he came home one Saturday evening, proclaimed undying love for his wife and told her he would do anything for her: he would punch a hole through the door if she asked him to. 'She told him not to be so daft,' says Kinnock, 'so he turned round and battered a hole into the back room with his fist.'

It was a life, for the most part, of great hardship. The family lived in a tiny terraced house, two rooms upstairs and two down, whose view was dominated by the pit head of the Tytryst colliery, fifty yards away across a small stream. This was the mine down which Archie worked (its name translates as 'House of Sorrow'). The six boys – Clifford, Gordon, Charlie, Harold, Wilfred and Bill – slept, three to a bed, in one bedroom, while Dorothy, the only girl, slept with her parents in the other. The ordinary, domestic details of their poverty are typical of place and period: there was not enough to eat, bread and jam and chips being the staple diet, a newspaper serving as the table cloth; there was no carpet to cover the bare flagstones of the floor; a visit to the lavatory meant carrying a bucket of water with you to the bottom of the yard.

In 1926 the mine owners cut the men's wages and tried to break up the power of the Miners' Federation, precipitating the General Strike. That was settled by mid-May, but the miners stayed out for a further seven months, until December. The Kinnocks, to use the phrase of the time, 'went on the parish' and had to borrow money to buy food. They were still paying it back six years later. Archie was a strong union man, and he also appears to have had a short temper. He fell out with the manager of the Tytryst pit and was transferred to the

Pochin colliery eight miles away, where Aneurin Bevan used to work. To be there in time for his shift he had to get up at 4.30 in the morning.

A myth, fashionable among some modern socialists, surrounds this kind of life. 'People were poor,' it runs, 'but at least they were happy in their class solidarity.' There was no such romantic working-class idyll under the roof of 125 Vale Terrace. Archie was a firm disciplinarian; his wife was strictly religious. Crammed together, lacking privacy, the family was drawn into incessant arguments. When, for example, Bill, the youngest boy, was born (unexpectedly, as Margaret Kinnock was over forty) one of his brothers exclaimed in exasperation, 'Not another one', and refused even to look at him. According to another of the children, their mother eventually died in her sixties 'from fatigue as much as anything else' brought on by 'the stress and the rowing – she was absolutely worn out.'

Apart from Bill, all of the sons worked in either the mining or the steel industry; two of them ended up working in both. Conditions were harsh. The men of the Kinnock family had between them an appalling collection of maimed and broken limbs. Archie had to brake the trucks which carried the coal underground by sticking pieces of wood on the rails, and he lost the tops of the first and second fingers on one of his hands in doing so. Clifford, the eldest boy, born in 1904, was hacking at the coal face with a pick when a piece of flint flew up and struck him in the face, permanently blinding him in one eye. Gordon contracted dermatitis on his hands. Harold, who worked in a steel mill in Ebbw Vale, had to have a pin put in his leg: his femur was broken when a lorry reversed into him. 'He had a hole in his leg you could put your fist into,' recalls Kinnock. Wilfred, a tough and loud-voiced extrovert, began his working life underground, where in various accidents he broke both his arms and his legs. He was then employed in a steel works. One day, when he was in his mid-forties, his left hand and forearm were trapped and severed in an unguarded piece of machinery: the men beside him fainted, so the story goes, and he had to pull himself free. He eventually contracted glaucoma and went blind and deaf. 'How he kept going,' says one of his brothers, 'God only knows.'

It was this heritage that was to shape Neil Kinnock as a politician. His speeches, especially his early ones, are filled with references to his family and upbringing. He did not exaggerate when, in a speech on workers' safety and health in 1973, he told the House of Commons:

> I am the first male member of my family for about three generations who can have reasonable confidence in expecting that I will leave this earth with more or less the same number of fingers, hands, legs, toes and eyes as I had when I was born.
>
> I am unlikely to know the infuriating itch of dermatitis, and if my lungs or my limbs do not function properly when I am fifty, it will not be because I have been forced to work in an atmosphere in which I am obliged to breathe filthy air in cramped and unnatural working positions. My father, my grandfather, my uncles have all suffered from various industrial injuries and diseases. . . .
>
> These injuries and diseases have been inflicted not as a consequence of some dreadful cataclysm but simply because the male members of my family, like most other male members in families throughout the country, have done nothing more adventurous than go to work in the coal, steel and engineering industries.[1]

The depression of the 1930s broke up the Kinnock family. Unemployment forced Harold, the most retiring and philosophical of the brothers, to seek work in London where, like thousands of others in the same predicament, he fell upon hard times. 'He hit a bad patch', recalls Dorothy Kinnock. 'He had no work. In order to get benefit he was means tested. They told him he couldn't have anything and that he should go home and live off my father. He wouldn't do that, so instead he did menial jobs for a time. He wouldn't tell anyone about it and we never did find out what he did.' Eventually, after a period which included casual labour selling icecream from a tricycle and working as a prizefighter in a fairground booth, he got a job as a steelworker in Scunthorpe. Charlie also emigrated to England. Bill, the only one of the children to have a good education, was rescued by the war. He became an officer in the gunners, later took a degree and became a schoolmaster in Surrey.

Archie's wife suffered from a variety of ailments, including diabetes, and Gordon, who stayed behind in South Wales with his parents, first got to know Mary Howells when she came to nurse his mother. He was a stocky, powerfully built man, physically the strongest in the family, a keen cricketer and footballer. He was also quiet, regarded by the family as a confirmed bachelor. But then, in the late 1930s, he took to walking Miss Howells back to the nursing home in Tredegar after her visits to his mother.

The Howells family felt about Mary much as the Kinnocks felt about Gordon: that she would never marry. 'She was a very independent woman,' recalls someone who knew her at that time, 'and she stood out against this working-class background.' Mary's background was even poorer than Gordon's. She was one of six children, only four of whom had survived. Her grandfather, father and two brothers, Tommy and Islwyn were all miners. They lived in East Avenue, Aberdare. Mary was a clever girl (she had passed her Higher School Certificate, the equivalent of today's A-levels), but she had been forced to leave school during the General Strike. 'There's no doubt that nowadays she would have got to university,' says Kinnock. That opportunity denied her, she became a nurse. Competent, hard-working, sympathetic, she had a remarkable command of both English and Welsh, which she occasionally used to devastating effect. She and Gordon made a good partnership. 'I've never seen two people happier together – a real love-match,' recalls one of Gordon's brothers; he admits himself to a youthful passion for Mary, 'a striking figure' with her trim good looks and her nurse's uniform. In 1940, when they were both in their thirties, they married, and in 1942 – to the delight of their families and also, it seems, slightly to their own surprise – Mary had a baby.

Neil was fortunate in the circumstances of his birth. He was brought up close enough to his father's family to appreciate the harshness they had endured, to absorb its lessons and later to transform that experience into the core of his own political beliefs. At the same time he was spared the privations of poverty and the shame of being poor which crippled the self-confidence of his uncles. Being an only child meant that he was the sole focus of his parents' love as well as the recipient of many of the family's resources. 'Gordon worked all the hours God sent,' recalls one member of the family, 'doing overtime in the evenings and on Saturdays and Sundays, all to get money for Neil.' His parents were determined to give him the best possible start in life.

Shortly after the end of the war the three of them moved from Vale View in Tredegar to a prefabricated council house in nearby Brynbach. 'I was brought up in a prefabricated bungalow,' Neil Kinnock once told MPs in a debate on Welsh housing in 1974. 'Sadly, those bungalows are still standing, seventeen years after they were supposed to be knocked down.'[2] They may have been dilapidated by 1974, but at the time they were built they were palaces compared with the sort of terraced house in which his grandparents lived. 'It was like moving to Beverly Hills,' Kinnock recalled. 'It had a fridge, a bath, central heating and a smokeless grate. It was on a mountain outside Tredegar and people used to come just to look at it.'[3]

When Neil was about four years old the dermatitis on his father's hands finally forced him to give up his underground job at the local pit. He was unemployed for a year. Eventually he took a new job in the steelworks in Ebbw Vale, ripping out the linings from the blast furnaces and from the buckets which carried the molten metal. Each day before his father set off for work, Kinnock recalls, his mother had to dress and bandage his hands. As a result of her husband's disability and their lack of money Mary, who had given up work when she married, went back to her old job. 'It was part-time to begin with,' says Dorothy Kinnock, 'then it became full-time.'

As Tredegar's district nurse, Mary Kinnock is affectionately remembered in and around the town to this day as

'Nurse Kinnock'. Not long after she resumed work, in 1947, when Neil was five, Britain was gripped by one of the coldest winters in its history. In Tredegar the snow piled up to depths of four or five feet. Through it all Nurse Kinnock kept on going, walking along the tops of garden walls through the snowdrifts to reach some houses. In the process she did permanent damage to her health. A bronchial complaint, aggravated by her heavy smoking, later turned into emphysema. But the family needed the money that her job brought in. According to Bill Kinnock, 'she stayed at work when she should've been at home. She did it for Neil.'

What sort of a child was he? According to Dorothy (Neil's Auntie Dor, who still lives with Clifford in their father's old house in Tredegar), he was playful and very lively, a 'happy boy'. He was an extrovert even then, with a fondness for wearing various sorts of hats – a passion which used to put Dorothy Kinnock in mind of that other famous lover of strange headgear, Winston Churchill. When his Uncle Bill was home on leave from the army, Neil liked to borrow his cap and swagger stick and march around the house giving orders. By the age of eight he had a fixed idea of what he wanted to do in life. 'Auntie Dor,' he frequently exclaimed, 'I want to be a private 'tec when I grow up.' Although it takes a considerable effort of the imagination to picture the present leader of the Labour Party as a private detective, this ambition apparently persisted for some time. He was a talented mimic, specializing in impersonations of James Cagney, jet aircraft and a popular coloured singer who used to perform something called 'The Banana Boat Song'. When he was badly behaved, which was fairly often, the punishment would depend upon which parent caught him. His father would often give him a good hiding: one of his uncles still recalls the beating Neil got on a family holiday when he repeated some swear words he'd picked up. His mother would never hit him but instead 'put him down verbally, which she could do very well. In fact I think he preferred to be smacked by his father.'

According to Alan Fox, a resident of Tredegar and a friend of the family, Nurse Kinnock was ambitious for her son:

> She took care to see that he went to the best junior school in Tredegar – Georgetown – even though it was the other end of town from where they lived. And she dressed him rather prim and proper, which was a matter of some discomfort for a Valley lad. I think as a result he tended to become a bit rebellious. He was idle and resentful of authority. In a funny way, by forcing him to rebel as she did, his mother did her best day's work for him.

In 1953 Neil passed his eleven-plus and was offered a place at Lewis School, Pengam, almost fifteen miles from Tredegar. The local grammar school was co-educational. Lewis School, which was considered one of the best in the area, was a traditional establishment catering solely for boys, and his mother insisted that he accepted its offer. It was a pretentious institution, and Neil hated it. He had a particular loathing for the headmaster. 'We were the heartiest of enemies,' Kinnock once said in a Commons debate on education. He was apparently something of a disciplinarian; at any rate, Kinnock called him a 'gauleiter'.[4]

His schooldays are remarkable for their utter lack of distinction. 'He never shone at all,' says his economics teacher. 'He was a lazy sod,' says one of his friends.[5] 'It was not their fault really,' admits Kinnock today.

> I'm not sure that I would have got on with any school at the time. It was a place that only recognized very narrowly defined forms of success, and if you didn't fall into that, then there wasn't too much concern about you. It wasn't my fault particularly or their fault particularly. It was just the kind of school that rated a particular form of success. I didn't conform to that, and so it meant that I developed no great affection for the school.
> Common to many schools at that time, they had this daft system of deciding on your allocation to forms by measures of average ability: adding up all the marks together and dividing by the number of subjects. And it meant that even if you did pretty well in English, history, geography, humanities, you could have that smashed to pieces by a disastrous result in maths or physics. And so a group of us nestled nicely in the 'B' stream and never did a stroke, not a stroke, never did any homework, and could just get along fairly respectably by the seat of our pants. I think the school lost a lot of talent as a result. Just lads who, had they been permitted to play to their strengths, would have done much better than they did.

Card

Sixteen-year-old Neil obtained only three O-levels, failing everything except the three subjects he liked – English, history and geography. He was miserable and determined to escape. His parents were horrified. 'I wanted to leave school,' recalls Kinnock. 'I wanted to go down the pit and they went absolutely – God, I wouldn't want to live through that three or four days again. And then I wanted to join the police force, and there was a similar response. I wanted to join the Army and there was a similar response. . . .' This was one battle that Neil Kinnock lost. His parents flatly refused to let him leave school, and he was made to re-sit his O-levels. He ended up with 'eight or nine', and in 1959, a year later than the rest of his class, he entered the sixth form to take his A-levels. His experiences at Lewis have left him with an abiding dislike of the whole grammar school system, with its emphasis on selection and its narrow categorizations of success and failure.

He seems at that time to have led something of a double life, the halves of which were separated by the hour-long daily journey to Pengam. At school he wore the uniform his despised headmaster insisted upon, and he conformed – even to the extent of becoming a prefect in his sixth form. At home in Tredegar he went around with his local mates and got into the usual scrapes of youths of his age. At sixteen, officially too young to be served in pubs, they would go off in search of sympathetic landlords in the local area. On one occasion, Kinnock recalls, 'a whole crowd of us' went to the Quarryman's Arms, 'miles away from the main town of Tredegar, in this lovely village called Trevil'. It must have been around 1958. 'And I went in to buy a pint with my mates – and Nye Bevan was in there. And this is the sense of deference that one had . . . we all turned round and ran out of the pub. I can remember Nye and the man who ran the pub, Evans – whom I know very well – laughing like hell behind us as we scattered out of the pub.' By that time, Kinnock was a member of the Labour Party in Tredegar and becoming politically active.

*

The myths surrounding Neil Kinnock's political awakening are now rising in the valleys of South Wales like morning mist. Go to Billy the Barber's in the centre of Tredegar, in the square by the town clock, and you will hear stories of how the Infant Kinnock, son of Mary, would dazzle local miners with his oratory at the age of eight. 'Kinnock stories have become a cottage industry round here,' claims Alan Fox, who watched Neil grow up. 'I certainly can't recall any ginger-headed waif at the end of the council estate flogging *Tribune*.'

What *is* clear is that Neil Kinnock did not, like most of his colleagues, acquire his socialism. He was born into it. Politics is discussed in South Wales with the enthusiasm and spontaneity which in England is devoted to sport or the weather. This was especially true in Tredegar in the 1950s, where the MP since 1929 was Aneurin Bevan. All the Kinnocks supported the Labour Party: Neil once called his mother 'a tungsten-coated socialist' and recalled how she 'used to make a practice of using a Tory car to take her to the polling booth, kindly inviting the driver in for a cup of tea and keeping him talking for anything up to an hour on the tactical grounds that "while he's taking my tea, he's not taking anyone else's votes" '.[6] Mary was well read; she knew what she was talking about. When Kinnock at sixteen briefly considered joining the local Communist Party, he later claimed that his decision not to 'was very directly influenced by my mother, who was a very radical socialist with a Christian tradition who didn't like the elements of the Communist Party that she encountered'.[7]

With both of his parents working, Neil necessarily had to spend a large part of his childhood in the company of his numerous relatives. Through the older Kinnocks he was made aware at an early age of the sorts of hardship that they had suffered. 'My grandparents,' recalls Kinnock, 'especially the old fellers, they were people who wouldn't just give you yes and no answers, they'd give you a full answer. And if they could decorate it with a joke or a story, then it was even better. I don't think that was untypical, you know. Without romanticizing it, it was that kind of environment.' Kinnock once proudly told the House of Commons that Archie, who 'spent fifty-two years in the coal mining industry', had warned him as a child against the corrupting powers of the Tories: 'He said, "If they cannot beat you, they will try to make you soft." '8

Kinnock's earliest memory of politics is of marching around as a child during election time, banging a biscuit tin and yelling, to the rhythm of 'Tramp, Tramp, Tramp, the Boys are Marching':

> *Vote, vote, vote for 'Neurin Bevan,*
> *He's the boy to beat the band.*
> *If you're workers, now's the day,*
> *To make the bosses pay,*
> *And Labour rule throughout the land.*9

The figure of Bevan dominated politics in Tredegar at that time – as to some extent he still does today. 'He was always there, as a sort of general background,' Kinnock was to recall a few weeks after his installation as Labour's leader.

A guy was driving me the other day in this nice official car that I've been given – he was a relief driver – and he was referring to the fact that he'd been somebody's servant in 1951 when the Tories won. And the lady of the household turned round – and, as he said, a real toff wouldn't have stooped to this, but she wasn't a real toff – and she said to him 'We are the masters now.'

And that set me in mind of that 1951 election. I was in Aberdare, staying with my grandparents, on the Friday and my grandmother and my grandfather were weeping. Now, my grandfather was a really hard nut. They don't come any harder. They were weeping at the fact we'd lost. When the radio said Mr Aneurin Bevan had been returned in Ebbw Vale, that was the only thing that cheered them up in the whole day. He was always there, you see, as part of the general background.

Today Bevan is commemorated by four slabs of stone on a windswept hill just outside Tredegar. 'It was here,' records the inscription, 'that Aneurin Bevan spoke to the people of his constituency and the world.' He has been dead for almost a quarter of a century, but the force of his personality seems to have marked indelibly most of the people who came into contact with him. 'The first meeting of his that I went to – I must have been about ten, I should think,' recalls Kinnock.

'It would be around 1952, 1953, something like that. And then I doubt if I missed a single meeting he did in Tredegar after that, because my father used to take me.' Kinnock met him to shake hands with only twice: 'one occasion was after the Sunday school marches through Tredegar, and the other occasion was when I was a Young Socialist delegate to the Tredegar Trades Council and he came briefly to one meeting.' Around the time that Kinnock went with his father to his first Bevan meeting, *In Place of Fear,* Bevan's only book, was published. Young Neil was 'only aware of it then because a main display window in the Tredegar Industrial and Co-Operative Society was crammed with the maroon and black of the first-edition cover'. He read it when he was fourteen, 'and I have been reading it ever since'.[10] 'Bevan,' Kinnock said once, 'in speech and writing, articulated exactly what I was feeling. I experienced the thrill that people do when they've heard what they believe to be their secret and innermost feelings endorsed by people of what they consider to be great sophistication.'[11]

Bevan begins *In Place of Fear* with a description of how he came to be a socialist: 'A young miner in a South Wales colliery, my concern was with the one practical question: where does power lie in this particular state of Great Britain, and how can it be attained by the workers?'[12] Kinnock, like Bevan, arrived at his political beliefs not through theorizing but through practical experience, albeit mainly at second hand. Bevan was one of ten children, three of whom died before the age of eight. He was entirely self-taught – he was working down the mines at the age of fourteen – and he was unemployed for three years. Kinnock escaped a similar fate by at least a decade and, with both his parents working, he had what in Wales is known as a 'tidy' home life. But his great good fortune was to have been born at a time, in a family, in a community, where it was still possible naturally to drink in a radical, pragmatic form of socialism without having to suffer the poverty and hardship which originally produced it. His mother, his father, his grandparents, his uncles were formative influences upon him. So too was a local miner, a friend of his father called Bill Harry.

Kinnock first met him when he was fifteen; 'my mother was nursing his mother-in-law, and I must have gone there and got chatting to him. He was a thirty-year-old Labour councillor, a very nice guy.' Kinnock remembers him as the man who first persuaded him to join the Labour Party: 'There were lots of other fellers around who were active – shop stewards, lodge officials and so on – but Bill had read more widely and has got a natural articulation. He was quite an impressive character, and in barn-storming speaking he was pretty good because he was very forceful and a good guy to be with, especially in trouble. He was generous-minded, articulate and had a very appealing political line.' Together they used to go to classes run by the National Council of Labour Colleges, held in a back room of the Tredegar Arms. About a dozen used to attend, among them some of the original members of Bevan's 'Query Club', founded in Tredegar to discuss socialist ideas in the 1920s. 'They were very smart fellows, very smart,' Kinnock once recalled. 'The older fellows could genuinely claim to be Marxist scholars. . . . We'll never see fellows like them again because such people today are all graduates. Learning was a lifelong thing to them. If you had asked them, "Where were you educated?", they would have said, "Why are you using the past tense?" '[13]

This was the world to which Bill Harry introduced the fifteen-year-old Neil. In later years, as Kinnock rose in national politics, a shadow fell upon the relationship between the two men which is only now slowly lifting. But for many years this self-taught miner was one of the mainstays of Kinnock's commitment to the Labour Party, and during the leadership election in 1983 he wrote to Bill Harry, paying him a warm tribute:

> I so much share your regret that Mam and Dad aren't around to see all of this. One way and another I didn't give them very much success until the last couple of years of their lives and they always stuck with me. I only hope I can show the same understanding of my kids.

Anyway, the only success that really matters is to help people like my mother and father – and there are millions of them. That's what I go on trying to do, just like you – yes, you more than anyone other than my folks – started teaching me to do all those years ago.[14]

Chapter Three

UNIVERSITY, GLENYS AND THE WEA

'People of my age,' Neil Kinnock once said in Parliament, 'belong to a nation of inheritors. We have, relatively speaking, been brought up with golden spoons.'[1] For working-class children perhaps the greatest inheritance of post-war Britain has been the widening of access to higher education: a quarter of a century ago in South Wales it was almost the only ladder out of a life down the pit or in the steel plant. Specializing in subjects which interested him, Kinnock did far better in the sixth form at Lewis than he had done lower down the school. He got A-levels in economics, history and English. His grades (two Bs and a C) were good enough to win him a place at University College, Cardiff, where in 1961 he enrolled for a degree in history and industrial relations.

He proved to be no more disciplined or academically gifted at Cardiff than he had been at school. 'I never rationed my time,' explains Kinnock. 'In retrospect, I understood that I could have done all the things that I wanted to do and possibly got even quite a decent degree. But I just permitted myself to be distracted by sport or debates or politics or going to the cinema in the afternoon.' He was to stay at Cardiff for five years, until 1966. He failed his finals the first time round, sat them again the following year and scraped home with a bare pass degree. His extra years at school and university meant that he was twenty-four by the time he got a job. 'I got a very good liberal education,' he says disarmingly.

University, Glenys and the WEA

Despite his undistinguished academic record, Cardiff was the making of Kinnock, for it was there that he developed the skills which have been the foundation of his fortune ever since: a tremendous quickness of mind and tongue and an aggressive, self-confident style of debate. Kinnock is not a particularly good writer. His articles are often turgid, the ideas smothered by layer upon layer of adverbs and adjectives; reading them is like being taken on a route march through a thesaurus. But on the platform, released from the confines of his prose style, Kinnock's ideas can take wing. On a good day he can bring to a subject not only passion but also an ability to relate it to a wider frame of historical reference or shared experience, a gift which can raise his speeches high above those of most average politicians. 'His horizons,' as Alan Fox, Kinnock's old friend in Tredegar, puts it, 'are wide. Like Nye's.'

Kinnock's training ground was the university canteen, where on Friday nights anything up to 600 or 700 people would crowd in to listen to debates. According to Kinnock:

> It was a very rumbustious house. It wasn't like your Oxford or Cambridge Unions . . . it was much more a cross between a mass meeting with pretty formal rules basically of proposition and opposition and speeches from the floor. It was a good atmosphere in which to speak, so that when I or others used to go to speak competitively elsewhere in more restrained houses we were like fish out of water.
>
> It was in the cafeteria, rather grandly called the 'refectory', in the students' union. But a cafeteria it was, with formica table tops and the whole thing and the only thing that turned it into a debating chamber was to have the tables cleared and a rostrum stuck up on a table at the end. And then it was a free-for-all, and if you couldn't hold the house, they were merciless, absolutely merciless. I was always very fortunate and I used to knock around with a crowd of lads who could hold their own. But anyone who couldn't – God, they used to get ripped to pieces. It was a good place to learn.

The students invited speakers from outside the university. James Callaghan, a local MP, was one visitor in the early 1960s. He never forgot the power of one of Kinnock's early speeches. Even in 1974, as Foreign Secretary, he was still reminding Kinnock in the chamber of the House of Commons

35

of the debate over ten years before 'in which together we destroyed the Conservative Government'.[2]

Kinnock did not speak in a debate until his second year. He might never have spoken at all had it not been for the influence of a young first-year student whom he met in the autumn of 1962. Glenys Parry, eighteen years old, freshly arrived from Anglesey to read for a degree in history and education, was standing in the lunch queue at the refectory, when 'suddenly, above all the hubbub, I heard this very loud voice and there, coming along the line, was a ginger-haired, freckle-faced man handing out leaflets on behalf of the Socialist Society. My first impression of him was simply how *loud* he was.'

Glenys was already active in politics. Her father, Cyril Parry, had originally been a merchant seaman. Unable to find work on board ship during the Depression, he had moved to North Wales and become a signalman on the railways. He was constituency secretary and chairman of the Anglesey Labour Party, and Glenys was taken campaigning as a small child. 'I grew up surrounded by canvass returns,' she says. 'I can't remember a time when I wasn't involved.' She joined CND at its inception when she was fourteen. By the age of sixteen she was a card-carrying member of the Labour Party. So when Neil Kinnock, working his way along the lunch queue in 1962 reached Glenys, he found a willing recruit.

She was – and is – strikingly pretty, more so even than her photographs suggest, for her attractiveness lies in her animation. Kinnock was taken with her at once and soon afterwards contrived to meet her at the students' union dance held on a Saturday night. He had been knocked about playing rugby that afternoon, drank too much and was violently sick. 'It was a case of me taking him home rather than the other way round,' recalls Glenys. Kinnock was understandably anxious to improve his image and a debate seemed the best way.

I'd been at Cardiff for a year [says Kinnock], but I hadn't spoken in a debate because I was in the rugby club and having a hell of a good time. I was involved politically – it was just politics and rugby and clowning around. And then I met Glenys . . . and in the course of our early conversations it became obvious that she admired people of fluency. So in order to impress her I made a speech in a debate and it went from there. It was about the reign of Queen Elizabeth – 'This House Hails the New Elizabethan Age' or something daft like that. I don't remember what I said or anything. I made an effort with that one, to impress her. It had the desired effect.

The relationship which developed between them was strong, if not always especially smooth. 'It was on and off,' says Glenys. 'I saw other men. Occasionally we drifted apart. But we always spent a lot of time together. He was a very good friend more than anything else. Each of us has always been the other's best friend.' It was politics as much as anything else that kept them together. Neil was chairman of the Socialist Society and Glenys became secretary. She still keeps a pink leaflet they wrote in collaboration headed 'Do You Believe?' They were both active members of CND. They organized protests against apartheid and the imprisonment of Nelson Mandela. They also campaigned for Callaghan in his constituency during the 1964 and 1966 elections – an activity not without its hazards. On one occasion, Kinnock recalled, they were 'drenched by a bucket of window washing water thrown by a lady screaming her hatred of Jehovah's Witnesses. When my helplessly amused girlfriend . . . laughingly explained that we weren't from the *Watchtower* but from the Labour Party, she was set upon by the outraged lady with a wet chamois leather.'[3]

Everyone who knows them maintains that Glenys is the dominant influence on her husband and highly ambitious for his success. 'She wants it more than he does,' says one Labour MP who knows them well. Throughout their marriage he has sought her advice, and many friends feel that, in the words of another MP, 'he'd never do anything if she was against it.' Kinnock has a hot temper; she cools it. He can be impetuous and rash; she counsels caution. He can also get carried away by the sound of his own voice; Glenys has developed a neat line in heckling. Kinnock, in his early years, could never see a roomful of people without wanting to organize it into a discussion group which he could dominate. One member of his audience remembers her keeping up a running commentary: 'Look at him, off he goes again, bloody fool.' 'Glenys is not a typical politician's wife,' insists Barry Moore, one of the couple's closest friends. 'She is an individual with very definite views. She often shuts him up by mimicking him – exaggerating whatever it is he's saying in a mock-pompous voice. Neil stops in mid-flow and looks furious until he can't help it and bursts out laughing.' 'It's a sign of Neil's strength,' believes Jill Craigie, the highly independent wife of Michael Foot. 'A less secure man would not like to defer to his wife as much as he does.'

Her husband's rise to prominence has not altered Glenys's attitude. She continues to work as a remedial teacher, and much of her energy is spent on trying to preserve as normal a family life as possible for them and their two children. She is mistrustful of the media and has made it a rule rarely to give interviews. 'I don't have anything much to say,' she insists. 'I don't want to push myself into the limelight. I want to try to protect the kids. I also don't want to do anything which might embarrass Neil.' Sometimes she teases him about what she could tell the press. 'I say to him: "You watch it, Kinnock – " ' she holds out her hand, palm upwards, and suddenly clenches her fist – ' "I've got you right *there!*" ' Most of all, Glenys dislikes being portrayed in the role of a supportive and dutiful political wife. When a television crew was making a profile of Kinnock during the leadership contest, she relented to the extent of allowing them to film the family at breakfast. The crew tried to use this concession to coax her into speaking: 'We've got a picture of you making coffee. We just want to ask you what it will feel like to be married to the leader of the Labour Party.' 'That,' snapped Glenys, 'is the verbal equivalent of making coffee.'

According to Dorothy Kinnock, Glenys is the only girlfriend Neil ever brought home to introduce to his family. Less than two months after their first meeting, they boarded a bus for what Glenys calls 'an eye-opening journey' along the winding valley roads to Tredegar. Glenys and Mary Kinnock, two strong characters, circled one another warily. 'I was intimidated by her,' says Glenys. 'I was frightened of putting a foot wrong. I wasn't allowed to breathe a word of criticism of Neil – she wouldn't accept that he had any bad habits and she'd often misinterpret things that I said.' Glenys came to have great respect for Mary:

> She was enormously proud of Neil, which was quite understandable because she was about thirty-eight when she had him. She'd had a tough life. She was very strong and very, very intelligent. She could obviously have got a lot further than just being a nurse if she'd had the opportunity. I got the impression she relied on Neil for intellectual stimulation. She really did enjoy having him about the house, and they'd have long discussions about Christianity – she was very religious – and that sort of thing.
>
> His father often wasn't there. He always seemed to be out working at weekends.

Mary quickly realized she had met her match. 'She was always very choosy about Neil's girlfriends,' recalls a member of the family, 'but after she met Glenys she said, "This is the one. I'll have to give him up now." ' Even so, Glenys believes that Mary remained slightly jealous of her, 'and that didn't really disappear until Stephen was born [in 1970]. It took that long for me to be accepted.'

They used to go home to Tredegar fairly often. Kinnock managed to pass his driving test at his third or fourth attempt and bought an old Standard Ten. 'I hated that car,' says Glenys. 'I spent more time pushing it than sitting in it. I never got in without kicking it.' The car was traded in for a battered bright green van, which was christened The Neilomobile – a mode of transport heavily subsidized by Nurse Kinnock until she eventually tired of paying out for it continually. At that point Auntie Dor stepped in with a 'loan' ('still unrepaid') of £15.

In 1965 Kinnock was elected president of the students' union, campaigning on the slogan 'Kinnock for Efficiency, Initiative, Approachability, Experience'. At the same time, with Kinnock's backing, Glenys became the National Union of Students' secretary in Cardiff – a carve-up of jobs which provoked some bitterness among other student politicians. Kinnock lived in a flat which he shared with Paddy Kitson, Callaghan's election agent. They wallpapered it with a variety of differently patterned rolls, and each strip clashed with the ones next to it. Part of the flat was used to store the costumes of an amateur dramatic society, and exotically clad actors were perpetually floating in and out. It overlooked the headquarters of the Cardiff Conservative Party. Glenys remembers that when meetings were on Paddy and Neil used to tiptoe around outside it in stockinged feet to try to discover the enemy's tactics. According to a friend who at one stage had a room next door, Kinnock lived in a room 'where the sheets were changed every month – or was it every two months?' While others lay nursing hangovers, Neil would

> wake up at around 7 a.m. in the morning and lie in bed singing hymns to himself. . . . A hurricane of energy, he, if anything, tried to do too much while the rest of us sat around doing too little. President of the union, haranguer-in-chief in debates, Labour Party activist – South African oranges never got past the union's door when he was boss – he did manage to fit in the odd lecture which, perhaps, explains his none too brilliant academic record.
>
> He was also oversensitive to any form of criticism and extremely emotional. In a party once, an ex-collier told him about his pit injuries and Neil burst into tears.[4]

Kinnock was at Cardiff for five years, Glenys for four. Both of them spent their final year, 1965–6, when Neil was the students' union president, studying for teaching diplomas. Kinnock had been offered a post at the Ebbw Vale College of Further Education. 'But before I could take that job up there was an advertisement for a Workers' Educational Association post, which was what I really wanted to do. I applied and got the job. The Ebbw Vale people were very reasonable about it.'

The Workers' Educational Association (WEA) is an educational charity jointly run by the trade unions and the Department of Education and Science. Its aim is to teach men who work on the shopfloor, and its classes range from languages to science. At the age of twenty-four Kinnock was made the full-time tutor and organizer responsible for East Glamorgan. He became a close friend of Allan Rogers, a former geologist and Labour district councillor, who looked after the adjoining area of Monmouthshire. They pooled their efforts, and many of the WEA courses in local factories were run between them. Most days the two men would pass one another in their cars on one of the narrow valley roads and flash their headlights in recognition, each on his way to teach at a factory the other had just left.

Teaching seems, at first sight, a surprising choice of career for someone who had so far shown such an aversion to organized education, but Kinnock appears to have been naturally gifted for the job: when he took his diploma at Cardiff he only managed a grade C for teaching theory but for teaching practice he won an A. He specialized in economics, and his classes offered him a perfect opportunity to hone his skills as a speaker. Rogers, now the Labour MP for the Rhondda Valley, remembers how impressed he was by his young colleague: 'He was a superb teacher. Very often I'd take the same class after he'd finished with them, and if I could, I used to arrive early so I could sit around at the back and listen for the sheer joy of it. He had a marvellous ability to communicate, to describe things. He could draw pictures in words.' One of his biggest classes, Kinnock told Simon Hoggart of the *Observer* in 1983, was for the workers in Aberfan: 'You had to work damned hard because they would take you to pieces if you didn't. You could be sounding off about China, then discover that someone had served with the Army in Hong Kong for six years and knew all there was to know about the Cultural Revolution.'[5]

It was, according to Rogers, a demanding job. The latter half of the 1960s saw a resurgence in trade union activity. 'We spent a great deal of time discussing the Government's plans to curb union powers, and Neil was one of those who helped lead the opposition in South Wales to the Government's White Paper, *In Place of Strife*.' It was a period of great hostility to the Wilson Government. Kinnock once recalled a branch meeting on *In Place of Strife* that 'made the chariot race in *Ben Hur* look like *Blue Peter*'.[6] As activity increased, so did the length of their working day. 'We'd leave home at eight in the morning,' recalls Rogers, 'teach all day, get home at six in the evening, grab something to eat, go out again at seven to take evening classes, and not get back again until eleven or twelve. That would happen perhaps three days a week. And then there'd often be weekend schools to go to.' 'I happily did an eighty-hour week,' Kinnock claims, 'forty hours teaching in factories and the rest on organization and weekend work. They were the best four years anyone could spend.'[7]

Hardly surprisingly, not all the local employers welcomed the WEA's activities. According to Rogers, in 1967 the shop stewards at one large engineering factory asked them to lay on a course, and he and Kinnock had to go and make arrangements with the personnel manager. 'I remember Neil and I sitting in his office. He was a really arrogant bastard. He leant across his desk and said: "What you're asking me to do is to give time off in order to turn those dull bastards into bright bastards." Neil flashed back at him straight away: "Oh no, sir, it's not our intention to raise them above your level." '

Prejudice was not confined solely to management. Kinnock has always detested racist remarks. Back at university, when the wife of one of the lecturers made a derogatory comment about blacks at a reception, Kinnock clearly recalls telling her to 'piss off', thus bringing the function to an abrupt end. On this subject he could lose his temper equally sharply inside a factory. 'One incident has always stuck in my mind,' says Rogers. 'We were in a class at GKN's factory in Dowlais, and one of the shop stewards said that the blacks were taking all the jobs and we ought to get rid of them. That was the only time I've ever seen Neil really angry in a class. He really tore this man apart – something he'd never normally have done.' Some months later, Kinnock was heavily involved in the opposition to the Springboks rugby tour and helped to picket their matches in South Wales – a hazardous activity in such fanatical rugby country. Kinnock remains to this day a committed supporter of the anti-apartheid movement.

'There was never any point at which Neil proposed to me,' says Glenys. 'Somehow it gradually became accepted while we were at Cardiff that we would eventually marry.' The first priority was to look for somewhere to live, and soon after they left university they found a suitable place: a new, three-bedroomed, end-of-terrace house in a village called Pontllanfraith. 'We borrowed the deposit from Neil's dad,' recalls Glenys. Other relatives helped them with decorations and furniture. When the house was ready, at Easter 1967, they were married in chapel ('for the sake of our parents') in Anglesey.

Moving to Pontllanfraith brought them into the Bedwellty constituency, and soon after their arrival they both joined the local Labour Party. There is a school of thought which holds that Kinnock, barely twenty-five years old, came to the area because he saw an ageing MP and scented the possibility of replacing him. Kinnock's own explanation is that they moved to Pontllanfraith to be midway between his WEA work and Glenys's job as a teacher at Abersychan Grammar School. Kinnock loyalists also point out that if he had been scheming for a seat, he would, in Barry Moore's words, 'have done far better to have gone to Merthyr, where much of his work was done, and where the sitting Member was in his seventies'. Kinnock confirms this: 'I'd had much more formal thoughts about what I'd better describe as another South Wales constituency, where I'd actually been approached by trade unions and by party members to consider having a go.'

Nowadays Kinnock is scathing about ambitious young men and women who try to get into Parliament. 'When I meet kids at the universities today,' he has been quoted as saying, 'who say they intend to "make a career" in politics, I want to kick their arses. People who think of politics as a "career" are repulsive.'[8] This is disingenuous, whether or not one believes that Kinnock came to Bedwellty in the hope of getting the seat. According to the university friend who used to be woken by his hymn singing, even at Cardiff Kinnock 'always knew he'd be an MP; there wasn't the slightest shadow of doubt in his mind – though there was plenty in ours.'[9] (This is a story that Glenys confirms: 'Neil always wanted to be an MP. We used to talk about it at university.') Unquestionably, therefore, by the time Kinnock arrived in Pontllanfraith he had parliamentary ambitions of a sort, however vague. His work in the WEA was providing him with the opportunity to make all the right contacts among influential trade unionists and Labour Party workers, and in April 1967, a month after his arrival in Pontllanfraith, he set about forming a local WEA branch in Bedwellty's main town, Blackwood. Through these activities Kinnock met many of the people who were to feature prominently in his life during the following years.

Barry Moore was an apprentice in a local engineering firm. A quietly spoken man, he tends, on his own admission, towards pessimism rather than optimism. His phlegmatic personality is a perfect foil for Kinnock's ebullience, and he is perhaps Kinnock's closest friend. 'It's a brotherly relationship,' says Moore. 'There are no real secrets between the two of us.' By coincidence, he and his wife Doreen were married on the same day as Neil and Glenys, and the two couples still see much of one another. He has always been Kinnock's election agent, was the constituency secretary for a decade beginning in 1972 and has since, under Kinnock's guidance, followed him into the WEA; today he actually has Kinnock's old WEA job. He remains the main power in the constituency and guards Kinnock's local interests with care.

In contrast to the steadfast Moore are three men who, fifteen years later, were to combine to try to topple Kinnock from the seat that they helped him win: Ron Davies, now the MP for Caerphilly; Ray Davies, a white-collar worker in the local steel industry who stood against Kinnock for reselection in 1982; and Terry Burns, now a supporter of Militant. Of the three, Burns, in the early days, knew Kinnock best:

I first met him in 1967 when I was twenty-one. I was an apprentice fitter. He came to one of our union meetings to discuss the formation of a WEA branch. At that time I was assistant secretary of the Bedwellty Labour Party, as well as youth officer.

If there was a left wing within the constituency in those days, I was it. So I was a natural ally of any other left-winger – which Neil certainly was. I'd say his political position at that time was like mine: midway between *Militant* and *Tribune*.

Burns, who in 1967 held two jobs on the General Management Committee, promised Kinnock that if he won both of them again at the next local party election, he would give up one of them and see that Kinnock took it over. 'That's what I did,' says Burns, 'and Neil became youth officer. That was the first position he held in the Bedwellty party.' Kinnock, in return, encouraged Burns to try for higher education. Like Moore, he was one of a number of young people in the area whose lives were changed by Kinnock as a teacher.

Kinnock's views placed him on what was then the far left of the Labour movement. He had a particular dislike for the Prime Minister, Harold Wilson. The day after Wilson had been elected leader of the party, in February 1963, he had visited South Wales, and Kinnock had chaired a meeting at which he had spoken to Cardiff's Labour students. Three years earlier Kinnock had heard Wilson speak on behalf of Nye Bevan in Tredegar and had been impressed; now he was appalled. He found the new leader indescribably pompous. At one point Glenys, who was on the platform with him, leaned behind Wilson's back while he was speaking, put her thumb to her nose and wiggled her fingers. 'He ignored the students,' she recalls, 'and only bothered to speak to the cameras. It was the first of many disappointments from Harold Wilson.'

No taunt angers Kinnock so much as the accusation of some on the left that he is a 'new Wilson', Labour shorthand for a man who masquerades as a socialist as long as it suits him and then abandons his former beliefs when he acquires power. He was particularly stung by a comment to that effect from Ken Livingstone, the leader of the Greater London Council, who joined the Labour Party around the time that Kinnock went to live in Pontllanfraith:

> There were only a couple of occasions when I thought of leaving the Labour Party [says Kinnock]. The last was in 1968. That was when Labour had devalued the pound and introduced a freeze, Wilson had attacked communists in the seamen's union, there was *In Place of Strife* on the horizon, Michael Stewart [the Foreign Secretary] had made that appalling speech on Vietnam – that was the moment I thought of leaving, and that was the moment when Ken Livingstone decided to bloody well join.

Terry Burns clearly recalls that in 1968 Neil Kinnock did indeed consider quitting the Labour Party:

> At the time of the incomes policy and *In Place of Strife* I remember sitting in Neil's house and discussing packing in Labour and forming a new party, to be founded on the trade unions. We even got as far as talking about a title. You wouldn't believe the one we chose – it has a certain irony about it in the light of later events – the Social Democratic Party.

Kinnock confirms the story, but according to him the proposed title was the 'Democratic Socialist Party'.

While Kinnock toyed in private with fantasies of a new trade union party, in public he began turning into something of a local celebrity. Every Saturday in Blackwood he would hold a day school on economics. So popular were these that by the end they were drawing audiences of between eighty and a hundred. It says something for the Welsh reverence for learning, and for Kinnock's popularity as a lecturer, that people were prepared to come from places like Rhondda and Merthyr to listen to him – not only giving up their day off but also travelling for an hour or more to get to Blackwood. As his reputation spread, so too, for the first time, did the rumour that he intended to try to become an MP. Ray Davies, then thirty-eight and an active member of the constituency Labour Party, later recalled his impression of Kinnock at that time:

> The first time I clapped eyes on Neil was at a WEA lecture in late 1968. I'd heard what he was trying to do and I wanted to see him for myself. He struck me as brash, extremely ambitious: there was a great determination about him that he was going to get what he wanted. He seemed

somehow to have that ruthless streak about him. But I didn't mind that.
You often have to have that to get to the top.

It was obvious to me and to others on the left that he was preparing to
try and get Finch's seat. We didn't mind. He was saying all the right
things.

There was no single moment at which Kinnock declared,
even to his new friends in the constituency, that he intended
to seek the local party's nomination for Parliament. It somehow gradually became accepted that he was interested and
would be a candidate. No one then knew when an election
would come – one was not due for three years. Most believed
that Finch, who was in good health, would go on for at least
one more term. That meant that Kinnock would be in the
running some time around 1975, when he would be well into
his thirties – a conventional timetable for an ambitious would-
be MP. Kinnock's life, however, has never worked like that.

A couple of months after Ray Davies went to see Kinnock
lecture, Harold Finch suddenly announced his retirement.

Chapter Four

BATTLE FOR BEDWELLTY

In 1974 Neil Kinnock gave the House of Commons an affectionate and accurate portrait of the constituency which, in 1969, he set about trying to win:

> Bedwellty is not Welsh by language, although Welsh by character and by temperament. We have all the essentials of Welsh valley life – clubs and choirs and chapels, and a 22,000 Labour majority. We are also situated in the Bible belt of rugby football. In the fifteen towns and villages that make up the constituency there is also the unique quality of life in South Wales, and that is a competitive self-sufficiency in each of these communities of such a degree as to make Marshal Chauvin seem to be like Florence Nightingale.[1]

For over four months, between Finch's announcement at the end of January and the selection conference at the beginning of June, Kinnock and his young supporters conducted a guerrilla war over the exotic political terrain of Bedwellty to wrest control of the seat from the miners. It was a battlefield made up of dozens of idiosyncratic and often remote outposts, each of which was entitled to a vote in the selection meeting. There were village Labour Party branches with names like Bedwas and Trethomas, Maesycwmmer, Ynsyddu, Pengam and Fleur De Lis, Cefn Fforest and Risca (three Riscas, in fact – South, Central and North). There were local trades councils in places like Mynyddislwyn and Rhymney Valley. There were the trade union branches: NUM Britannia, NUM Bargoed Surface, NUM Bedwas Cokemans, AUEW Crosskeys, TGWU Courage and ISTC

48

Special Number 3. There were affiliated organizations, Co-ops, young socialists, women's branches. . . . The list eventually produced 150 elected delegates who were sent to help pick the new MP. If Kinnock ever becomes Prime Minister, there will be a good film to be made about the eighteen-week Battle for Bedwellty, a mixture of *Clochemerle*, *The Godfather* and *How Green Was My Valley*: 'We made a list,' recalls Barry Moore, 'and systematically went round and tried to see them all. I remember we couldn't find one man – he lived halfway up a mountain. Eventually we found his address and drove out there. I got out and went up to the door to ask for his support, while Neil hid behind a hedge. All this, you must understand, was before we tightened up the rules.' 'It was a ludicrous scene,' says Kinnock, 'with me sort of hiding round the corner while they went off to get this nomination form signed. There were lots of things like that. Daft.'

Kinnock tried to speak at as many meetings as possible. Each area had its own local issues, and Kinnock is remembered for the skill with which he adapted his remarks to suit the particular concerns of his audiences. His greatest handicaps were his age (hence the need for his supporters to pretend he was twenty-eight rather than twenty-seven) and his inexperience. 'I was asked at one meeting,' Kinnock recalled, 'about the fact that I'd never worked with my hands. I had, during holiday jobs, but I knew that wouldn't impress anyone. I asked them to imagine me going to the manager of the colliery, wearing my cap and gown, and asking for a job, and told them that if I did that they wouldn't be nominating me, they would be certifying me. This got a big laugh. I felt that was the turning point in being accepted.'[2]

Sometimes branches turned out to have their own 'favourite sons'. Ray Davies, for example, organized a meeting of members of the Bedwas and Trethomas ward. Kinnock went, and he spoke well, but the ward chose to support Dengar Evans, the local chemist. 'Neil was very upset,' says Davies, 'and rang me up and insisted on spending a long time analysing what had gone wrong. It wouldn't have mattered if he had been Nye Bevan incarnate. Dengar had that nomination sewn up.' In what was a fairly right-wing seat Kinnock also had to watch his radical opinions. Terry Burns alleges Kinnock told him that he would be glad when it was all over and he could put his CND badge back on.

Kinnock's main rival was the National Union of Mineworkers' (NUM) nominee, Lance Rogers, then in his fifties. According to Davies: 'Lance was the best possible candidate to oppose Neil – from Neil's point of view. He was old, he was associated with the Finch era, whereas Neil was young, spoke a lot about the need to bring new technology to the valleys, that sort of thing. He appealed to the younger members.' Even so, says Moore: 'We didn't think we'd win. The NUM looked too strong. But Rogers was getting on, and we thought that at least we'd be putting down a marker for the future.' The strength of the miners was reflected in the nominations. Kinnock received only nineteen, whereas Rogers had thirty, twenty-one of them miners; in all, the selection conference finally included forty-four NUM delegates.

The meeting to determine who would be Bedwellty's next MP took place in Blackwood church hall on 6 June 1969. The 150 delegates included Glenys Kinnock (then pregnant with their first child), who was representing the constituency's Young Socialists. Her husband was one of a short list of four; the others were Rogers, Evans the chemist, and Keith Griffiths, a local councillor. Each man had to speak for fifteen minutes and then answer ten minutes of questions. They drew lots to determine the order of appearance. 'Neil,' Gwyn Evans remembers, 'spoke fourth. He was very nervous. When he first stood up, his voice started cracking. But then he found his feet and he was all right.'

Kinnock, in his words, 'didn't expect to get it, but we didn't expect to fall ignominiously short'. They were hoping for thirty-four votes on the first ballot. The result, when it was announced, was as great a shock to them as it was to the miners:

KINNOCK	64
ROGERS	59
GRIFFITHS	16
EVANS	11

Griffiths and Evans were eliminated, and the conference immediately went on to a second ballot. Kinnock now knew he was close to victory. When the result was announced there was a gasp from the delegates:

KINNOCK	75
ROGERS	75

By then the meeting had been going on for over two hours. People wanted to get home. Some of the miners had night shifts to go to. Moore, who was stationed at the back of the hall where the votes were being counted in order to guard against any last-minute chicanery, thought the tide was running in Kinnock's favour and wanted the meeting to continue. He and Kinnock's other supporters looked to Glenys to see what she thought. 'I made a signal that we ought to get on with it,' she says. 'I couldn't bear the prospect of going through it all again.' Moore persuaded one man who was halfway out of the door to resume his seat – only to discover immediately afterwards, to his horror, that the man was one of Rogers's miners. The meeting eventually decided, by eighty votes to sixty-eight, to invite each of the two candidates to make a second speech.

Outside it was growing dark, and a curious crowd of people, wondering why the meeting was taking so long, were peering in through the lighted windows. Inside, in what his supporters portray as an episode from some Welsh edition of 'Scenes from the Lives of the Great Socialists', Neil Kinnock's moment had come.

Lance Rogers, caught unprepared, was unable to do much more than repeat once again the line which had been his refrain in his first speech: 'I am from the grassroots of this movement.' It was a poor performance, recalls Ray Davies,

51

who was one of Kinnock's delegates: 'Lance came back and said, "What can I say? I appeal for your support." Neil came back and started off on a completely new tack about how we needed a new hospital in the middle of the valley. We never got that bloody hospital. We're still talking about it to this day. But that doesn't matter. The important thing is that it sounded good and he said something new.'

After Kinnock had finished speaking, there was a third vote. The ballot papers were carried to the back of the hall, and Moore watched the counting. 'It was obviously going to be close. If they'd tied again there was going to be a second selection conference.' The final vote was:

KINNOCK	76
ROGERS	74

At least twenty people, Moore estimates, have come up to him in the years since and claimed that they were the ones who switched their vote. Most are probably telling the truth. After the second ballot some Kinnock supporters almost certainly went over to Rogers, thinking, as Moore puts it, 'Well, Lance deserves it. Neil's young. He'll get another chance.' But, correspondingly, some of Rogers's supporters had been impressed by Kinnock's spontaneous oratory; enough of them switched their allegiance to give Kinnock the nomination by two votes. Public speaking, Kinnock's greatest skill, an inborn talent discovered at Cardiff, nurtured in debate, practised at the WEA, had won him the seat. 'The youngsters gathered round and started slapping him on the back,' says Davies. 'Glenys was in tears. It was just like the day of the revolution.'

In one sense, indeed, it was the start of a revolution. For this was more than just a personal triumph. It was the victory in Bedwellty of a new generation with a new style of politics. Kinnock's success signalled the start of a takeover of the entire constituency party. Over the next couple of years his campaign team captured most of the important posts on the GMC and in the local wards, and the party moved sharply to

the left. Such scenes were to become familiar in constituencies throughout the country over the next ten years, as
the influx of teachers, lecturers and local government officials
transformed old-fashioned working-class parties. Kinnock's
victory was an early example of a trend which would later
rock Labour's national leadership. Among other things, that
trend would lead to a demand for greater democracy and for a
shift in power away from MPs in the House of Commons to
party members in the country. Ultimately it would lead to
changes in the party's constitution and to Kinnock's own
election as leader.

Such implications were in no one's mind on that June
evening in 1969 when Kinnock, his wife and a dozen of their
campaigners went to the working men's club in Pontllanfraith
to toast his victory. Kinnock, drink in hand, climbed on to the
stage and, to much applause, thanked them all for their help.
At closing time everyone went on to the Kinnocks' house for
further celebration.

That night the prospective parliamentary candidate for
Bedwellty rang his parents and told them what had happened.

> His father [recalls Glenys], who was always unbearably cautious, just
> said, 'Don't count on it, lad. You've still got to get elected.' Of course,
> we laughed – Neil was sitting on a 25,000 majority. His mother was also
> anxious. I don't think she ever really wanted him to do it. She was
> worried about what it might do to us and about the sort of things people
> do and say to you when you're in that position.
>   She saw things we didn't. And she was quite right.

News of Kinnock's surprise capture of the Bedwellty nomination was greeted with astonishment by many Labour Party
activists in South Wales. He was so young. 'To be honest,'
says Alan Fox, 'most of us just thought of him as a bright
university student at that time. He was considered politically
very naive in Valley terms. It must have been an amazing
campaign that he and his supporters conducted.' A few miles
north of Bedwellty, in Tredegar, Michael Foot, who had
succeeded Aneurin Bevan as the MP for Ebbw Vale, was

equally amazed. 'We always thought Bedwellty a bit of a strange place. Even though it's next door to Ebbw Vale, it has a reputation for being right-wing. It was a great feat for a left-winger like Neil to have won. I was delighted.'

A great deal of speculation surrounds Kinnock's relationship with Foot. They had first been introduced by Bill Harry some time around 1963, when Neil was still at university. 'We used to go on long walks together over the mountains,' remembers Foot. 'Right from the beginning, he made an impression on me with his wit, his good humour, his enjoyment of life.' It has often been said that Foot, thirty years older than Kinnock, childless and with a deep affection for the people of Ebbw Vale, looks upon Kinnock as the son he never had. 'Balls,' says Foot. 'The only member of the Kinnock household with whom I have the slightest fatherly relationship is Stephen.' (Foot often takes Kinnock's son to soccer matches.)

If anything, the relationship is perhaps the other way round. In temperament Foot is one of nature's perpetual children. His favourite quotation is from Hazlitt:

> Happy are they who live in the dream of their own existence, and see all things in the light of their own minds; who walk by faith and hope; to whom the guiding star of their youth still shines from afar, and into whom the spirit of the world has not entered. They have not been 'hurt by the archers', nor has the iron entered their souls. The world has no hand on them.

Kinnock's favourite author during the 1960s was Jack London.

It was Kinnock who loved to organize, to take on the paternal role. 'A whole group of us used to go on these picnics with Michael,' says Fox, 'and Neil just couldn't sit still. He'd bring along a ball, divide us into teams, insist we all got up and played.' This mildly authoritarian streak persisted. Alan Fox knew him well around the time when he first won the Bedwellty seat:

> If he and Glenys were going out, they often used to come and dump their kids here. I remember once they sat around with my children playing toy

soldiers – all very peaceful and contented. Then Neil arrived. He completely transformed this childish game. He imposed a huge series of rules: this cannon could fire so many yards, this number of soldiers could advance when you threw this number on the dice. It was chaos. He insisted on taking the armies over. The kids ended up leaving him on his own.

His friends also call Kinnock 'the world's worst chairman' when it comes to public meetings. Not long after he took over at Bedwellty, as part of his drive to liven up the constituency, Kinnock and his supporters introduced an annual Chartist Rally, designed to draw to the area prominent speakers from the Labour movement. It has become an important event in the political calendar of South Wales and attracts audiences of several thousands each year. From the first year Kinnock has been chairman. His introductions to each speaker are sometimes as long as the actual speeches themselves. 'Glenys's reactions used to be something to watch,' says Fox. 'She'd pull on his coat tails, drum her nails, look at her watch, yawn – it was so pointed, it could have been embarrassing, but you had to laugh.'

The exasperation is invariably tinged with affection. Kinnock's good humour generally disarms all but his most severe critics. Fox tells a typical Kinnock story about that first Chartist Rally. The two speakers invited were Michael Foot and Derek Childs, the Bishop of Monmouth. Fox was having a drink at the Kinnocks' house in Pontllanfraith just before the first rally when there was a knock on the door. Kinnock opened it, to reveal the imposing figure of Childs standing on the doorstep, holding his crozier. 'Oh, Christ,' said Kinnock. 'It's the bishop.' As Childs stepped over the threshold, Kinnock seized his bishop's staff and asked him why he had brought his Crook-lok with him.

Chapter Five

YOUNG MP

Kinnock was twenty-eight and had been the prospective candidate for less than a year when Harold Wilson suddenly decided to call an election in June 1970. After the excitement of winning the Bedwellty nomination, the election itself was a formality. Kinnock wanted to win by the biggest majority ever and attracted some criticism locally for not doing more to help the party's campaign in any of the more marginal seats around the Labour fortress of Bedwellty. According to Ray Davies: 'He was bound to get a huge majority. He was completely safe. I asked him if he and his youngsters – about twenty Young Socialists – would spare a day to help in neighbouring constituencies which were marginal. Monmouth was the one we were thinking of. He made a firm promise to help, but nothing happened. Finally I rang up and it was Glenys who told me on the telephone that they couldn't spare anyone.' Kinnock, fighting his first election, wanted to establish himself firmly in his own seat. Besides, it looked to almost everyone as though Labour would romp home that summer. In fact, Monmouth turned out be one of seventy seats that Labour lost. The final result of the election turned Labour's 1966 lead over the Conservatives of 110 seats into a Tory lead over Labour of forty-three. But the swing to the Conservatives which swept the Wilson Government out of office could hardly make any impression on the Labour hold on Bedwellty. Kinnock was returned by a majority of 22,279.

In London that summer he lived out of a suitcase in a hotel near Paddington Station. Dennis Skinner, the newly elected MP for Bolsover, stayed in the same hotel for a short time, and in the early days the two were quite close. Together they immediately joined the Tribune Group of left-wing MPs. 'We were the first in at the first meeting,' recalls Skinner. 'We thought it was fantastic. We couldn't wait to get started.'

Kinnock was also quick to make his maiden speech. He chose to speak during an Opposition debate on the National Health Service on 13 July and was called third, after Barbara Castle and Sir Keith Joseph. Like his great hero Bevan, almost forty years before, the young Welsh MP chose, in his very first speech, to defy tradition. It is a custom in Parliament to keep a maiden speech non-controversial, confined largely to a description of the constituency and the virtues of the previous member. 'I was aware of the tradition,' says Kinnock, 'but I wouldn't know how to make a speech like that.' He dispensed with polite convention in his first few lines, then went for the Tories with a vengeance:

> First, there has been a lot of talk about compassion, and this from a party whose very existence is an illustration of rapacity and selfishness. To me and to the people of South Wales that is what Conservatism means. I make no apology for giving their definition, because they are the people whom I represent.
>
> Secondly, we have had the pious palaver of the creation of 'one nation', and this from a Government that is prepared in the name of the god 'choice' to encourage the development of private alternatives in education, welfare, insurance and health –

At this point, Kinnock was halted by angry interruptions from the Conservative benches. The Member for Bedwellty was undeterred:

> There is no order of the House that demands that I make a non-controversial speech. I am talking about a controversial subject, a matter of life and death, and nothing is more controversial than that. ...
>
> Perhaps I have a suspicious mind, but the South Wales valleys breed suspicious minds, and I have reason to believe that the 'one nation' party is conducting a survey of the Welfare State system and the

National Health Service with a view to undertaking extensive mining operations.

Kinnock described a National Health Service in which doctors and nurses were about to be 'sucked out of the pool of medical manpower into private medicine' and quoted the NHS's creator, Bevan: 'we shall have a nation divided by the salt, some above, some below.'

I am in this House, and I hope that other hon. Members on this side are, to knock the salt off the table. . . .

. . . Compassion is not a sloppy, sentimental feeling for people who are under-privileged or sick, to be used as a tear-jerker or as an expedient at the time of an election. It is an absolutely practical belief that, regardless of a person's background, ability or ability to pay, he should be provided with the best that society has to offer. That is compassion in practice; anything less than that is sheer sentimentality.

Kinnock warned against any plans to make the Health Service partly dependent 'on voluntary donation and philanthropic management':

The slightest step in that direction will earn the fury of the people of this country, and I shall be in the van of that fury.[1]

It was a startling parliamentary debut. Christopher Mayhew, then the Labour MP for Woolwich East, described it as a maiden speech 'in what I would call the modern form. It was made with the fluency, confidence and aggressiveness which we older hon. Members have been trying, without success, to cultivate over the years.' That afternoon George Thomas, a fellow Welsh MP and a shrewd observer of the House, later to become one of its most successful Speakers, paid Kinnock a remarkable tribute: 'He spoke with a fluency that is typical of the valleys from whence he hails. He abandoned the tradition of the non-controversial speech as other great people have done before him.'

When Kinnock was elected leader in 1983 it was widely remarked that he was not a 'House of Commons man'. By then it was certainly true. From the mid-1970s onwards Kinnock increasingly devoted his time and energy to travelling the country and addressing constituencies and unions.

But in the early days, with no national reputation to win him invitations and audiences, Kinnock had no forum other than the Commons chamber, and he used it extensively. It is the traditional arena for a young politician trying to make his name. 'Speak often,' Benjamin Disraeli was advised on his election to Parliament almost 150 years ago, 'but speak shortly.' Kinnock observed the first half of this traditional prescription for success, while generally ignoring the second. During his first eighteen months in the Commons he spoke on, among other subjects, the coal industry, pensions, brewing, the Health Service, Rolls-Royce, school milk, unemployment and Wales. His contributions were frequently followed by a request from the Speaker that MPs should try to keep their speeches shorter.

Some of the older Labour MPs seem to have had their doubts about this brash young Welshman; they were not used to being harangued by someone less than half their age. It took Kinnock some time to win them over. About six months after his maiden speech, Kinnock says, 'A very senior member of the House of Commons – a very senior member – came up to me and said that he'd just listened to a speech I'd made on some industrial development order or something, and he'd listened to my previous three speeches, and he wanted to say that a lot of the things that they'd been led to assume about me were inaccurate.'

A style of speaking which works well on a public platform can often ring embarrassingly hollow in the chamber of the House of Commons. Members of Parliament are a difficult audience. They know all the tricks of oratory; they have heard all the arguments before. It takes something outstanding to impress them. Even so, Kinnock's natural fluency won him respect. During a debate on the right-wing coup in Chile, for example, he made a speech which was both effective and dramatic:

> Those men did not drive their tanks, fire their guns and rockets or drop their bombs in the cause of saving the Chilean economy from destruction. They did it for the reason for which any usurping fascist power or

59

any usurping militaristic power has done it at any time, at any place, in history, whether we are talking about the Norman barons, Soviet tanks in Central Europe, or the invasion of Chilean civil rights in September of this year. They are classic examples of what happens when tyranny is exerting itself. . . .

I had prepared notes for my speech, but I have been so appalled by the attitude of Conservative Members that something more than a rehearsed speech is called for. If hon. Members wish to call it emotion, they can do so. I call it history and a sense of decency. . . . we must vote with our stomachs and hearts in saying whose side we are on. Are we on the side of brutality and the suppression of civil rights, or are we on the side of maintaining our own parliamentary traditions and freedom of speech. . . . ?

. . . the Junta has taught people in Chile and the rest of the Third World that they will not beat forces of that kind with ballot boxes. They will not be able to build a guard against militarism with piles of ballot papers. The language which the militarists, ITT, and the multinational corporations understand is not the language of democracy and peace. People will have to learn the lesson of Chile in the hardest possible way.[2]

Even Julian Amery, the junior Foreign Minister who replied to the debate and a noted right-winger, was impressed by Kinnock's performance. He told MPs that the Member for Bedwellty had made a speech which he admired for 'its forcefulness and oratory.'

Other speeches that Kinnock made at about this time were also praised. After he had moved a motion on safety and health at work (part of which is quoted on p. 23), Jeremy Thorpe hailed Kinnock's contribution as 'extremely lucid, cogent and valuable'. 'I congratulate him,' said Reg Prentice, 'on the very powerful speech he has made.' To passion and fluency Kinnock also began to add deftness and humour. In 1972 he called Edward Heath's offer of talks to the TUC a 'poisoned carrot'. During a debate on prices and incomes John Stokes, a Conservative MP, rose to complain that Kinnock was implying he had advocated fascist policies: did the hon. Member for Bedwellty not know that he had fought in the war against fascism? Kinnock's reply charmed his opponents: 'I appreciate that I owe my freedom in some measure to the hon. Gentleman. My only contribution to the war effort was in giving up bananas for the first three years of my life.'[3]

*

Kinnock was still building his reputation at Westminster when he was suddenly overwhelmed by tragedy at home. In the winter of 1971, while on his way to work, Gordon Kinnock collapsed with a heart attack. Kinnock was rung in London by his mother and drove straight home. He picked her up, and together they went on to the hospital, where he looked round the door into the ward and saw the doctors giving his father heart massage. For some time there was hope that he might recover. 'Then the telephone rang,' says Dorothy Kinnock, 'and it was the hospital to ask whether we would all go down at once.' Neil and the other members of the family arrived just before Gordon died. He was sixty-four.

Gordon is remembered as a gentle man, less assertive than Neil's mother who, most people feel, was the dominant influence upon him. But strong character though she was, Mary Kinnock seems not to have been able to cope with the loss of her husband. 'She was distraught, devastated when he died,' says Glenys. 'You couldn't comfort her.' Mary had been in poor health for years, but she had never retired to bed, however ill she felt. Gordon's death broke her spirit. 'He died,' says Barry Moore, 'and she literally took to her bed. She got up only once, for the funeral, and that was it. About a week after his burial she died as well.'

It was, understandably, a terrible blow to Kinnock. 'We had been out shopping for Christmas presents,' remembers Glenys. 'We got back and his aunt called to say Mary was dead.' 'He was absolutely beside himself,' says Allan Rogers, who helped out by driving him around at that time. Alan Fox recalls how he and his wife Megan used to visit Kinnock: 'I think it took Glenys a long time to convince him that that aspect of his life had gone, and gone dramatically.' Kinnock's family and friends are unanimous in their agreement about the importance to him of his mother and father. 'He was always very conscious of his parents,' says Glenys, 'and of that whole family background. He's still very conscious about not letting them down. He's a great believer in roots and background and decency and clean shoes and looking smart and all those aspirations for their children which his parents and my parents represent.' 'His mother gave Neil his fluency,' believes Bill Kinnock, 'his father gave him his determination, and both gave him his idealism.' 'They were always very reasonable people,' says Kinnock. 'Oh, we used to have bust-ups like everybody does, especially teenagers with their parents. I mean, I wasn't a terrible tearaway, but I used to conduct parts of my life in a way which my parents strongly disapproved of. So we used to have disputes . . . but basically they were very, very reasonable people who would always give you a straight answer.'

One measure of how important Kinnock's parents were to him is the frequency with which he speaks of them. Things that they said, things that happened to them are brought into conversation and speeches repeatedly, just as he often refers in a similar way to his own children.

> I'll give you an example [he says], typical of my mother. She ensured that the first letter I received as a Member of Parliament in this place was from her and my father. It was a short letter, a mixture of pride and frivolity. And so I went into the library to reply to it with due formality. . . . And whilst I was there, Winston Churchill walked across in front of me, and Jeremy Thorpe went in the other direction. And so I wrote to them saying: I wasn't sure what I was going to say to you in this letter, but a Churchill and a Thorpe have just walked past, and it's the first time a Kinnock's sat here.
>
> I really did feel – as I still feel, very, very profoundly – that this place is for us, for our kind of people. I suppose that's why I refer to them such a lot in my speeches.

A few days after Mary Kinnock's funeral Glenys gave birth to their second child, Rachel. The baby was two weeks overdue, which Glenys put down to the strain they were going through. She and Neil spent the week following the birth at Gordon's and Mary's council house, clearing out their possessions. 'Books to old people's homes, clothes to hospitals. It was an awful, awful experience.' At first the baby was a welcome distraction from grief. 'It was a massive compensation,' recalls Glenys. 'It meant that Neil could talk about his parents, how they would have liked to see her. It helped to get it out of his system.' But soon Rachel became an additional burden in what was increasingly an intolerable situation. 'You see, we were very young,' says Glenys, 'we didn't really know what being an MP entailed. We'd only been to the House of Commons once before he was elected. So it was a real shock, after years of always being together, when he suddenly started going off to London on a Monday morning and coming back on a Friday night with a bag full of washing.'

For eighteen months prior to Rachel's birth Kinnock had been commuting between his work in Westminster and his family in the constituency. He had moved into a tiny bedroom in the north London home of Ann Swingler, widow of a former Labour Minister – a house he shared with two other MPs, Kevin McNamara and Don Concannon. He had only a single bed. Glenys could rarely come up to stay. The weekends were the only opportunity he got to see his family, and after Rachel's birth Glenys slipped into a deep depression. 'He went back to the Commons and left me alone in the house with two babies. The place had mice, which terrify me. I had no friends nearby, no work. I was very, *very* miserable.' The situation was beginning to threaten the marriage: 'I wouldn't like to say what might have happened. I had to stop it.' Barry Moore and his wife now became very close to the Kinnocks.

After his parents died [recalls Moore] Neil hated going off to London and being separated from his family. I think he had this irrational feeling that he'd be away and he'd come back to find that he'd lost them too. For a couple of months he tried to come home about twice a week. He was practically commuting between here and Westminster.

Glenys couldn't stand it. Doreen and I used to get telephone calls from her at all hours of the day and night. She once rang about one o'clock in the morning to say she could hear mice. We went round, and I shall never forget the sight of her, standing on a stool in the middle of the kitchen with Stephen in her arms.

It was obvious that things couldn't go on like that.

The domestic situation took its toll on Kinnock's work. He was restless and felt he was wasting his time in London. 'I wasn't very happy,' he says. 'I was quite seriously contemplating not running again. We were a young family and we never saw each other. . . . It was worth making that sacrifice if there was some sense of achievement, both for Glenys and for me. But if there was no sense of achievement, then it wasn't worth doing.'

The only solution was to move the family to London and Kinnock began looking for a suitable place. At around the same time he changed the telephone number of the house in Pontllanfraith because Glenys was being bothered by what Moore calls 'odd calls'. Rumours in the local party that he was leaving and that he had gone 'ex-directory' blew up into a full-scale row. 'He found a place in Kingston-upon-Thames,' says Moore, 'and he had to explain to the GMC that he was going to move out. There was some criticism. It lasted about six months. The problem was that he'd said in the past that he'd always live in the constituency; that, for example, he'd always be passionately interested in education in the valley because his kids would be at the local school.'

The climax came at a meeting of the General Management Committee on 28 April 1972. According to the minutes, Kinnock confirmed that he was moving out but 'explained that he intended to buy a house in the constituency where his family would come during weekends and long recesses from Parliament. His reasons were primarily that his young family were growing up without their father.' Members of the GMC demanded to know why they had not been told earlier. Had he not also pledged at the selection conference that he would always live in the constituency? That he had made such a promise on his selection Kinnock denied, but he 'accepted that he should have informed the Executive of his intentions earlier'. He excused himself by saying that 'things were so tentative that it did not occur to him at that time.'

It was more a matter of bruised pride than anything else, and Kinnock soon rode out the storm. In London the family chose to live in Kingston, and later in Ealing, mainly because they were close to the main road link with South Wales, the M4. He visited the constituency and held surgeries as regularly as before. Even his opponents concede that Kinnock is a particularly conscientious constituency MP..

Perhaps the most revealing moment of the whole episode came when Kinnock argued that there was at least one benefit to be gained by his moving out: 'he could undertake more engagements to Tory or marginal constituencies.' He told his GMC that he had so far spoken at three meetings around the country. He had been invited to twenty-six.

Chapter Six
'ATTACK, ATTACK, ATTACK'

In the decade that followed Kinnock was to show himself at his most effective politically when operating within the Labour Party. He had made his first speech to a party conference in the summer of 1971, a few months before his parents died. It was a special one-day conference convened on 17 July in Westminster's Central Hall to debate the party's position on entry into the Common Market. It provides an interesting glimpse of Kinnock in action in his early years, as well as an insight into the essentially pragmatic nature of much of his politics.

Kinnock began by describing the Government's White Paper advocating entry as 'comic cuts'. He urged opposition to it, but not because he necessarily agreed with the anti-Marketeers who held that the EEC offered no economic advantages (he merely said that in his view 'that case is not proved, whether it has been adduced by the Conservatives or whether it has been adduced by ourselves'). Instead the argument he advanced was a straight domestic political one:

the man who is leading the British nation, or trying to lead us, into Europe in 1971 is not Harold Wilson. It is not even Roy Jenkins. It certainly is not Michael Foot. It is Edward Heath.
For 364 days out of the year on every issue – on school milk, the freeze on public employees, the lot – in Parliament and outside we stridently, without reservation, attack, attack, attack. We have called the Conservatives everything we can lay our tongue to. And then we are prepared to go before the British people on the 365th day – not on a

marginal issue, not on a minor non-contentious issue, but on the biggest issue of our generation – we are going to put our arms round him and say, 'After all, Ted, although we hate you for the rest of time, we think you are right on this one.' It is not on.

Kinnock's remarks drew applause from the delegates, and he went on:

we cannot with one tongue be the enemies of this class-ridden Government and with the other tongue embrace them and follow their policies. . . . And it is because I am a member of the Labour Party, and because I am a trade unionist, and because I want to see the Tories beaten, and because I am willing to use any weapon to beat them, that I am against EEC entry *on these terms at this time.* [Author's emphasis][1]

It was a pragmatic argument which neither Harold Wilson nor James Callaghan would have found trouble in endorsing.

Kinnock was warmly applauded. Michael Foot was impressed by Kinnock's conference style. 'He spoke from the floor for five minutes and he did it very well. That sort of conference speech is a very difficult thing to do.'

'Attack, attack, attack': the phrase could almost stand as Kinnock's political motto. Like Aneurin Bevan – who on one famous occasion proclaimed that he carried in his heart 'a deep burning hatred for the Tory Party. . . . they are lower than vermin'[2] – Kinnock showed more than merely a professional distaste for Conservatives. He really did on occasions seem to 'hate' them. Up until the beginning of 1972 Kinnock claims to have been seriously considering 'chucking it all in' at Westminster. His disillusionment was not solely the result of the problems posed by living apart from his family. He also felt confined and frustrated by his role as an Opposition backbencher in a House of Commons easily controlled by a large Conservative majority. It is revealing that the episode which he says changed his mind was the one which brought a fresh note of class warfare into British politics – the miners' strike of that winter. '[It] brought home to me the fact that it was important for people to have articulate spokesmen in this place [Parliament], that part of the battle was to be fought in here. . . . And though I wouldn't say that after 1972, after the miners' strike, I never looked back, it did impress upon me there was a real function . . . in this place.'

Kinnock, like Bevan before him, stands squarely in the pugilistic tradition of politics: it is, he is fond of remarking, a 'blood sport'. Friends say he relishes a fight. The bitter crises in industrial relations during the last two years of the Heath Government provided him with plenty of opportunities to deploy his invective. 'Conservatives,' he said in 1972, 'are past practitioners of the confidence trick; of giving the impression that they are not such bad chaps; that they are on the side of the working class; that they favour a one-nation policy. So they become the Government, and that gives them the opportunity to use the disgusting and doctrinaire policies of the last two years.'[3]

Kinnock is normally a good-humoured and approachable man. But for all his charm there is about him on occasions a hint of suppressed violence, of anger waiting for an outlet. It is there in the way he delivers his speeches, rocking like a boxer on the balls of his feet, his head tilted back, his chin jutting forward. It is there in his language. It is to be seen repeatedly throughout his career, most commonly in spontaneously savage responses to heckling or interruptions, of which 'guts at Goose Green' during the 1983 general election is merely the most famous example. It is even there in his passion for sport: as Simon Hoggart has observed, 'there's an urgency about his feeling for soccer, rugby and even cricket; it's an emotional need rather than just a recreation.'[4] 'He feels very strongly about things,' says Glenys, 'and he makes people angry. People either really like him or they hate him. Not many are indifferent to him. It's the way he speaks, the language he uses. He shouts at hecklers. He gets very angry.'

Allied with the passion which can so easily bubble over into anger is a streak of machismo. His love of rugby is not confined to the playing field (where he regularly coaches his son and other teenagers); he is equally at home in those citadels of masculinity, rugby club dinners. A Welsh colleague remembers him as the guest speaker on one occasion, staying to drink and joke into the small hours. 'Neil's very much a man's man,' says Allan Rogers. 'He can walk into a local working man's club and be instantly at home. He's got a typical Valley working-class mentality. It's a very masculine environment. The men go out for a pint, the women stay at home and do something else. It's a macho society.' According to Alan Fox, 'he slots effortlessly into crude and earthy conversations. There's something of the beer-swilling, rugby-playing Valley boy about him.' Some left-wingers complain about his alleged lack of interest in, or understanding of, modern sexual politics. He enraged feminists at one Tribune rally by telling what they regarded as 'sexist' jokes. At the time of the row over the parliamentary candidacy of Peter Tatchell, whose homosexuality attracted much attention, Kinnock claimed to be on the 'balls wing' of the party.[5] Jill Craigie has heard him refer to an MP slightingly as 'unmanly', and be reproved for it by Glenys. Her first recollection of the young Neil is of an argument with him about long hair; Kinnock felt strongly that young Labour Party supporters should look neat and tidy and that long hair was offensive to the average voter: he keeps his own hair cropped to a length endorsed by the regulations of the army or the police – those two organizations he wanted to leave school to join when he was sixteen.

This is only one facet of Kinnock's political outlook. But it is an important one, and it can be traced back to those first years in the House of Commons. Perhaps the clearest example occurred during that miners' strike of 1972, when Kinnock attempted to defend some of the violent scenes on the picket lines:

Hon. Gentlemen opposite have bemoaned picketing. If they had been on strike for five weeks, if their families' total income was seven pounds a week social security benefit, if they were worried about smoking their next cigarette, if they were worried about paying the rent, and they saw some cowboy coming along driving a bald-tyred wagon without a road-fund licence, what would their reaction be? What would be the instinct of any red-blooded man in this House, having put his family to all that inconvenience and near-misery, if he saw someone riding roughshod over his picket line? I know what my attitude would be. In fact, I should be worried if it were not the case.[6]

It is impossible to imagine Tony Benn or virtually any other middle-class socialist delivering such a speech at that time and carrying any conviction. But Kinnock's roots are not middle-class, and socialism for him is not a matter of intellectual conversion. When he talks about industrial injuries, he talks about his own family. When he talks about poor housing, he describes the home in which he was brought up as a child. His defence of picketing, appealing to the 'red-blooded' instincts of any normal man, is authentic Kinnock: aggressive, masculine, the political commitment drawn from his own experience as a miner's son and as the proud head of a close family. Michael Meacher, epitome of the compassionate middle-class socialist, a public schoolboy converted to the faith by his discovery of poverty, recalls watching Kinnock in this early period and being 'stunned' by the force of his speaking. 'The speeches he made in the Commons between 1970 and 1974,' Michael Foot believes, 'were the basis of his reputation.'

Perhaps the prize for prescience should go to Chris Mullin, a young freelance journalist, later to be the editor of *Tribune*. In 1973 he was Labour's prospective parliamentary candidate in Kingston-upon-Thames where Kinnock lived, and the two men became friends. 'He had charisma, he was full of jokes, he told stories – he could do all the things I can't,' says Mullin. 'I remember thinking very early on that he was bound to be leader unless he was hit by a bus.' After one dinner at Kinnock's house Mullin rang round various bookmakers trying to put a bet on Kinnock's eventual leadership of the Labour Party. But in 1973 hardly anyone outside Westminster had heard of the young MP for Bedwellty. To Mullin's eternal disappointment, no bookmaker would offer him odds.

Kinnock's speeches brought him to the attention of the party leadership, and Harold Wilson decided to send him as part of a small delegation to the Soviet Union. The group comprised 'hand-picked people', says Kinnock. 'Young members, new members . . . at that stage it was a sort of informal signal that the leader of the party was making his light to shine upon you.' When Labour was returned to power as a minority Government in March 1974, Wilson thought sufficiently highly of Kinnock's ability in the House of Commons to ask him to second the Queen's Speech, an honour which traditionally goes to a young and promising MP. Kinnock describes it as 'a number 12 shirt, as it were'.

Kinnock was enthusiastic about the return of a Labour Government. Six months earlier he had been impressed by Denis Healey's speech at the party conference in Blackpool, during which the Shadow Chancellor had boasted that there would be 'howls of anguish' from the rich as Labour brought about 'a fundamental and irreversible shift in the balance of power and wealth in favour of working people and their families'. Walking out of the conference hall with Glenys and Neil, a colleague recalls Kinnock talking excitedly of all that Labour would do after the election. 'Glenys brought him down to earth at once, saying, "Don't be stupid, Neil. These are the people who sold us out last time and they'll do just the same next." ' Glenys remembers the occasion. 'It's true. I was always more cynical about the leadership than Neil.'

Despite his wife's doubts, in his speech on 12 March 1974 Kinnock hailed the Government's legislative programme, set out in the Queen's Speech, as a 'blueprint for democratic socialism'. He also spoke proudly of his membership of the Tribune Group, which he called the 'light cavalry of the Parliamentary Labour Party'.[7] In reply Edward Heath graciously described Kinnock as having 'delighted us' by delivering one of 'the most attractive and effective speeches that we have heard made for this purpose in recent years'.

For Kinnock the triumph was slightly overshadowed by the fact that he had managed to land himself in a potentially embarrassing situation. He had been approached separately by two Ministers, each of whom had asked him to be his Parliamentary Private Secretary. 'I didn't want to be anyone's PPS,' Kinnock recollects, 'but I didn't want to

71

offend them, so I just said the first thing that came into my head, which was that I was doing it for Michael Foot.'

Foot, who had just been appointed Secretary of State for Employment, was unaware of this, and Kinnock passed the afternoon of 12 March in an agony of apprehension in case either of the two Ministers should happen to mention it to him. That evening the young MP went to the special reception in Downing Street where, he remembers, 'I spent all my time hanging around the door, hoping to grab [Foot] when he walked in. Luckily he was busy trying to sort out the coal strike, so he was late. I told him what had happened. He said, "But I don't want a PPS." I said, "That's all right. I don't want to do it." ' Much against his better judgement, Foot took him on.

A Parliamentary Private Secretary keeps a senior Minister informed about the mood of MPs and acts as his master's emissary in the Commons. 'A chap has to subordinate his own way of doing things to some extent,' says Foot. 'Some are born to it, some are not. Neil was not made by nature to be a PPS.' Indeed, Foot goes so far as to call him 'one of the worst PPSs in history'; only Bevan, he believes, who was PPS to the Labour leader George Lansbury for a year, was worse at the job than Kinnock; like Bevan, Kinnock only did it for a year.

The significance of the period is that it provided Kinnock with what has proved to be his only glimpse of the inner workings of government. 'As one of Michael's team,' he recalls, 'I went to a lot of the meetings relating to the operation of the social contract [the bargain under which the unions pledged to try to hold down wage demands in return for concessions from the Government]. That impressed me, because there round the table were the TUC and Ministers who wanted it to work – and they went to great lengths to try to ensure that it did.' Yet, impressed though he was, Kinnock was not tempted to try to be anything more than a spectator.

The only part which Kinnock could have played in the 1974–9 Government would have been a lowly one, in which the accent would have been on grind rather than glamour. Most people who know him well believe (as his poor academic record at school and university suggests) that Kinnock's mind is not best employed coping with run-of-the-mill detail. 'I can't pretend that he was our hardest worker,' says Russell Kerr, at that time chairman of the select committee on nationalized industries, of which Kinnock was a member. 'He was very intelligent and very witty, but he was a bit lazy and his attendance was thin.' He was not a great reader. Indeed, it was around this time that an MP recalls Kinnock jokingly telling him that although he made regular speeches on economics, 'he'd only ever read one book on the subject, *The Affluent Society* by J. K. Galbraith.' 'He's a teacher,' says Ian Mikardo, 'and teachers don't always make the best scholars.'

Kinnock therefore had little hesitation, either at this point or later when James Callaghan offered him two ministerial posts, in turning his back on the traditional route to power. It was not just that the work (like being a PPS) would have been humdrum. It would also have robbed Kinnock of his greatest political asset: his voice. For even the most junior office in government gags its holder and binds him with the doctrine of 'collective responsibility' – anathema to a man who had so far built his career on his ability as a speaker and whose interests ranged across the whole spectrum of politics.

Kinnock's decision to keep clear of office, which was to be such a powerful part of his appeal when he ran for the leadership in 1983, may have been predominantly the result of ideological disagreement. But it was a choice to which he was temperamentally as well as politically suited. He had a growing reputation; he was now relaxed with his family around him in London; he had no responsibility; and he was free to speak as he wished. Kinnock looks back on the four or five years which followed as among the happiest of his life.

Part Two
REBEL

Chapter Seven
KINNOCK AND THE OUTSIDE LEFT

Quick-witted, aggressive, independent, Neil Kinnock was perfectly equipped to be a rebel, and the Labour Government of 1974–9 was a perfect target for rebellion. Among socialists a record of opposition to it carries the cachet which in the Conservative Party fell to those who followed Churchill and opposed appeasement in the 1930s. 'Harold,' said James Callaghan when Wilson announced his resignation, 'I believe history will treat you more kindly than your contemporaries.'[1] This may be the case. But there are as yet no revisionist histories of Wilson or Callaghan or their administrations, and for a large section of the Labour Party, there never can be.

If any one thing can be said to have been the making of Neil Kinnock, it was his repeated and documented opposition to the policies of that period. It won him popularity in the party. It gave him a power base. It meant, during his opposition to Tony Benn, that the so-called hard left could never finally succeed in pinning upon him the damning label of 'careerist'. Ultimately it left Kinnock with clean hands, while his main rivals for the leadership were, in the eyes of many, irretrievably sullied by their association with a period of failure. For five years, untrammelled by ministerial responsibility, he was free to follow his political instincts.

From this point on it is impossible to understand Kinnock's growing success without placing the man and his actions in the context of the events which were happening around him. Between 1974 and 1979 the old structures of power within the Labour Party first buckled and finally broke. The political forces responsible for that dislocation were the ones which eventually pitched Kinnock into the leadership nine years later.

Even before it took office in 1974, many on the left half-expected that the Labour Government would fail to live up to its manifesto commitments. Lip-service might be paid to radical policies, but, as Glenys Kinnock put it, those making the speeches were those who had 'sold us out last time'. The Labour Government of 1964–70 had been a deep disappointment to the left. It was 'essentially a Gaitskellite Government,' wrote Eric Heffer in 1972, which 'soon went into headlong retreat'. He went on:

> Once bitten, twice shy! One has only to cast a quick eye over this year's Conference resolutions to see how distrustful the Party is at grassroots level. They feel that too often they are ignored. They were so ignored during the lifetime of the last Labour Government. Conference decisions were flouted, the PLP [Parliamentary Labour Party] appeared to live in a different world. . . . It is this issue above all others that the Party must get right before it can make any serious progress. . . . Today, and rightly so, pragmatism is a dirty word.[2]

It was felt that Harold Wilson had tried to fight presidential-style election campaigns in the 1960s and that the party had neglected policy. Accordingly, after Labour lost office in 1970 the party's National Executive Committee (NEC) set up a series of working parties to devise fresh policies. Supervised by Tony Benn, the radical proposals produced included a commitment to nationalize twenty-five of Britain's leading companies.

On 30 May 1973 the new policies came before a special meeting of the NEC that was supposed to approve Labour's pre-election manifesto. The discussion, held at the Churchill Hotel, in London, turned into a bitter twelve-hour wrangle, with the right especially concerned about the proposed increase in nationalization. 'We'll find it very difficult,' Wilson is reported to have said at one point, 'to explain to the voters that simply by taking over Marks and Spencer we can make it a efficient as the Co-op.' It was, he said later, 'an outlandish proposal'.[3] When the final vote was taken, shortly before 10 o'clock that night, seven NEC members voted in favour of the nationalization plan (among them were Tony Benn, Judith Hart, Joan Maynard and Joan Lestor); six, including Denis Healey, James Callaghan and Shirley Williams, voted against. Wilson, who had abstained, promptly announced to the press that whenever the election came, he would simply veto the commitment's inclusion in the manifesto.

This single event, which did much to crystallize the left's hostility to the leadership, had one particularly significant consequence. A few weeks after what became known in left-wing demonology as 'the Churchill Hotel NEC', a small group of about a dozen activists assembled in a committee room of the House of Commons to establish a pressure group which they called the Campaign for Labour Party Democracy (CLPD). The moving spirit behind it was Vladimir Derer, a quietly spoken, scholarly man in his early fifties who had come to Britain from Czechoslovakia in 1939. His wife, Vera, a polytechnic lecturer, was also among the original twelve. The CLPD had one central object: to ensure 'that policy decisions reached by annual conference should be binding on the Parliamentary Labour Party'. Its 'Statement of Aims', drawn up at the meeting, called on Labour's NEC to 'carry out fully its responsibility'; 'to be responsive to rank-and-file opinion'; 'to report back in writing' to local parties and trade unions; to open up their meetings to 'representatives from constituency Labour Parties'; and, finally, to ensure 'that Labour's election manifesto accurately represents party policy as expressed by annual conference decisions'.

Kinnock was one of the earliest members of the CLPD. In the summer of 1973 the left-wing MP Frank Allaun had canvassed for support on its behalf among his colleagues in the House of Commons. 'I saw a circular with Frank's name on it,' recalls Kinnock. 'The general propositions about democracy had a strong appeal for me, as they had for others.' According to Derer, Kinnock was one of ten MPs who signed the original 'Statement of Aims'. Kinnock does not appear to have given the matter much thought. He was always willing to put his name to a good cause, and the CLPD's stated aims were at first sight fairly innocuous.

The CLPD's 'Statement' may not have appeared particularly revolutionary; its implications were. It was the manifesto of a new political force: the 'outside left', operating among the activists outside Labour's traditional centres of power who were committed to changing the party's direction by first altering its constitution. The CLPD was to be no obscure and short-lived pressure group. It succeeded in channelling a general dissatisfaction with the performance of Labour Governments into a demand for specific constitutional changes.

In October 1971 eighty-nine Labour MPs had ignored party policy and either voted in favour of Britain's entry into the Common Market or abstained. Feelings against the pro-Marketeers ran high. According to Benn, it was this vote 'against the three-line whip . . . that started the pressure for democratic change in the party'.[4] One constituency, Lincoln, sacked its MP, Dick Taverne. In 1973 Taverne resigned his seat, forced a by-election and won as an Independent by a margin of 13,000 votes over the official Labour candidate.

That autumn the CLPD held its first fringe meeting at the Labour Party conference. Eight or nine members of the Lincoln party turned up wanting to know how individual MPs could be made accountable to their local parties without the issue's turning into a media field day if they were sacked. It was the first mention of mandatory reselection, of altering the constitution of the party to ensure that all MPs, right, left and centre, had to be readopted as candidates midway through a parliamentary session. From 1974 onwards this became the CLPD's primary aim, and in 1975 its campaign received an unexpected boost. The right-wing views of Reg Prentice, Labour's education Minister, led to an attempt by his left-dominated constituency to dismiss him. Twelve Cabinet Ministers and 160 Labour MPs signed a letter in his support; Harold Wilson publicly endorsed him. Two years later he joined the Conservative Party. The CLPD exploited the issue for all it was worth. On the night of Prentice's sacking its supporters were photographed parading outside the meeting with placards reading 'Labour MPs – Must be Chosen – By Labour Party – Not by Prime Minister – Not by Fleet Street – Not by Themselves'.[5] That year the number of organizations affiliated to the CLPD jumped from six to thirty-two; its membership more than doubled; and twelve constituencies submitted resolutions to the party conference calling for mandatory reselection.[6] 'I have spent thirteen years so far trying to hold this party together,' Harold Wilson told the NEC that November, 'and I do not like what is going on.'[7]

One reason for the CLPD's success was its tactical skill. Derer, supported by his wife, devoted himself full-time to the organization. Their home in north London became its head-quarters. From the living-room of their house they sent out thousands of copies of the CLPD's *Newsletter*. Derer pion-eered the use of 'model resolutions'. Each constituency was entitled to put forward one resolution to the party con-ference; if enough were received on the same subject, it was likely to be given a full debate. The CLPD would send out a 'model' to every constituency in Britain. 'What was novel,' said Derer afterwards, 'was not circulating the resolution but circulating *massively*. We sent out to each constituency some twenty, twenty-five, thirty copies of the *Newsletter* asking the secretary to pass it on for discussion in the wards, and that's how we got on.'[8]

Until 1981 hardly anyone outside the Labour Party had heard of the CLPD. For seven or eight years it was largely ignored by the leadership and by the right. Its preoccupation with the minutiae of resolutions, amendments, references back and the other technicalities involved in changing the Labour Party's constitution effectively masked its importance. As David and Maurice Kogan put it in *The Battle for the Labour Party:*

> Their documents seem to the inattentive outsider to contain a great deal of boring material rather than a call to arms. Members of the right might have asked themselves: who wants to bother with this stuff and can it really be harmful? Yet its technical competence diverts the reader from the fact that its authors' objective is to change society by changing a party's constitution.[9]

Kinnock was hardly the sort of man to get excited by this tedious, behind-the-scenes style of politics, and from the outset his relationship with the CLPD was an equivocal one. Although he paid his subscription, he took little interest in it. 'He attended an early meeting, I think in about June 1974,' recalls Derer, 'but I wasn't there, and I certainly can't remember coming across him until a financial meeting in 1976.' He supported the vague 'Statement of Aims', but of the three issues which eventually provided the thrust of the CLPD's attempts to change the constitution he was for a long time opposed to one (reselection) and at best lukewarm about another (giving the final say over the contents of the election manifesto to the NEC). Only on one issue, that of widening the franchise for the election of the party leader, was he wholly in sympathy with the organization of which he was a founder member.

His attitude towards mandatory reselection is particularly revealing. He thought it was an unjustified attack on the rights of the PLP, an attempt to reduce MPs to the status of little more than puppets that would have a damaging effect on the party's public image. His opposition to reselection lasted for almost four years, until May 1977, by which time its acceptance was virtually inevitable. He was slowly converted after a long series of late-night arguments with Chris Mullin and others. Even after he had changed his mind, he told Mullin that it was 'only one element' of what was needed to be done in the party. He had no stomach for the aggressive way in which the outside left occasionally pushed reselection. In 1977, when Mullin wrote a provocative article in the CLPD

Newsletter mocking the attendance records of a dozen mainly ageing Labour MPs and advising party members to 'question your MP on his record in voting', Kinnock angrily came to the defence of his colleagues, telling Mullin that his article was misinformed, ill-researched and had nothing to do with socialism.

In its highly organized campaign to transform the constitution the CLPD later came to be compared with Cromwell's New Model Army. But if it represented the Roundheads of the Labour Party, Kinnock remained a Cavalier. His opposition to Labour's leadership between 1974 and 1979 was flamboyant, his style of revolt essentially traditional. It was founded on a familiar kind of emotional appeal to the sentiment of the left. The other rebellion, being masterminded at the same time from London NW11, was an altogether more calculating one, and in so far as it sought to change policy by first changing Labour's constitution, it was also more far-reaching. 'I have been coming to this conference for the last six years,' said Terry Hunt, a constituency delegate to the 1976 Labour Party Conference,

> and each year we have been passing good resolutions on everything from unemployment to the Health Service. . . . And each year those policies have been ignored by our leadership. This is bound to continue. We are wasting our time here this week, sitting through the debates, passing resolutions, because our MPs are not accountable to us. . . . *we do not want again this year to waste our time debating policy matters*. [Author's emphasis][10]

For the CLPD changing the constitution had a higher priority than debating the issues. It was a view of the Labour Party which Kinnock never shared, and although the divisions between him and the outside left did not emerge fully for another five or six years, the ambivalence was there from the start.

Kinnock's first brush with the new Labour Government, within months of its election, illustrates the point. The issue was one of his favourite causes, Britain's policy towards South Africa. Royal Navy warships had visited the port of

83

Simonstown in the autumn of 1974, and Kinnock had criticized the decision to send the ships during a clash with James Callaghan, the Foreign Secretary, on the floor of the Commons.[11] A few weeks later, in November, he was on the attack again at the Labour Party conference.

By then an extra dimension had been added to the affair. Tony Benn, Judith Hart and Joan Lestor, three members of the Government who were also members of the NEC, had voted for an NEC resolution condemning the visit. Harold Wilson, always quick to smell rebellion and increasingly worried about the conflict between party and Government, had reacted sharply, sending each of the three a personal minute warning them that their NEC vote was

> clearly inconsistent with the principle of collective responsibility. . . . I must ask you to send me in reply to this minute an unqualified assurance that you accept the principle of collective responsibility, and that you will from now on comply with its requirements. . . . I must warn you that I should have to regard your failure to give me such an assurance, or any subsequent breach of it, as a decision on your part that you did not wish to continue as a member of this administration.

'I doubt,' wrote Wilson afterwards, 'if so strong and unequivocal a minute as this has been issued before – certainly not since.'[12] Wilson considered the initial replies he received 'unsatisfactory and equivocal'. Eventually, rather than resign, the three were forced to meet his terms in full.

It was against this background, on 28 November, that William Curtin of the Liverpool Toxteth Constituency Labour Party moved an emergency resolution at the Labour conference supporting the three censured NEC members. It was an early indication of the way in which opinion was moving in the Labour Party. Mr Curtin asked questions which many others were to take up in the coming years:

> if a Labour Government continues year after year to disregard the wishes of the overwhelming majority of the people of the Party, then what the hell are we doing in the party? Why should we flog ourselves to death working for it? Why should we go out night after night canvassing? Why should we go raising money to work out policies which, when we come to power are completely ignored? We might just as well go and join the Young Liberals and at least have a bit of fun![13]

Kinnock, who made the last speech from the floor, bluntly welcomed the motion as an opportunity 'to look at three ministers . . . to look at what they did and the reasons why they did it, and as a movement to say: "We find no fault with these people." ' It was a remark which drew loud applause. Kinnock, as a member of the CLPD might then have been expected to concentrate on the constitutional aspect of the affair; but, on the contrary, he went out of his way to sidestep it:

> I am sure that neither the people from Toxteth nor Ray Buckton from ASLEF . . . nor anybody in this hall wants to see the great effort being made by the organized labour movement in this country to strike blows against Vorster's regime dissipated in an argument about constitutional technicalities. So the main issue and the main purpose that must still stay before us is not the relationship between the National Executive and the Government, or the Party and the National Executive, but this question of how most effectively do we make our contribution to the worldwide struggle against this legalized racialism which is the South African state?

Having thus neatly dismissed what 'the people from Toxteth' clearly *did* regard as the central purpose of their motion, Kinnock then turned to what *he* saw as the main point of the matter and proceeded to make a rousing attack on those who attacked Labour's policy as being 'unrealistic':

> I say to those people: what is so realistic about an investment-hungry Britain seeing its capital drained off continually to South Africa and anywhere else in the world where the state will put jackboots at the disposal of capitalists in order to safeguard their investments?[14]

Kinnock's speech, highly regarded by Michael Foot and by others, demonstrated that nine months into the life of the Government he was determined to pursue an independent line. It also showed how much less a priority, for Kinnock, was the issue of the Labour Party's constitution.

Chapter Eight

LIFE AND SOUL OF THE PARTY

Kinnock never had much affection for the Royal Family. In 1953, when he was eleven, he was taken to a neighbour's house to watch the Coronation on television. 'It gave me my first really long look at television,' he said later, 'my first unlimited dose of sweets and my first glimpse of a pineapple. And that, for me, was the Coronation. I was sick. It is a feeling which has stayed with me ever since.'[1] (This was one issue on which he would have disagreed with his grandfather. Archie was a staunch working-class royalist. 'If the monarch ever goes,' one of his sons remembers him frequently remarking, 'so does the Empire.') Later, as an MP, after Prince Philip had made one of his controversial pronouncements on the state of Britain, Kinnock attacked him as a 'professional prophet of doom' and added: 'All that is doomed is the system of purchased privilege that he has enjoyed all his life.'[2]

In February 1975 the Wilson Government proposed to increase the allowances paid to the Queen and other members of the Royal Family in the Civil List. Kinnock was angered at such behaviour from a supposedly socialist Government, and less than two months after his attack on the leadership over South Africa he rebelled again, this time on the floor of the House of Commons. Kinnock called the Queen's various relatives 'senior executives in what I may call "The Crown Limited" ' and claimed that they were 'outrageously overpaid', citing in particular the £22,000 given to

Princess Alice of Gloucester and the £65,000 paid to the Duke of Edinburgh.

> We are now considering paying an extra award to the richest woman in Britain, one of the richest women in the world. . . . I seriously consider it is time we undertook a job inspection of Her Majesty as an employer.

Kinnock's conclusion provides an insight not only into his opposition to the Government but also into that faculty which makes his repartee so swift – and so potentially self-destructive:

> My right hon. Friend the Prime Minister drew attention in his statement on 12th February to the fact that the Queen was disposed to make a £150,000 contribution towards the expenses of the Civil List in 1975. *The thought that sprang immediately to my mind and to my lips* was 'What a magnificent example to us all'. . . . I cannot accept that Her Majesty's contribution is a source of virtue or that it is particularly praiseworthy. And in the circumstances of our nation at this moment, with the social and economic problems we face, we can do nothing other than make our protest and make our opinions felt by voting against the order tonight. [Author's emphasis][3]

Kinnock was one of ninety Labour MPs who went into the Opposition lobby in a vain attempt to deny the Queen her increase. The following week, he resigned as Foot's PPS.

The 'social and economic problems' which Kinnock cited as his reasons for voting against the Civil List were rapidly worsening. In 1974 Britain's gross domestic product was shrinking; the country had a balance-of-payments deficit of almost £4,000 million; and unemployment was already on the way up. The worst problem of all was inflation: 17 per cent in the last quarter of 1974, 19.9 per cent in January 1975, 21.7 per cent in April, 22.3 per cent in July. Professor Anthony King has written:

> From the vantage point of the early 1980s it takes an effort of will to recall the atmosphere in Britain towards the end of 1974 and in the early months of 1975. The British had never known before what it felt like to be, say, a German during the Ruhr occupation and the great inflation of the 1920s. They began to feel the ground shift, ever so slightly, under their feet, and they behaved irrationally, as people often do when they are afraid.[4]

The inflation rate soon had a disastrous effect on the foreign exchanges.

On the morning of Monday, 30 June 1975, Harold Wilson was opening the Royal Agricultural Show at Stoneleigh, eating strawberries and making a speech, as he later put it, 'on the theme of "no panic" ', when word reached him, 'from the Treasury via No. 10, that the foreign exchange markets were in turmoil'.[5] The pound had lost more than five cents against the dollar. Government Ministers discussed the crisis that afternoon and late into the night. At one o'clock in the morning the Ministers emerging from the Cabinet room were advised by the Treasury that an incomes policy had to be introduced immediately. 'Without a legal framework, indeed one backed by criminal sanctions, we were told, sterling would go.'[6] The Government shied away from so drastic a step. Instead the unions were persuaded to agree to limit wage increases to a maximum of £6 per week; the Government enforced the limit in its own capacity as an employer by threatening to cut off funds to nationalized industries that breached the policy and by restricting payment of the rate support grant to local authorities which threatened to do likewise. It was the first in a series of steadily tighter deflationary measures which Labour took over the next few years.

The morale of the left was already low. On 5 June the British people had voted in a referendum, by a majority of two to one, to stay in the EEC. Neil Kinnock had been among those active in the anti-Market campaign. Four days later Harold Wilson had moved to break up the left-wing team at the Department of Industry. Eric Heffer, the Minister of State, had already been sacked for speaking out against the EEC before the referendum. The Under-Secretary, Michael Meacher, was moved to the Department of Health and Social Security. For the Secretary of State himself, Tony Benn, long a thorn in Wilson's flesh, the Prime Minister had devised a special fate, the equivalent of exile from the Kremlin to a power station. He was told to go to the Department of Energy, and he was given a few hours to decide whether or not to take the job. 'He took it extremely hard,' said Wilson.[7] The main reason for dissolving the Industry team, recorded

Marcia Falkender, Wilson's political aide, was the 'considerable erosion of confidence in the City'.[8]

For Benn it was a traumatic experience, and in so far as it fuelled his distrust of authoritarian leadership, it was to prove a traumatic experience for the Labour Party as well. He pondered resignation. Barbara Castle has left a vivid impression of him 'sitting at his desk, a figure of tragedy, surrounded by a cortège of political advisers: Michael Meacher, Joe Ashton and other figures I could hardly make out because the curtains were drawn against the brilliant sun. The heat was stifling.'[9] Benn decided to take the Energy post, but there was no doubt in his mind that it was 'an absolutely major political reverse. . . . From the point of view of the Party and the country, it was a position of disgrace, or intended to be.'[10] What made the humiliation all the harder to bear was that Wilson had leaked his intention to move Benn well in advance – to the *Daily Telegraph* – and had ostentatiously ignored the warnings not to sack him that the stories had prompted from Ron Hayward, the party's general secretary ('Sack Benn at your peril') and Jack Jones, leader of the TGWU ('Any move of Mr Benn away from the Secretaryship of Industry, and I think I can speak for the TUC, would be a grave affront to the trade union movement').[11]

In the debate on the Government's deflationary package in the Commons on 23 July, Kinnock therefore spoke for many when he claimed:

> The radical part of the Labour Party is bruised, and the bruise extends way beyond the Tribune Group, to which I belong, to fellow members of the Parliamentary Labour Party and right out into the trade union movement. . . . I fear that the Government are well on the road to changing their personality.

The Prime Minister had warned that if the new measures were not accepted, 'the British people will be engulfed in a general economic catastrophe of incalculable proportions.'[12] Kinnock did not accept that the only cure was the traditional policy of holding down wages and public expenditure. He insisted:

> Scattered throughout the Labour movement, there are various alterna-

tive strategies to the orthodoxy which the Government once again seem to be embracing like a nervous virgin.

And he finished with this warning:

> It has been explained to us that the previous Labour Government were blown off-course. We could attribute that to inexperienced navigation, but if the present Labour Government are blown off-course it will not be inexperienced navigation but downright piracy. If that happens we will not be forgiven.[13]

However unpopular his attacks made him with Labour's front bench, Kinnock's standing among ordinary party members began to rise dramatically. There were few MPs attacking the Government as vociferously as he was. None had his flair for communication. Gradually he was building himself a base of support in the country, and 1975 proved to be a turning-point in that process. What he needed was an opportunity to make an impression on party delegates. That autumn he was given his chance.

The annual rally organized by the *Tribune* newspaper has become one of the great rituals of Labour politics. In the week of the party conference, on a Wednesday night, 2,000 left-wing delegates gather in a revivalist atmosphere to listen to the left's leading speakers of the day. It was Bevan's platform when he was in revolt against the party leadership in the 1950s. To the radical wing of the party, an invitation to address it is an important mark of distinction.

On the night of 1 October 1975 the rally was held in the Spanish Hall inside Blackpool's Winter Gardens. 'The hall was packed,' recalled Barbara Castle, 'the TV lights picking out the baroque moulding at the back of the platform, which gave the whole scene an air of dramatic intensity. The plaster Spanish villages towering on the walls above the speakers' heads added a final touch of incongruity.'[14] On the platform, along with Michael Foot and Ian Mikardo, was Neil Kinnock.

Kinnock was not billed as one of the main speakers. His task was to make the customary twenty-minute appeal for funds. Before 1975 Mikardo had traditionally made the collection appeal, but that year Mikardo had decided that he wanted to make a major speech. 'So,' recalls Kinnock, 'Dick Clements [then editor of *Tribune*] had to find somebody to speak. I'd gained a little reputation for being the life and soul of the party so he asked me to do it. I was terrified.' Three years earlier Clements and his wife Bridget had taken Neil and Glenys under their wing when the couple had first arrived in London, introducing them to people and trying to make them feel at home. Now, by inviting him to address the rally, Clements performed possibly his greatest service to Kinnock. With so many constituency and trade union activists in the audience, it was an important moment for the thirty-three-year-old MP. Such chances come rarely. Kinnock rose to the occasion superbly.

Earlier in the week Michael Foot had made a speech about the problems of the economy. Exhorting the labour movement to hold together, he had drawn upon one of his favourite quotations. 'We face an economic typhoon of unparalleled ferocity,' Foot had said. 'Joseph Conrad wrote a book called *Typhoon*, and at the end he told people how to deal with it. He said, "Always facing it, Captain McWhirr, that's the way to get through." Always facing it, that's the way we have got to solve this problem.' At the *Tribune* rally on Wednesday Kinnock took the opportunity to tease his old mentor: 'You can imagine Michael delivering that. So I did a sort of semi-mimicry of him. I repeated the line and that got a response from the audience and then I left a little pause and then said, "Of course, the bloody ship sank." It brought the house down. From then on, of course, if you know you've got 'em, then you can tell jokes, so I told a few and we got a record collection.'

Bizarre as it may seem to build a political career in part on a reputation for being 'the life and soul of the party', there is no doubt that this *Tribune* speech was a watershed in Kinnock's fortunes. Mrs Castle wrote in her diary that it was 'the funniest collection speech I have ever heard. He's a find, that boy.'[15] 'He had the whole place in uproar,' remembers

91

another member of the audience. According to Joe Ashton, a fellow Tribunite MP, 'He went a bomb. He was the star of the show. And there were 500 constituency votes sitting in that audience.' Michael Foot, with characteristic generosity, told Glenys Kinnock that it was the greatest speech he'd ever heard at a *Tribune* rally. She was, he told her, married to a future leader of the Labour Party. 'I think my retort was, "Don't be silly," ' says Glenys. The collection that night raised an unprecedented £2,000.

It was soon apparent why Mikardo had declined to do the collection. It was his turn to speak after Kinnock, and he immediately launched into a tremendous attack both on the Government and on the union leaders who were underpinning its pay policy. Halfway through his speech Jack Jones – the architect of the £6-per-week policy, who had been at a reception and had happened to hear what Mikardo was planning to say – came striding down the aisle from the back of the hall, leaped on to the stage and stood for a full minute jabbing his finger at Mikardo 'like an Old Testament prophet pronouncing his doom . . . jab following jab with inarticulate shout after inarticulate shout. . . . there was pandemonium.'[16] 'There was I,' says Kinnock, 'sitting on the platform feeling very pleased with myself, when Jack jumps up.' Kinnock thought at first he was looking for somewhere to sit. 'I thought, "Oh, here he is," so I moved an empty chair across for him to sit on. Whereupon he burst into this great tirade of accusations against Mikardo. It was just as though someone had hit you in the face with a telephone directory – wham!'

Not surprisingly, the press the next day, concentrating on the public row between Mikardo and Jones, missed the significance of Kinnock's debut, but from that night onwards he was a regular attraction at the *Tribune* rally and increasingly in demand to speak around the country. The following year, 1976, he decided to stand for the constituency section of the NEC. 'I had thought I'd leave it for a couple of years, but people said, no, might as well get your name down. So I put up.' Nearly every local party casts a block of 1,000 votes. On behalf of Bedwellty Barry Moore sent a letter to each constituency asking for support. 'We didn't want him to get a humiliating vote,' says Moore. He need not have worried. Kinnock's *Tribune* speech, along with his attacks on the Government, had clearly lodged in people's minds. That autumn he won 155,000 votes. 'A hell of a good vote,' says Kinnock. 'Much better than I'd expected.'

Meanwhile, despite the urgings of Kinnock and others, the Government drifted steadily rightwards. Its most radical piece of legislation should have been Tony Benn's Industry Bill, but Wilson's reaction on seeing an early draft of it was that it was 'a sloppy and half-baked document, polemical, indeed menacing, in tone'.[17] By the time it eventually became law, in 1975, it had been drastically watered down. 'Planning agreements' had been a central feature of Labour's election manifesto. 'Major companies,' explained Benn, 'would have to clear their corporate strategies with those they employed, [otherwise] they would not get a release of public money, via investment grants or regional employment premiums or anything else.'[18] By the time Wilson had finished with the Bill planning agreements were made voluntary rather than compulsory; as a result, in the private sector not one planning agreement was ever concluded.

The underlying problem, as so often for Labour Governments in the past, was the strength of sterling. The economic package of July 1975 produced only a temporary respite. The pound resumed its slide. From $2.20 before the summer crisis its value slumped that autumn to $2.02. In December, after a traumatic series of meetings, the Cabinet agreed to cuts in public expenditure totalling about £3,600 million: Wilson called it 'by far the most hectic and harrowing month I experienced in nearly eight years as Prime Minister'.[19] Sterling resumed its slide the following spring, falling below $2.00 for the first time in history.

On 10 March a general motion approving the proposed spending cuts was placed before Parliament. To the Government's surprise and outrage, thirty-seven left-wing Labour MPs, among them Neil Kinnock, abstained. The Government's motion was defeated by 284 votes to 256. Wilson was furious. He called the combination of Conservative votes and Labour abstentions 'one of the most unholy Parliamentary alliances' in history. It was, he said, 'arsenic and red chiffon'. When Eric Heffer insisted that the thirty-seven had abstained 'precisely because the Government had pursued Conservative policies in relation to expenditure', Wilson shot back that it was 'always an arguable question about promiscuity whether one is more open to criticism for going into the bedroom or being the lapdog outside the door'.[20]

Kinnock was unrepentant and not in the least intimidated by Wilson's anger: 'I think there are basically two kinds of people: those who give the impression they can be warned off and the ones who give the impression they can't. . . . In the second case the whips and the leadership don't waste energy on trying to persuade them because they know they would not have arrived at this position without being serious about it. . . . Nobody ever put the pressure on me.' Kinnock knew that his view of the public expenditure cuts was the one which was shared by most party members, if not by the Prime Minister and the Government. Just over a week after the revolt, on 19 March, he delivered his Parliamentary Report to his General Management Committee in Bedwellty:

> It was not the task of Labour to salvage and re-establish capitalism. The [expenditure] White Paper, was, he said, one of the most reactionary ever to be introduced by a Labour Government. [It] was too much to take. . . . He would not, and could not, stand by and see unemployment used as an economic tool. . . . The backbenchers demand loyalty to be two-way – the thirty-seven were the best friends this Labour Government had – they said you must change your policies before it is too late. He was aware that people would be critical. But the people would not forgive if he and his colleagues sat back and saw the basic treasures of the labour movement destroyed.[21]

The Bedwellty party backed his stand.

Remorselessly the slide in sterling went on. In May it hit an all-time record low of $1.76. There it stayed until the autumn.

Then, on 30 September, with Denis Healey at Heathrow preparing to fly to a Finance Ministers' meeting in Hong Kong, news came that once again the pound had fallen more than five cents in a single morning. After worried consultations with his advisers, Healey got back into his car and left the airport. He went to Blackpool, where the Labour Party conference was in session, arriving in time to speak in the afternoon's debate on sterling. 'I do not come with a Treasury view,' he began, 'I come from the battlefront.'

The reception accorded Healey, who was howled at and heckled, is dispassionately recorded in the official transcript of the debate. It gave a dramatic indication of the gulf which was opening up between the Government and the party. Healey announced the Government's intention to go to the International Monetary Fund (IMF) for credit 'not to finance more spending, public or private' but to stave off 'speculative attacks on sterling'. He dealt bluntly with the idea of import controls, the so-called 'siege economy' being advocated by the left. It was, he said,

> a siege economy of a rather odd type, a siege in which we stop the imports coming in but we demand total freedom for the exports to go out. Now I have never heard of a siege in which you keep the enemy out of the castle, but the enemy allows you to come and go as you please through its ranks. And yet that is the sort of siege economy that some of our critics are asking for [*Shouts from the floor*] . . . that would be a recipe for a world trade war and a return to the conditions of the thirties. [*Cries of dissent*]

Healey shouted over the hecklers that he intended to negotiate with the IMF a policy that would mean sticking to 'things we do not like as well as things we do like':

> It means sticking to the very painful cuts in public expenditure [*Shouts from the floor*] on which the Government has already decided. It means sticking to a pay policy which enables us, as the TUC resolved a week or two ago, to continue the attack on inflation [*Shout of 'Resign'*]. . . . That is what it means and that is what I am asking for. . . . [*Applause*][22]

The IMF imposed stringent conditions in return for its support. Labour was forced to make substantial increases in taxes and to cut public expenditure by a further £2,500 million. The left was bitter. In a debate on public expenditure the following spring Kinnock pilloried Healey and his team of Treasury Ministers:

> They treat the City of London as if it were some kind of winnable Tory marginal constituency. . . . They think, generation in and generation out, as their predecessors have done, that somehow there is some deal, some kind of understanding, that can be reached with people who are sworn ideological enemies. The sooner my right hon. and hon. Friends understand that, the sooner we shall have the policies that we need if we are to have a Labour Government that we can be proud of.[23]

The leadership continued to plead for patience, insisting that this set of cuts would be the last. 'There have been so many last ditches,' remarked Kinnock after one PLP meeting, 'that these days the Labour Party looks like a ploughed field.'

By the time of the IMF cuts the Labour Party had a new leader. Harold Wilson had resigned on 16 March 1976, a week after Kinnock and the other thirty-six rebels had abstained in the vote on public expenditure. There were six candidates for the succession: four right-wingers (James Callaghan, Roy Jenkins, Denis Healey and Anthony Crosland) and two from the left (Tony Benn and Michael Foot). Only Labour MPs were eligible to vote.

Kinnock strongly backed Foot, working as one of the leaders of his campaign team. 'We do not want a heavy,' he claimed, in a clear reference to Callaghan and Healey. 'We want a heavyweight, someone who does not confuse Fleet Street with the man in the street.'[24] When the result of the first ballot was announced, the vote for Foot surprised many; he came top of the poll:

FOOT	90
CALLAGHAN	84
JENKINS	56
BENN	37
HEALEY	30
CROSLAND	17

The flicker of hope in Foot's camp that he might possibly win was dashed by the result of the second ballot on 30 March. Crosland had been eliminated, and Jenkins and Benn had both stood down. Callaghan had picked up most of these votes and now led Foot by 141 to 133. Healey was eliminated, and in the final ballot on 5 April Callaghan won easily, by 176 to Foot's 139. Shortly after six o'clock that evening Callaghan became Prime Minister.

At the time of the leadership election it was frequently and complacently remarked that the Parliamentary Labour Party was 'the most sophisticated electorate in the world'. Kinnock, after several weeks of trailing around the House of Commons trying to work up support for Foot, was unimpressed. At the height of the campaign he wrote to *Tribune* to express the view that the franchise should be widened to embrace not only MPs but the whole of the labour movement. 'Some MPs had consulted their constituency parties,' recalls Kinnock. 'Many more wanted to be consulted. It seemed a good way of getting more participation. The idea took off fast. My view then was that there should be a special one-day conference to be called when the need arose. I hadn't thought through all the refinements.'

As a result of his experience in 1976, Kinnock can take the credit for being one of the first – several believe the first – to raise the idea of an electoral college, the constitutional change which enabled him to win the leadership seven years later.

Chapter Nine

DEVOLUTION

Politically, Kinnock regarded the new Prime Minister as at least as great a reactionary as the old one. But on a personal basis he much preferred Callaghan to Wilson, a link strengthened by the fact that one of Glenys's closest friends at university had married Callaghan's son, Michael. Callaghan, on his side, seems to have felt a certain exasperated affection for the young Welshman who had canvassed for him in the 1960s. This, coupled with Michael Foot's increased influence over appointments, and Kinnock's own standing on the left of the party, meant that in the course of the next two years Callaghan tried on several occasions to entice Kinnock into the Government. The most definite offer was of a junior ministry at Prices and Consumer Protection, to serve, ironically, under Roy Hattersley. Kinnock is reluctant to talk about the second offer. 'He was prepared to be very accommodating, I've got to tell you that.' It was probably a post at the Department of Industry. On each occasion that Callaghan telephoned, Kinnock consulted the people he has described as his 'safety belt':[1] Glenys and a couple of close friends, including Barry Moore. Glenys actually took the call on the first occasion. 'When the operator said it was Downing Street,' she recalls, 'we fell about laughing.' Her view on both occasions was that it was an attempt to shut him up. Kinnock turned the jobs down.

In addition to all the other arguments against going into the

Government there was, by 1976, a new one. Labour was bound by its manifesto of October 1974 to 'create elected assemblies in Scotland and Wales', and a fresh word entered the political vocabulary: devolution. Kinnock was passionately opposed to any growth of separatism in Wales and from 1976 onwards devoted increasing amounts of his energy to fighting the Government's proposals, both in Parliament and in the country. On economic policy Kinnock had been one of a few voices in the wilderness. On devolution he proved a force to be reckoned with.

He was strongly supported by Glenys. Dick Clements remembers early on in the devolution debate a conversation over dinner at the Kinnocks' in which he indicated vague approval of the Government's proposal. 'My God, she bit my head off,' he recalls ruefully. 'She soon put me straight.'

Although some Labour Ministers later tried to affect a deep philosophical interest in separate development and local democracy, the policy in reality lived and died as a political expedient to buy off nationalist votes, both electorally and in the House of Commons. In 1970 the Scottish National Party (SNP) had only one seat; in February 1974 it won seven; in October 1974, with over 30 per cent of the popular vote in Scotland, it won eleven and pushed the Conservative Party into third place. By the side of the SNP, the Welsh nationalist party, Plaid Cymru, was a much smaller phenomenon; nevertheless, by 1974 it had three seats in Parliament. Scotland and Wales are Labour's heartlands: without them it can never hope to form a Government. Worried about the inroads the nationalists might make into their vote, the party set out to placate them.

Kinnock had first outlined his arguments against a separate assembly for Wales in a long and detailed speech as early as February 1975. Devolution, he claimed was 'nonsense and a distraction from the main theme and from the political and economic struggle in 1975 and for many years to come'. His principal argument against the Government's policy was a Marxist one:

99

I believe that the emancipation of the class which I came to this House to represent, unapologetically, can best be achieved in a single nation and in a single economic unit, by which I mean a unit where we can have a brotherhood of all nations and have the combined strength of working-class people throughout the whole of the United Kingdom brought to bear against any bully, any executive, any foreign power and bureaucratic arrangement, be it in Brussels or in Washington, and any would-be colonizer, either an industrial colonizer or a political colonizer.

'Their misfortunes,' he declared of working people, 'are not the result of being British, Welsh or Scottish.' He was challenged by Gwynfor Evans, the leader of Plaid Cymru: if he wanted to see a more just society, did he not feel that Wales, with its 'great tradition of social justice' and its 'sense of community', would be an ideal place to start? Kinnock dealt with that notion with the bluntness which was to make him hated by the more romantic Welsh nationalists:

If the hon. Gentleman is suggesting that the Welsh people's facility or desire for or competence in social justice is any greater or smaller than any other nation, he is making an immense miscalculation of both the niceness and the nastiness of the Welsh people. I do not think that we are any more or less in love with social justice or practise it better or worse than any other nation.

He gave equally short shrift to the idea that devolution would in some way 'contribute to resolving the problems of alienation and frustration':

These problems do not derive from distance as such. If it were the case that proximity to Parliament spawned confidence and affection for Parliament, the people of Ealing, Watford and Wimbledon would feel differently about Parliament than those who live in Cardiff, Edinburgh or anywhere else, but they do not.

Kinnock accused the Government of failing to undertake any real analysis of the underlying problems of Britain's democracy. Yet, he concluded:

it is this analysis that takes place at every party ward meeting, at every Saturday morning 'surgery', on every occasion when we bump into someone in a pub, in a club, on the street or in a shop. He looks up and says 'Politicians!' – I hope I shall be excused for saying this – 'They are all the bloody same.'

This is the crisis that we have to resolve. It will not be resolved with or without legislative powers, with or without executive powers, with or without the single transferable vote, with or without new Parliaments, with or without changes of address, merely by the introduction of a constitutional Bill. It requires a different will and a different attitude to government, and not merely a change of address for Parliament.[2]

The speech is worth quoting at some length not only because, by the time Kinnock sat down after twenty minutes on his feet, he had outlined practically all of the main arguments he was to deploy over the coming years but also because devolution, arcane though it seems now, was an important issue in Wales at that time, and in opposing it Kinnock showed considerable political courage. His campaign against devolution is powerful evidence against those who accuse Kinnock of careerism and opportunism.

Kinnock opposed devolution because he believed it would lead inevitably to the separation of Wales from the rest of Britain. He had an intense dislike of Plaid Cymru which, some of his friends believe, had its origins in the 1960s, when he ran across a particularly strong contingent at Cardiff University. Certainly they grew to loathe him as he mercilessly caricatured them as mournful Druid fanatics bent on inflicting their obsessions on the average Welsh citizen. He cited the Welsh television channel as an example:

Ninety-nine per cent of my constituents have no command of the mother tongue like my wife and cannot even rub along like me. They fume with mid-Atlantic cultural resentment. And even those like my family in other parts of Wales who speak *yr iaith* as their first language think that the Friday Western had the drop on the fascinating story of Roman gold mining in Dyfed as told in Welsh. . . .[3]

'He was rough on anyone from Plaid Cymru who interrupted his speeches,' says Alan Fox. 'He would put them down very crudely.' Gwynfor Evans once accused him of being anti-Welsh. Kinnock lost his temper and told the Commons that he would 'like to issue a warning to the hon. Gentleman which I would be glad to deliver personally if he were here in his usual sedentary position. If he says any such thing outside this House again, I will sue him to the point of bankruptcy.' If he repeated his accusation within Parliament, Kinnock threatened to 'ensure that he receives . . . ignominy'.[4] One gets the impression that in an earlier age Kinnock would happily have challenged Evans to a duel, and occasionally the mutual antagonism between the two sides did come close to physical violence. One night, when Kinnock was at home in his cottage in Pontllanfraith, there was a loud hammering on the door. Outside were five Nationalist supporters who had reeled over to find him following a local wedding reception. After a heated argument on the doorstep, one of them produced a gun. Kinnock hastily slammed the door and called the police. On another occasion the door was kicked in.

It was not only the Welsh nationalists whom he angered. Fighting devolution also put Kinnock in opposition to many of his old political friends and allies. The man responsible for piloting the devolution legislation through Parliament was the new Lord President of the Council and Leader of the House of Commons, Michael Foot. 'It was a major difference between us,' says Foot. However, 'It didn't injure our friendship at all. I respected the way he put his case – I couldn't have failed to be impressed. From the point of view of his ambition, it would have been far easier for him to have kept quiet, especially as the Transport and General – his own union – was a strong supporter of devolution. . . . He upset some of his natural allies in Wales and elsewhere.' At one point, George Wright, General Secretary of the Wales TGWU, put Kinnock's union sponsorship in question for his failure to follow the party line. In Foot's constituency of Ebbw Vale Kinnock's name became a dirty word. 'It was partly the issue of devolution,' Foot says, 'partly because they were loyal to me.' Foot tried his best to protect him. 'He's all right,' he used to say when Kinnock came under attack, 'leave the boy alone.'

One rift particularly distressed Kinnock. Bill Harry, the miner in Tredegar whom Kinnock has acknowledged as the greatest political influence upon him after his parents, was incensed by his friend's stand on devolution: 'He not only betrayed Michael,' says Harry, 'he betrayed the party. He allied himself with groups like the Tories, the Welsh landowners, the National Front. I was shocked once to actually see him on a platform with a Tory MP opposing his comrades.' Not a man to hide his feelings, Harry told Kinnock what he thought of his action. He even heckled him at meetings. It was a rift which upset Kinnock, for their relationship up to then had been a close one. Harry had been approached to be a possible candidate for the Bedwellty seat in 1969 but had refused because he wanted to see Kinnock win it. On his side, Kinnock saw Harry as a link with his past in Tredegar, as the kind of socialist Michael Foot had in mind when he wrote of Ebbw Vale, 'against this rock all the prissy values preached by the BBC, all the tinsel tuppenny-half-penny ideas filtered through television, all the snobbery and smug complacency associated with a Tory-directed affluent society beat in vain.'[5] Shaken, Kinnock tried to use Alan Fox, a mutual friend and Labour councillor in Tredegar, as a mediator. 'When he fell out with Bill,' recalls Fox, 'he got in touch with me several times by letter, by telephone and in conversation, asking me how the rift could be healed. . . . When he opposed devolution he did it at the expense of a number of personal friendships in Tredegar which were dear to him.' 'Bill was very conscious of the decentralized democracy argument,' says Kinnock, 'and if that's all the devolution proposals had meant, I could have supported them without any difficulty at all. But I thought that they had different implications and that the financial relationship between Wales and Westminster would have been disastrous for Wales, absolutely disastrous. He saw it as evidence of severe divergence from the party's policy and got worked up about it, then personalized it. . . . It became extremely bitter.'

Undaunted, in the autumn of 1976 Kinnock took on Foot at the Labour Party conference, accusing the promoters of devolution of 'indecent haste', 'illogicality' and 'appeasement': 'It seems to be the case, as the great Welsh poet Shakespeare said, that some like Michael Foot are born devolutionists; some like the rest of Her Majesty's Government by various means achieve devolution; for the rest of us –

for 85 per cent of the people of this country – devolution will be thrust upon us.' No one, he claimed, 'not even the most radical devo-fanatic,' could claim that devolution was especially popular: 'we have not had a riot in Ebbw Vale for lack of any direct elections to the Wales Tourist Board.'[6]

Six weeks later Kinnock tabled a resolution in the Commons calling for a referendum on the subject. It attracted seventy-six signatures. Kinnock claimed that opponents of the Bill could muster forty Labour backbenchers to vote against it unless a referendum were granted. 'We are saying to the Government that there is no chance of getting this Bill through unless there is a referendum at the proper time.'[7] The following month the Government agreed to the demand.

The fighting dragged on for more than two years. A guillotine motion to speed up progress was defeated. A clause was written in stating that the Act would not come into force unless the proposals were accepted by at least 40 per cent of the eligible electorate. Kinnock was so confident that his judgement would be vindicated and that the Welsh people would reject devolution that he opposed a Conservative attempt to delete Wales from the Bill altogether: 'if we take Wales out of the Bill, [devolution] will remain alive and twitching; if we defeat it in a referendum, we shall kill it and long may it lie dead.'[8]

He opposed devolution in the press ('questions of autonomy, independence, home rule, devolution [are] distractions from the main course of necessary change'),[9] on television ('at best irrelevant, and at worst pure expedient cowardice')[10] and in the form of his own 15,000-word pamphlet, *Facts to Beat Fantasies: The Detailed Reasons for Voting NO in the March 1st Referendum and Answers to the Claims of the Yesmen and Guessmen*. 'He stated his views with great persistence and skill,' admits Foot. 'He was the most powerful opponent we had in Wales.'

Kinnock appears to have made only one serious mistake. On 2 March 1978 he alleged in the Commons that English-speaking children aged between five and six at an infant school in Gwynedd, in North Wales, had to ask to go to the lavatory in Welsh 'or suffer the consequences'. He refused to name the school in case the children were 'further victimized'. The story was extensively reported in the national press and subsequently picked up by local papers. A Welsh Nationalist MP called it 'hysterical nonsense'. Kinnock replied that 'the fact remains that in the name of nationalistic zeal there are people, members of [Plaid Cymru] and others, who are making this kind of warfare against children': it was one of 'the characteristics of nationalism'.[11]

Kinnock got this curious story from his sister-in-law, Barbara Parry, an English girl who was married to Glenys's brother. It was an embarrassing situation, an example of Kinnock's quickness of tongue outstripping his caution. Five weeks later he tried to substantiate his accusation by forwarding to the Gwynedd County Council eighteen letters of complaint from parents with children at local schools. The Gwynedd authorities reacted by ordering three senior officials to conduct an inquiry. On 6 July their report exonerated Gwynedd of the charges. All eighteen letters 'bore dates later than [the] allegations in the House', claimed the report. Only four letters had specifically supported Kinnock's story about children being prevented from going to the lavatory, and of these 'two were withdrawn, a third parent declined to give further particulars and asked that the matter be dropped and the fourth complaint was denied by teachers to the satisfaction of the investigators.' The report concluded that it was 'most unlikely that there is any teacher in the county who, in Mr Kinnock's words, "undertakes warfare against children who are not capable of defending themselves". As a result of his remarks the County Council, the teaching profession in Gwynedd and indeed Wales have been grossly libelled in the Press.'[12] One of the letters turned out to have been written by his sister-in-law.

Any embarrassment the incident may have caused to Kinnock or to his campaign was certainly not reflected a few months later, on 1 March 1979, when the people of Scotland

and Wales went to the polls to vote in the referendum. In Scotland there was a tiny majority (51.6 per cent) in favour of devolution among those who voted – far short of the 40 per cent of the electoral roll needed to give Scotland an assembly. In Wales the Government suffered a crushing humiliation. Scarcely one eligible voter in ten voted in favour of devolution. Kinnock's own county of Gwent was the most hostile region: 88 per cent of those who voted rejected the proposal. Among the adult population as a whole, only one person in twenty supported the assembly. According to Anthony King:

> The damage done by the referenda to the Callaghan Government's prestige and self-esteem was enormous. Ministers had devoted the better part of two parliamentary sessions to the two devolution schemes. Now one of them, the Scottish, had received only the most tepid response, while the other, the Welsh, had been rejected with contumely. Even if many in the Government were not wildly enthusiastic about devolution, they had hoped for better results than these.[13]

It was a particularly hard blow for Michael Foot. 'On that issue, Neil was right and I was wrong. The referendum vindicated his point of view.'

Before the devolution battle Dick Clements believes that Foot, although fond of Kinnock, 'tended to patronize him a little'. The skill of Kinnock's campaign and the outcome of the referenda put a stop to that. The result had shown that Kinnock was more than just a good talker. He had judgement, a feel for what people wanted. He was right to say that devolution was a 'distraction': two months after the referenda the Scottish and Welsh Nationalists lost all but four of their seats. In the late-night sessions, ploughing through clause after clause of the Bill in Committee, he at last began to prove his capacity for the grind of politics.

He also demonstrated what Foot calls 'the supreme political virtue: courage'. Attacking Healey for public expenditure cuts was like shooting ducks in a barrel: Kinnock, after all, has yet to experience what it must be like to be told at midnight that the Treasury cannot guarantee to hold the currency the following day. Devolution was a different matter. 'It was like civil war,' says Glenys. 'Whatever has happened to Neil since and whatever may happen in the future, we have been prepared for it by that campaign.' Kinnock was on the receiving end of some dirty tricks. He had to endure threats to his life and property. Rumours were spread that he owned a farm, a mansion, a swimming pool, that his children went to public school. He upset many of his former supporters, and in some areas he has never been forgiven. 'If we had an elected assembly now,' argues Bill Harry, 'it would be Labour-controlled. It could have been a focal point for opposition to the Tories. As it is, Wales doesn't have a single voice to speak up for it.' The row between the two men over devolution was still smouldering even in the summer of 1983, when Kinnock was running for the leadership. Harry wrote Kinnock a hostile letter to which Kinnock replied: 'I can only insist to you that my opposition to the devolution proposals was conscientious and reasoned and pursued in what I thought – and still think – were the best interests of the Welsh people.'[14] Ebbw Vale was the first constituency party to which Kinnock belonged. Even so, because of the resentment caused by the devolution issue, he was not invited back to speak at the party's annual dinner until he had been elected leader.

Chapter Ten

THE PARTY MAN

By 1977 Kinnock was becoming one of the favourites of the Labour Party Conference. That year at Brighton he helped to organize, and starred in, a revue called *The End of the Peers Show*. The *Guardian* later reported that he 'brought the house down' with his rendition of 'Ole Man River', retitled 'Ole Man Callaghan': 'He must know somethin',' sang Kinnock, 'But he don't do nothin'. . . .' According to the *Guardian*, 'the Brighton Pavilion shook.'[1] That same year Kinnock stood for election to the NEC for a second time. 'My CLP [Constituency Labour Party] has nominated me for the NEC,' he wrote to a friend. 'Obviously I can't get elected for some time yet, but I would be obliged if you could persuade your conference delegate to vote for me. Naturally if your delegate and/or the party has any questions, I'll gladly give answers.'

On the day that the votes for the NEC were actually being cast, Kinnock spoke in the conference's main economic debate. The hall was packed with delegates, and the occasion gave Kinnock a perfect opportunity to demonstrate his continuing opposition to the Government's deflationary policies. He called for an expansion of public expenditure by £3,000 million, and he told Healey:

> There was an imperial emperor, you know, Denis, called Nero and he thought that if he presided and fiddled, then something would develop eventually in a new Rome. It is not going to happen like that. . . . we are

not asking you to let it rip, we just want you to tear it a bit for production, tear it a bit to fight unemployment, tear it a bit to win the next election and do it now.[2]

The following day, Kinnock's vote showed a dramatic increase, to 244,000. He was becoming a national figure. Shortly afterwards he was picked as one of Britain's 'young politicians to watch' in the *Sunday Times Magazine*. 'He's the left-winger every right-winger loves,' a colleague was quoted as saying. 'What next?' asked the caption beneath Kinnock's picture, and promptly answered its own question: 'A place on Labour's National Executive Committee. He's getting closer every year. . . .'[3]

As Kinnock's standing in the party grew, so his interest in the House of Commons lessened. He had outgrown the role of backbencher and was increasingly frustrated. This impatience with Parliament had first surfaced publicly in July 1975. 'All the pejorative descriptions of this place,' he told MPs, 'as a talking shop housed in a sausage machine are gaining justification.'

I go so far as to say – and I hope that my wife does not read Hansard tomorrow – that I would be prepared even to accept the present situation of our pay if someone could give me a guarantee that next week, the week after and the month after that I would not have to put up with the frustration and embarrassment of knowing that I cannot do my job properly because of the distractions of the way in which we try to work.

The list of grievances was a long one: the paucity of debates, the triviality of Question Time, the unread avalanches of paper produced by committees, the 'insane hours' which MPs were forced to work, the 'ludicrously inadequate facilities' . . . above all, perhaps, for Kinnock, the frustration of being a powerless Labour Member, constantly expected to support an administration with only the barest majority. 'What is required from backbenchers on the Government side,' he complained, 'is their vote and certainly not their voice.'[4]

The familiar litany, delivered during a debate on a guillotine motion to curtail discussion of an energy Bill, evoked a warm response. To Iain Sproat, a Conservative MP, it was a 'brilliant speech'; Jo Grimond for the Liberals found it 'most enjoyable'; Roger Stott, a Labour Member, called it a 'brilliant speech about the shortcomings of our parliamentary system' and suggested that every MP should read it.

Kinnock's outburst was born of more than just the frustration of the moment and had greater significance than was realized at the time, for it marked the point at which he gradually began to divert his energies away from Parliament. In his first year as an MP Kinnock had voted in nine out of every ten divisions; in the 1975–6 session he voted in six out of ten; in 1977–8, five out of ten.[5] The days he used to spend in the House he now increasingly spent away, speaking around the country to local Labour parties, trade unions and university societies. It was the start of a trend which would give Kinnock, by 1982, one of the worst attendance records in Parliament, voting that year in less than a quarter of the total number of divisions.

As the time which he devoted to Parliament dwindled, so his criticisms of the institution increased. 'Much of its time,' he wrote in 1977, 'is wasted.'

> The procedures and traditions of today's British Parliament were forged to supervise an Empire, referee Victorian capitalism, ameliorate the more embarrassing consequences of exploitation and provide a leather-bound supporters' club for Party leadership. . . . The advance of popular democracy, civil rights and accountability came in spite of all that, either through maverick radicalism or Establishment skin-saving.[6]

Occasionally he appeared to advocate what a few years later he would be associated in condemning as 'extra-parliamentary activity':

> We are at the dawn of the age when the power of democracy is moving out of its single base of the ballot box periodically on to the shopfloor. Opposition Members will throw up their hands in disgust and horror at that, in the same way as people of their convictions did when the vote first came to working men and women.[7]

Kinnock's falling rate of attendance did not reflect a decline in political activity. On the contrary, he was busier now than he had ever been. He was simply transferring his energy to a more appreciative audience – the party in the country, where his opposition to Wilson and Callaghan was turning him into the darling of the left. 'I've always considered that speaking around the country is an important part of being a Labour MP,' says Kinnock. 'You're a full-time, paid political activist.' To begin with his visits were 'entirely in Wales', but as his reputation grew he ventured 'further afield'.

He was becoming one of the left's most well-known figures. Apart from travelling and meeting party members in person, Kinnock was now reaching a mass audience through his frequent appearances on television. He took to the medium from the moment he first encountered it, and the medium took to him in return. Kinnock looks good on television – open and straightforward. Other politicians are told the tricks and try to learn them: hold still, speak simply and clearly, smile as often as possible, try to create an impression of intimacy with the viewer at home. Kinnock does it all naturally.

He had been interviewed on film a couple of times when he was president of the students' union at Cardiff, but his first major experience of television came in 1968. Harlech TV ran a regional programme, *Free House,* set in a pub called the Bridge. The idea was that the cameras would eavesdrop on a typical locals' conversation about current events. Kinnock, only twenty-six years old, was the programme's most loquacious participant. Wherever the cameras went, he followed; whenever there was a lull in the conversation, he was there to fill it. It was good experience, and when he arrived at Westminster in the early 1970s he was quickly discovered by the national networks. There were few who could match Kinnock's fluency in putting over the left's case against the Government on issues like devolution and public expenditure. With Tony Benn silently imprisoned in the Energy Department by collective responsibility, Kinnock began to emerge on television as the leading advocate of socialist alternatives to the policies of Wilson and Callaghan.

Rebel

'One thing I was lucky with,' recalls Kinnock, 'was a Robin Day programme called *Newsday*. It used to go out on BBC2 early in the evening and was watched by six old ladies and a dog, but it was sharp and you had to do it well. I remember doing a show with Dickson Mabon and seeing it played back on VT [videotape]. It was about the first time I'd seen myself and I remember thinking: yes, I can do this.' Kinnock became one of the programme's most frequent contributors.

Some sections of Labour's left regard people who work in television as devils incarnate. Kinnock gets on well with them, as he gets on with most journalists. In 1975 the BBC's *Tonight* programme hired him to contribute two film reports on that year's Conservative Party conference. Granada Television commissioned him to do the same on the Labour conference. Kinnock enjoyed the experience hugely. By 1976 he was appearing on television almost every week. It was unheard of for him to turn down an invitation. Kinnock was the man who could be rung up at midnight or pulled in at the last moment to talk in witty thirty-second bursts on any subject from Chartism to new technology and all points in between. The scale of his exposure on television helped him enormously in building up support in the country, and in 1978 he achieved a decisive breakthrough.

The results of the NEC elections are traditionally read out at the Labour Party conference on a Tuesday morning. In 1978 Kinnock, along with Glenys, Barry Moore and some journalist friends, was drinking in a bar in the Winter Gardens. The results were about to be announced. Gwyn Evans and Glenys went off to try to discover what had happened. 'I saw the results come through on one of the television screens just outside the hall,' recalls Evans, 'and I ran back to the bar – I got there before Glenys – and I shouted at him, "You're in," and he leapt to his feet and shouted, "Never," and everyone started clapping.'

Kinnock had not merely been elected: out of thirty-four candidates in the constituency section he had come fourth with 274,000 votes. He had moved ahead of Barbara Castle

112

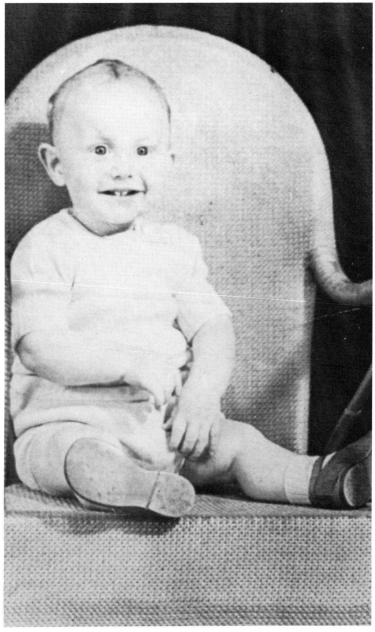

1 Neil Kinnock, born on 28 March 1942 – at ease in front of a camera, even as a baby. (Kinnock family)

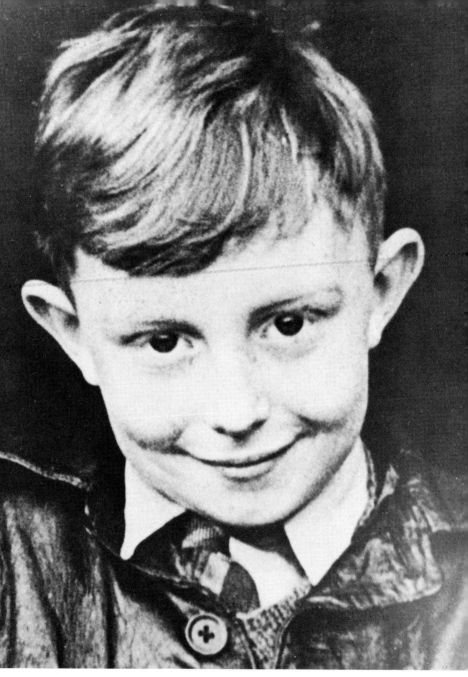

2 Aged eight. A 'happy boy' who wanted to be a private detective.
(Kinnock family)

3 *and* 4 Kinnock's parents had both known great hardship as children. They were determined to give Neil, their only child, a better start in life, and the family had regular outings to the country and the seaside. (Kinnock family)

5 In fancy dress, as a pirate. (Kinnock family)

6 Kinnock hated school. He tried to persuade his parents to let him leave early to join the army or the police. His one passion was sport. (Kinnock family)

7 The student politician: Kinnock at Cardiff University in the early 1960s. (Kinnock family)

8 In 1965 Kinnock was elected president of the students'
union, with the enthusiastic support of his girlfriend,
Glenys Parry. (Kinnock family)
9 (*opposite*) Easter 1967. Neil Kinnock and Glenys were
married in Chapel. (Kinnock family)

10 Kinnock's first experience of television was in 1968 as a 'regular' in *Free House*, a Harlech TV discussion programme, set in a pub. (Kinnock family)

and Joan Lestor, two existing members of the NEC, and knocked Ian Mikardo off the Executive altogether. Dennis Skinner had been elected at the same time, but with a considerably smaller vote than Kinnock's.

That lunchtime an eclectic group, including Ian Aitken and Julia Langdon of the *Guardian*, Jimmy Reid and Margaret Jackson, the Labour MP for Lincoln, together with Glenys and various Welsh friends, went off with Kinnock to Yates's Wine Lodge to drink draught champagne in celebration. A group of day-trippers lined up to shake him by one hand while he raised his glass with the other. 'My cup runneth over,' he joked. It was his political coming of age, the result of a combination of energy, charm and a reputation for rebellion. 'There are two interesting newcomers to Labour's National Executive Committee,' wrote the *Yorkshire Post,* a Conservative newspaper, the following day.

> Mr Dennis Skinner is a left-wing fanatic who looks and sounds like a left-wing fanatic: that makes him only half as dangerous as Mr Neil Kinnock, a left-wing fanatic who looks and sounds like a reasonable man. Mr Kinnock is a personable young MP with a knack for buttering up naive people in the news media ('Nice chap, Neil,' they say). He peddles left-wing rubbish with considerable charm in mellifluous Welsh tones.[8]

There was no doubting his popularity in the party. An hour after being toasted by his friends with champagne, he was called to speak in a conference debate on the election of the party leader. The moment his name was announced he was applauded. 'Comrades,' began Kinnock, 'first of all, thanks very much for one thing and another.' He turned to Mikardo on the platform. 'And thanks, too, to Mik – not just for this resolution, but for years and years of everything that has gone before.' This tribute to the man he had just replaced also produced applause.

Kinnock that afternoon was in high spirits. Reaffirming the ideas he had advanced in his *Tribune* letter of two years before, he urged a widening of the franchise for the election of leader. He professed surprise that the issue should even need debating after the experience of the 1976 leadership

113

election. Could anyone seriously argue that the PLP was somehow 'an elite and well-informed group' especially qualified to choose the leader? 'Let me tell you,' said Kinnock, 'as a campaign manager in the course of the last leadership elections . . . that that is not the case.'

> Without great disservice to my colleagues in Parliament, the fact of the matter is that part of the exercise was exactly equivalent to knocking up council estates at ten past nine on a wet and rainy winter evening. There appeared to be a comparable lack of knowledge of the exact issues at stake in the Parliamentary Labour Party as there is in that deserted and windswept electoral situation. The fact is that in the Labour Party there are only two areas of election in which the candidates produce no manifesto, give no undertakings, have no specific constituency and no direct accountability or responsibility. The two areas are leader of the Party and members of the National Executive Committee.

To the delight of the delegates, he then took what was to become a famous swing at the widely disliked figure of Roy Jenkins:

> in the course of that leadership election we were forced to certain electoral expedients. Nothing dirty, you understand, but there was among the candidates, for instance, one Roy Jenkins – Taffy as we used to call him. [*Laughter*] And there is a story told . . . about an elderly Yorkshire Member who was sitting in the tearoom, and was approached by one of Roy's acolytes – sorry, I mean supporters – and asked: 'Will you be voting for Roy Jenkins?' And the Yorkshire Member said: 'No, lad, we're all Labour here.' [*Laughter*] [*Applause*]

Kinnock ended by calling on the conference to ensure that in the future the constituency parties ('those who are disenfranchised, although they do the job') and the unions ('those that provide the money') had a say in the leadership election: 'it is a major, giant step towards democracy from what we have now.'[9] Nevertheless, despite the warmth of Kinnock's reception, the conference decided by a majority of four to one to leave the power to elect the leader solely in the hands of MPs, one of the last victories the right was to enjoy for a long while.

Chapter Eleven
THE WINTER OF DISCONTENT

The autumn that saw Neil Kinnock's election to the NEC also saw the start of the destruction of the Labour Government. Most people had expected an election in October 1978. The Prime Minister had done nothing to discourage speculation; indeed, he had fuelled it. According to Dick Leonard of the *Economist*, 'Tom McNally, the Prime Minister's political adviser, at a lunch in Rye in early August, specifically told Terry Lancaster, the political editor of the pro-Labour *Daily Mirror*, that the election would be in October. There is good reason to believe that McNally was personally authorized by Callaghan to do this.'[1] The date the Prime Minister had chosen, McNally assured Lancaster, was 5 October. This 'authoritative leak' quickly found its way on to the front page of every Fleet Street paper. On Friday, 1 September, Callaghan held a dinner at his Sussex farm for leading trade union leaders to discuss the forthcoming campaign, and the following Monday, 4 September, David Basnett opened the Trades Union Congress in Brighton with a rousing call to arms. It was a considerable shock to many, therefore, when in a ministerial broadcast three days later Callaghan announced that there would not be an election after all. To some this was 'Jim's little joke'. To many in the Labour movement it looked like a wilful demonstration of prime ministerial power, especially as Callaghan had broken with tradition and had consulted hardly any of his colleagues. It was an episode which was not forgotten the following May.

Callaghan's hubris was followed by an appropriate period of tragedy for the Government. In September, when there was a semblance of unity in the party, Labour had been virtually level with the Conservatives in the opinion polls. Then, at its annual conference in October, following the Government's announced intention of holding wage increases to 5 per cent in the following year, the party split. 'Let us make no bones about it,' said one delegate. 'If the Government persist in attempting to impose the 5 per cent limit, they will be committing political suicide. The 5 per cent limit will undermine their support amongst the working classes. You can only stretch an elastic band so far. Inevitably, it has to snap.'[2] The party voted by 4 million votes to 1.9 million to reject 'any wage restraint by whatever method'.

In November the Ford Motor Company agreed to pay its workers wage increases averaging 17 per cent. When the Government proposed to retaliate by applying sanctions against Ford, it was defeated in Parliament by an alliance of Conservatives, Liberals, Nationalists and Ulster Unionists. Two days later, on 15 December, Neil Kinnock told his GMC in Bedwellty that, in his view, 'we should have had an October election. Every four to six weeks we could expect to be beaten and confidence votes will depend on fringe parties. [Kinnock] stated that we have office but not power. . . . It was inevitable that the [policy] would break down because the 5 per cent norm was rejected both by the Labour Party and the TUC.'

Over the next few weeks Kinnock's predictions came true – with disastrous results for Labour. Strikes hit the National Health Service and operations had to be postponed. Tanker drivers stopped deliveries, causing petrol shortages. An unofficial strike by water and sewage workers led to the cutting off of water supplies in the north-west. Garbage piled up in the streets as the result of a stoppage by local authority workers; newspapers carried pictures of rats amid the rubbish in Piccadilly Circus. Even some gravediggers downed tools, leaving the dead unburied; pickets turned away funeral cortèges from cemetery gates. The impact of these scenes, especially on television, had a profound impact on public opinion: *Nationwide* began its programme each evening with a news round-up it called 'Britain in Crisis'. Opinion polls showed Labour trailing the Conservatives by 18 or 19 per cent. 'Militancy was seldom politically inspired,' wrote Anthony King. 'It was often a direct response to falling living standards and a deep sense that the Government's successive incomes policies had been unfair in their results.'[3] At the beginning of January Callaghan made a forlorn attempt to emulate Stanley Baldwin, a predecessor whom he increasingly resembled. He flew back from the sunshine of the Guadeloupe summit conference in the Caribbean and gave a press conference at the airport, of which the underlying theme was (as one newspaper headline put it) 'Crisis? What crisis?'

On 26 January 1979 Kinnock outlined the political situation to his local party 'with some dismay and concern':

> if we had an election now we faced slaughter and there was no assurance that the present problems would end in the near future. . . . Such is the position now that we have a Government totally operating Tory policies. We have the Prime Minister advocating [that] people cross picket lines. Neil Kinnock reminded delegates that the only reason we've come so far, that children stay in school after [the age of] 9, is because we've had picket lines. . . . An attempt at coalition is not impossible; certain Cabinet Ministers are already canvassing the idea. . . . He gave a clear commitment that if any coalition attempt were made, he would not support it. . . . Today's situation is the product of an opportunity lost . . . the Party must remind the leadership of where we come from or we die as a movement.[4]

Ten days later, on 5 February, Kinnock publicly attacked the 5 per cent pay policy in the House of Commons as 'inoperable' and 'insupportable': 'the kind of figure that throws negotiators into resentful, unproductive and unco-operative silence'.[5] So it proved, and Labour's ability to reach agreement with the unions, previously regarded as its strongest electoral asset, was irretrievably lost.

It was its defeat in the devolution referenda on 1 March which finally pushed the Government under. Once the results were known, the Scottish Nationalists withdrew their support from the Callaghan administration in the Commons, claiming that they had been betrayed by Labour. The Liberals announced that they would side with the Conservatives in a vote to bring the Government down. Despite a flurry of last-minute deals to try to buy off the votes of the remaining Ulster Unionists, Welsh Nationalists and Irish Catholic MPs, the Government lost a no-confidence motion on 28 March by a single vote. 'Now that the House of Commons has declared itself,' said Callaghan when the Conservatives' cheering had subsided, 'we shall take our case to the country.'[6] After the Prime Minister had made a dignified exit from the Chamber, Neil Kinnock formed an impromptu choir of Labour MPs in the gangway on the Government side of the House and led them in singing 'The Red Flag'.[7]

On the 3 May the electorate recorded its verdict on the Labour Government: a 5.2 per cent swing to the Conservatives, the highest since the Second World War. In Bedwellty Kinnock was returned by a majority of just over 20,000; the candidate put up against him by Plaid Cymru lost his deposit. But elsewhere in the country Labour was badly beaten. The final result gave the Conservatives 339 seats, Labour 268, the Liberals eleven and the rest seventeen.

Compared with the disaster which was to befall it four years later, the scale of Labour's election defeat in 1979 appears relatively unspectacular. In fact, its share of the vote – 36.9 per cent – was then the lowest recorded by either of the two main political parties in any of the ten general elections since the war. Not only was it the party's poorest showing since 1931, but it was roughly the same level of support that Labour used to enjoy in its political infancy in the 1920s. For the third election in a row Labour's share of the vote was below 40 per cent. This long-term decline had to some extent been masked by the two 'victories' of 1974: in each of those the party's share of the vote was actually smaller than it had been in the defeat of 1970. The working class deserted *en masse*. Only one manual labourer in three bothered to vote Labour. According to one political analyst, 'The only other European democracies in which the left does as badly are Eire, Switzerland and Belgium, but in these cases rurality or religious and linguistic cleavages can be cited in explanation.'[8] The postmortem was a bitter one. To left-wingers like Chris Mullin, the leadership had betrayed the party's most basic principles:

> by the end of 1974–9 the Labour Government was doing things that not even a Liberal Government would have done – the trying of journalists under a section of the Official Secrets Act that they were pledged to abolish, kicking out Agee and Hosenball at the behest of the CIA. In the end doing a sordid little deal with the Ulster Unionists, simply for the purpose of keeping the backsides of Ministers in the official limousine for another six months. And then in Ireland we had a Secretary of State for Ireland, Roy Mason, who was presiding over systematic torture which was a feature of the system then and has been demonstrated to be since then in the European Court of Human Rights.[9]

In office Labour Ministers had been able to argue that the party should rally round the Government; that opinion polls demonstrated how much the electorate distrusted the left; that if they left him alone, Callaghan – according to the polls the most popular figure on the political scene – would see them through to victory. After the Government had been rejected overwhelmingly by the electorate all these restraints on criticism fell away. At the party conference that autumn the leadership had to endure a succession of attacks: its 5 per cent policy had been a 'slap in the face'; the election had been lost 'not just because of a winter of discontent, but because of three years of discontent following the throwing out of the industrial strategy'. 'It was not a defeat for socialism,' argued one delegate, because the Government had not been socialist: 'Those of us who stood out against it were called the rebels. They were the rebels who refused to accept Conference decisions.'[10] 'The Lib–Lab pact,' Tony Benn subsequently maintained, 'was the worst period of government we have had.'[11] Now that the party was in opposition, the scene was set for an unparalleled shift in power away from Labour's centre and right and towards the left.

Neil Kinnock had castigated the Government over everything from its policy in South Africa in 1974 to its demise on the picket lines in 1979. The general election result seemed the final vindication of his stand. Logic and his track record suggested that he would now join the chorus calling for change in the party. But instead of participating in the criticism, he suddenly seemed to change tack. As Tony Benn announced that he would not be seeking election to the Shadow Cabinet, Kinnock announced that he would be. In order to be free to criticize the leadership, Benn divested himself of collective responsibility; Kinnock, for the first time, embraced it.

To begin with, no one seemed to notice. Only slowly was it realized that amid the clamour of recrimination and dissent one voice, once familiar, was silent. Kinnock's role as a rebel had come to an end practically overnight.

Part Three
LOYALIST

Chapter Twelve

PROMOTION

The scale of the 1979 election defeat was a shock to Kinnock: 'I thought it was a very, very significant defeat. There were few people who agreed with me. It just looked like any common or garden defeat: you know, you go through the swing doors one way in 1979, you're back through the swing doors another way in 1983 or 1984.' But the more he pondered the figures, the more alarmed he became. 'I thought, oh hell, we'd better get the act together somehow.' A few weeks later, to the surprise of many, he decided to stand for election to Labour's Shadow Cabinet. He did so not as a gesture, but 'seriously hoping to get elected'.

For a man who had spent relatively little time at Westminster in recent years, he did remarkably well. The election to Labour's Shadow Cabinet is confined to the Parliamentary Labour Party. The twelve MPs who poll the highest number of votes automatically get a place on the front bench. Kinnock came fourteenth. With such a respectable vote, he had a reasonable expectation of getting a minor post. Michael Foot thought he deserved better. 'I rang Neil,' recalls Foot, 'and told him that I proposed to go to Callaghan and suggest that he make him education spokesman. I said, "Look here, suppose he asks you, will you take it?" He said yes straight away. Others might have hesitated. He didn't. He saw the advantage immediately.' Foot then went and saw Callaghan, who was 'agreeable', and on 18 June Kinnock took the job.

Ian Aitken in the *Guardian* called it 'an astonishing leg-up to one of the most charismatic figures in the much-maligned Tribune Group'.[1] Kinnock was only thirty-seven years old. Apart from his one year as Foot's PPS, he had held no Government job. He had no specialist knowledge of education. His only reputation was as a critic of Callaghan's Government, and in so far as he had fought vigorously against devolution, he was one of those who indirectly had contributed to its fall.

In a miserable period for Labour in the aftermath of the election defeat, Kinnock was seized upon by the press as one of the party's brightest hopes. The *Daily Mirror* called him 'Labour's Likely Lad', a 'fiery red-haired Welshman . . . plucked from the list of also-rans': 'Friends and admirers, and there are many, say he will go right to the top in politics – perhaps even the very top in Downing Street. Others, and there aren't many, say that Neil Gordon Kinnock is "silver-tongued" and not much else'.[2]

Callaghan's motives for giving him the job were clear enough. He knew Kinnock, seems to have liked him and respected him enough to have offered him promotion when he was Prime Minister. Michael Foot's intervention must also have been an important factor. But, above all, he was in desperate need of a left-winger to help him placate his radical critics in the party. Roy Hattersley was said to have 'wanted the education brief more than virtually any other'.[3] Callaghan wanted Kinnock, and Hattersley had to settle for the job of local government spokesman.

News of Kinnock's advancement met with a certain degree of cynicism. Left-wing colleagues reportedly greeted him with remarks along the lines of, 'Now that you've arrived, Kinnock. . . .'[4] The faint smell of compromise was not lessened by the fact that the left was in the process of trying to take away the leader's power of patronage. Dennis Skinner was promoting a campaign to make all places in the Shadow Cabinet subject to election. Eric Heffer, who had won three more votes than Kinnock and had come thirteenth in the

Shadow Cabinet ballot, actually refused to contemplate an offer of a job. He told Callaghan that he wanted a front-bench place only if it was his by right of election; he did not want one purely because of the leader's patronage. Some on the left felt that Kinnock had undermined their campaign. At a subsequent meeting of the PLP he 'came under fierce and well orchestrated attack'. This had never happened to Kinnock before and he was said to be 'deeply hurt'.[5]

Kinnock's decision to take a job in the summer of 1979 proved to be the hinge upon which his career turned. It demonstrated that for Kinnock politics is not about striking heroic stances: it is about power. Between 1974 and 1979 he wielded more power by staying outside the Government than he would have had if he had taken up the offer to take a place inside. The election defeat altered that. A place in the Shadow Cabinet offers its occupant more scope to display his talent than a junior ministry. When the opportunity for advancement came, Kinnock grasped it. 'It was put up or shut up time,' he says. 'I couldn't spend the rest of my life saying how bloody right I was and how everybody else was wrong.' Almost all his political career had been spent in rebellion against his front bench, in particular against its timorous economic policies. 'But it was no good wingeing on about that unless I was prepared to try and influence affairs.'

Having made his decision, Kinnock stuck to it. He seems to have been guided by the biblical precept 'Whatsoever thy hand findeth to do, do it with thy might: for there is no work, nor device, nor knowledge, nor wisdom in the grave, whither thou goest.' His philosophy, he later explained, albeit in slightly more prosaic language, was that 'when you get something, you work like hell at it, and one of the reasons you get to the next step is because you worked like hell at the one you're on.'[6] He is a pragmatist in politics and has no time for those who refuse to compromise, who choose either 'death or glory': 'I've never seen a hell of a lot of glory in death, frankly, if you're not around to enjoy the fruits. That's the line I've always taken. . . . I don't mind fighting, but the fight in itself is not enough of a justification. You fight to win.' He believes that such pragmatism 'might be cultural'. For five years Kinnock had laid into the Government with all his strength. Having taken his place on the front bench, he now committed himself equally completely to his new position. Rather naively, he seems to have expected everyone else to fall into line behind him. He was increasingly upset and angry when they failed to do so.

On 19 June, the day after Callaghan had given him the education portfolio, Kinnock rose to make his first speech from the Opposition front bench. He did not pretend to assume a new gravitas. It was still very much the old-style Kinnock, slashing at the Conservatives from the dispatch box as if he were back on the platform at a *Tribune* rally. So Nicholas Winterton thought he could talk about education, did he? Kinnock told him he brought to the discussion 'the guile of a Panzer driver'. Another Conservative MP, Ray Whitney, had appealed to Kinnock to 'do the House and the country the service of leaving this issue of choice and comprehensivization out of politics'. 'I am as likely,' shot back Kinnock, 'to remove the question of comprehensive education from the sphere of political debate as the hon. Member for Wycombe is to send his children to a secondary modern school, a type of school which he so much admires.'

In his search for an image to sum up his defence of the comprehensive system, Kinnock characteristically reached back to his own schooldays in Tredegar. 'Nobody who has observed a community that operates a selective eleven-plus system can doubt that on the morning of the results there are not faces of schoolchildren wreathed in smiles. . . .' But, charged Kinnock, 'there are floods of tears in many homes.' He turned to Mark Carlisle, the new Secretary of State for Education. 'The guilt for those tears will remain on the backs of the right hon. and learned Gentleman and his colleagues.' He ended with a jeer at the social composition of the Government: 'It is what one expects from a party led by a Cabinet containing twenty-two people, nineteen of them public schoolboys. The Cabinet is more thickly populated with public schoolboys than the free bar at Twickenham on international day. I must not knock public schoolboys too much. They will be sucking their thumbs and shouting for matron before we know where we are'.[7]

This was just about acceptable stuff for a first speech from the front bench, but it was material better suited to a Labour Party conference than the House of Commons, and that autumn in Brighton Kinnock scored a notable triumph. His short speech from the platform at the end of the education debate – his first contribution to the conference as an NEC member – was interrupted more than a dozen times by laughter and applause. *The Times Educational Supplement* wrote of 'the startling red hair' and the 'musical Welsh voice' which 'sang out from the Brighton platform above the routine rantings of squabbling delegates and lifted the slanging match on cuts and standards into a more eloquent dimension'.[8]

The Conservatives were busily strengthening the private sector in education; Kinnock pledged that a future Labour Government would repeal all the Tory legislation, so that 'any governors, any parents, any teachers, any headmasters . . . recognize that when they allocate the Assisted Places Scheme, they are suckling a corpse; it is dead before it starts. We will ensure that it is buried for ever.' Kinnock called on the party to be 'at the fist point' of public anger against the Conservatives' cuts in education spending:

> We are the party of raising standards, but with cuts of this size you can as well raise the dead as you can raise standards. What sickens me is the daily reports from associations of Chambers of Commerce, from the CBI, from employers deploring the fall in standards of literacy and numeracy. . . . These are the people who were campaigning and spending hundreds of thousands of pounds supporting the Tory Party, begging for, demanding, tax cuts. I say to them, 'You can't have tax cuts and higher standards of education. You must make your choice.' . . . But they cripple our children and then taunt them for being lame.

Kinnock ended by quoting Mark Carlisle as having said that

'in the long term the education service and all the other public services depend upon the health of the economy':

> Typical Tory, he has got it absolutely the wrong way round. The health of the economy in this industrial and technological revolution, as in no other, depends on the health of the education service. We have in Britain four raw materials: oil, coal, gas and children – brains. He that in any of those areas deliberately and calculatingly creates waste, under-use and destruction destroys not only the chances of this generation, but poisons the well for all generations to come.[9]

Kinnock sat down to thunderous applause. According to the *Guardian* the following day, he 'captured the loudest and longest standing ovation of the party's conference'.[10] Standing ovations, routine in most political parties, are only occasionally, grudgingly, bestowed by Labour delegates. Tony Benn and James Callaghan each received one, but theirs were largely orchestrated by their supporters. Kinnock's was spontaneous. 'Knuckles clenched, red hair glinting. . . . Words of protest poured from him,' wrote the *Financial Times*: his speech was 'a performance in the Bevan tradition – fluent, fervent and forceful'; and the paper predicted that he was 'obviously destined for the same political stardom'.[11]

The only section of the audience which noticeably failed to rise to its feet was the PLP. But Kinnock can hardly have been bothered about them. He was at the pinnacle of his popularity among the rank and file. In the elections to the NEC that week he jumped to second place, collecting a massive total of 484,000 votes, only 3,000 behind Tony Benn. Praising 'the most passionate speech of the week' and 'real old-fashioned conference oratory', Terence Lancaster made a shrewd prediction in the *Daily Mirror*: 'Labour's left saw one of its members emerging as a future party leader yesterday – and it wasn't Tony Benn.'[12]

Chapter Thirteen

FRATRICIDE

Kinnock had a good week in Brighton. Most other members of Labour's parliamentary leadership did not. 'That conference,' wrote Austin Mitchell, the Labour MP for Grimsby, 'the tone, the bitterness and the hatred of MPs, came as a shock to most, helped frighten and cow them.'[1] Speakers from the right of the party were either heard out in silence or howled down. The loudest applause went to those, such as the party's General Secretary, Ron Hayward, who attacked the record of the last Labour Government:

> You have got to ask yourself: why was there a winter of discontent?
> [*Applause*] The reason was that, for good or ill, the Cabinet, supported
> by MPs, ignored the Congress and Conference decisions. It is as simple
> as that. [*Applause*] The Tories do it much better than we do. I wish our
> Ministers or our Prime Minister would sometimes act in our interests
> like a Tory Prime Minister acts in their interests. [*Applause*][2]

Shorn of office, Callaghan and his senior colleagues suddenly looked out of touch and vulnerable, and to the old catalogue of 'betrayals' – the jettisoning of the industrial strategy, for example, and the public expenditure cuts – the left now added a new grievance: the bowdlerizing of the 1979 election manifesto. 'We hardly recognized the manifesto we were supposed to be fighting on,' complained one party worker.[3] Gone was most of the detailed policy drawn up by the NEC over the previous five years. Gone was the commitment, approved by a majority of seventy to one at the 1977

129

conference, to abolish the House of Lords. Instead the party went to the country with *The Labour Way is the Better Way*, a document as bland as its title, devoted largely to a defence of the Labour Government.

It subsequently emerged that Callaghan, like Wilson before him, had simply vetoed any proposals he did not support. The manifesto was taken out of the NEC's hands and drawn up in Downing Street by two political advisers, Tom McNally (later to join the SDP) and David Lipsey. Tony Benn, the chairman of the NEC's influential Home Policy sub-committee and the architect of many of the vanished policies, later alleged that the leadership had cynically sat back and watched while the conference passed the House of Lords proposal, bided its time and then killed it, 'secretly, late, quietly, before the party could discover what had happened. . . . I have seen policies develop in the subcommittees, come to the Executive, go to the unions for consultation, be discussed in the liaison committees with the unions, come to conference, be endorsed; then I have seen them cast aside in secret by those who are not accountable to this movement.'[4]

Delegates to the 1979 conference were understandably indignant. Stuart Weir claimed that Callaghan's behaviour 'overturns and flatly contradicts the movement's central tradition of collective and democratic decision-making. But he got away with it. . . . Scores of party political commitments were killed or maimed.'[5] As it turned out, by ignoring the NEC and then losing the election Callaghan had delivered himself into the hands of his opponents. The left could now excuse itself from any share of the blame in the defeat. It was not the NEC that had lost the general election, Hayward was able to argue, because 'it was not the manifesto of the NEC that we put before the electorate.'[6] Tom Litterick, one of over fifty Labour MPs who had lost their seats, called the defeat a 'fiasco'.

Speaking of fiascos, I have in my hand a sheaf of documents. Each one is labelled 'Labour Party Campaign Handbook'. Each one on a separate topic – women's rights, the disabled, EEC, housing and so on, and each one drawn up by your NEC based on not one but many conference resolutions. . . . It was these documents that your NEC sought to incorporate in our election manifesto this year. Then, one day in April of this year, Jim Callaghan turned up, and that is what he did to your policies.

In a gesture which was widely televised that evening, Litterick then hurled the discarded documents from the rostrum and went on bitterly: ' "Jim will fix it," they said. Ay, he fixed it. He fixed all of us. He fixed me in particular.'[7]

The anger expressed at the 1979 conference was not merely a response to the election defeat. It was the culmination of almost a decade of increasing frustration and bitterness. The growth of the Campaign for Labour Party Democracy was a barometer of grassroots discontent. Between 1975 and 1979 the number of party organizations affiliated to it had increased almost tenfold, from thirty-two to 292. The important advance had been among the unions – 'where the votes are', as Vladimir Derer puts it. In 1975 only one union branch had supported the CLPD. In 1979 the campaign enjoyed the support of eighty-five.[8] Derer and the other leaders of the CLPD arrived in Brighton that October optimistic that their moment had finally come. 'The need for greater democracy within the Labour Party,' argued Derer in that year's conference *Newsletter*, 'was brutally emphasized by the shattering general election result.'

They were pushing for three constitutional changes which they believed would provide the necessary increase in 'democracy': mandatory reselection of MPs; a widening of the franchise for the election of the party's leader; and an amendment to ensure that the NEC would in future have the final say over the contents of the manifesto.

That the conference would adopt mandatory reselection was never in doubt. In 1978 the leadership had been reprieved by Hugh Scanlon, the engineers' leader, who 'accidentally' failed to cast his union's block vote in support of reselection; but for that it would already have been written into the constitution. In 1979 Callaghan was powerless. 'I gather the votes are in the bag, well, good luck to you,' he told the delegates in his main speech as leader, a few hours before the crucial vote. 'Of course,' he added forlornly, 'if any of you want to recall your delegations during the lunchtime and think again, I shall feel this speech has been worthwhile.'[9] Callaghan was the block vote made flesh. He had built his political career on the strength of his links with the unions. But even he could do nothing to stem the tide. On the afternoon of Tuesday, 2 October, reselection was passed, to loud applause, by 4 million votes to 3 million.

The fate of the other two constitutional changes was less straightforward. The motion calling for an electoral college to choose the party's leader was defeated once again. But it was not destroyed totally. Instead it was included among the subjects to be considered by a special Commission of Inquiry set up by the party to consider its internal problems and due to report back the following year.

The third issue was the manifesto. Under Clause Five of Labour's constitution the manifesto's contents have to be agreed at a final meeting between the NEC and the Cabinet (or Shadow Cabinet, if the party is in Opposition) immediately prior to the election. The left sought to give the last word to the NEC alone. Considering the mood of conference delegates on this subject in 1979, the CLPD believed there was a good chance of getting this change agreed. In the event it was foiled by the NEC itself. Faced with a choice between two motions – a 'hard'-left one, which would have given it immediate control of the manifesto, and a 'soft'-left compromise which merely called upon them to submit proposals for change to the 1980 conference – the NEC opted for the second course; the resolution favoured by the CLPD was not even put forward for debate at the conference.

The CLPD and its supporters were bitterly disappointed. (They were to be even more so a year later, for when the motion was finally debated the right, now on its guard, had organized to defeat the proposal.) The NEC had decided to support the compromise motion by a majority of a single vote. The man who was seen as having given the centre-right its victory was Neil Kinnock.

Kinnock had been present at the meeting in April at which Callaghan had vetoed the abolition of the Lords. He found it 'very disturbing. It was obvious that we had to move away from that.' But he was not convinced that control of the manifesto by the NEC was the answer. 'The party leader clearly has a veto before an election anyway,' argues Kinnock: no party, he believes, can realistically expect to force policies on to a reluctant leader only a few weeks before polling day. 'The important thing is to produce a system whereby we can ensure that policy is sustained without going through a Clause Five meeting a few weeks before the election.' He voted against the CLPD's motion.

However genuine Kinnock's reasons, it was at this point that puzzlement on the left over his decision to stand for election to the Shadow Cabinet began to turn into a general suspicion of his motives. 'In many ways,' pronounced Jon Lansman, a young member of the CLPD executive with a passing resemblance, in appearance and outlook, to Saint-Just, 'Neil Kinnock can be held responsible for the fact that the NEC does not have ultimate control for drafting the manifesto: that is a significant crime.'[10]

Kinnock had never been a typical supporter of the outside left. For four years, between 1973 and 1977, he had somehow managed to combine being one of the CLPD's founder members with a passionate opposition to its main aim, mandatory reselection. Now, as the divisions within the party intensified, this balancing act became impossible to sustain. For a few more years Kinnock continued to turn up at the odd CLPD rally; he would even make a point of contributing to the collection at the end. ('Thank you, Neil,' said the chairman on one occasion, 'perhaps next time you'll give us your vote as well.') But, in reality, from the day of his vote on the manifesto in 1979 Kinnock and the CLPD parted company. On such issues as the Benn campaign for the deputy leadership, the endorsement of Peter Tatchell and the expulsion of

Militant, he found himself repeatedly in opposition to the hard left, which began to speak of him as a Wilson figure, a man who had found it convenient at one stage to wear a left-wing mask in order to secure his advancement and conceal his self-interest. 'It must be said,' wrote *Tribune* in 1983, 'that his career shows disturbing signs of following that path well worn by ambitious Labour politicians. First he flirted with the left and got himself elected to the National Executive Committee in record time. Then he abruptly kicked away the ladder up which he had so deftly climbed and set about ingratiating himself with the Parliamentary Labour Party. . . . Kinnock's record defies rational analysis.'[11]

As far as Kinnock was concerned, it was the hard left that was behaving irrationally, and as 1979 drew to a close he began voicing his exasperation. The party had just been routed in an election, and in its place was the most right-wing Government Britain had had for years: 'At such a time,' he complained to the Bedwellty General Management Committee in November, 'you would think the Labour Party would unite but instead they invent a war. The [Commission of] Inquiry is an excuse for internal warfare. The PLP feel threatened. It is all a distraction from fighting Toryism. There should be no war in the Labour Party. There should be a willingness to adopt policies which are a real alternative to Toryism.'[12] This was the message he would continue to try, unsuccessfully, to put over for the next three and a half years.

The new year began badly. The Shadow Cabinet, whose decisions Kinnock was obliged to defend, had agreed that it would be impossible to guarantee that a future Labour Government could restore all the cuts in education spending being made by the Conservatives. On 8 February 1980 Kinnock had to defend this position at a meeting of the PLP. It was his first experience of the painful consequences of collective responsibility. The former scourge of Healey and the IMF now warned MPs that it would be 'hopelessly dishonest' to promise a full restoration of the cuts which, he said, could amount to £10,000 million by the time of the next general election. The spectacle of Kinnock, of all people, defending expenditure cuts was not well received by left-wing MPs. He was given a rough reception. The PLP's meetings are supposed to be confidential, but afterwards there were plenty of MPs eager to describe Kinnock's discomfiture. His speech was said to have been 'disastrous in content, style and delivery'. He was accused of 'doing the dirty work' for the party leadership. Someone told him he was in the wrong job: he ought to be the shadow Chief Secretary to the Treasury.[13]

The criticism did not end there. Two weeks later, on 22 February, Kinnock was questioned about the reports of his speech at a meeting of the Bedwellty General Management Committee. He repeated the same views: in five years' time a Labour Government would inherit what amounted 'virtually to a war economy'; it would be 'stupid and dishonest' to say 'four years before the next election' that every penny of the cuts would be restored. 'We have too often in the past made promises we could not keep and we must not do so again and destroy our credibility.'[14] The left-wingers in his local party were amazed at the change in Kinnock's tone that had taken place in the course of only a year. 'We couldn't comprehend Neil's line on it,' remembers Tony Wilkins, a local organizer for NUPE, the public employees' union. 'In the past he'd have put his hand up with the rest of us. . . . We said to him, "It's a commitment." But he wouldn't go up that road.' 'He startled everyone,' says another GMC member.

The row continued for several months. In June the Bedwas and Trethomas ward of the constituency put forward a motion to the Bedwellty GMC for submission to the 1980 party conference: 'This Conference condemns Mr Neil Kinnock's statement . . . to the effect that he would not undertake to restore the education cuts carried through by the present Tory Government.' It must have been an unpleasant jolt for Kinnock, who had had no criticism from his constituency since 1972, when he had announced his intention of moving to London. He maintained his position on the cuts: 'We must not make a hostage of our integrity. We cannot restore the cuts merely by saying we will do it. We will need the means to carry it out.' The fifty or so GMC delegates voted overwhelmingly to remove the specific condemnation of him from the motion. The amended version, calling simply on the 'leadership' of the party to restore all the education cuts, was then put to the vote. It was defeated, but only by twenty-seven votes to twenty – hardly a ringing endorsement of Kinnock's position. For the first time he was under fire in Bedwellty not from the right but from the left.

There were now plenty of people, especially at Westminster, who were longing for Kinnock to make a slip. Conservatives scented a dangerous, if prolix, enemy. Labour MPs were jealous of his talent for combining rapid promotion in Parliament with enormous popularity in the constituencies. In the *Daily Mail* Andrew Alexander wrote:

> It has for some time been very difficult to listen to Mr Neil Kinnock, Labour's education spokesman, without experiencing very uncharitable sentiments. It is time, one feels, for that young man to be cut down to size. Yesterday (we rejoice to say) the cutting down took place. Indeed, the fellow was quite sliced off at the knees. Moreover, it was fascinating to observe that pleasure in this process was by no means restricted to the Tory side.[15]

The circumstances of the 'cutting down' were curiously similar to those surrounding the controversy over Kinnock's allegations of 'victimization' in Welsh schools two years earlier. At a Labour Party conference on education on 7 June he had attacked the cuts in school spending and claimed that 'headmasters are being turned into touts and children are drawing lots to use books and equipment and parents are becoming flag sellers.' The 'allegation' had been prominently reported on the front page of the *Observer* on 8 June. Two days later Mark Carlisle – whose placid, understated manner was ideally suited to take the wind out of Kinnock's aggressive rhetoric – gently pushed the shadow spokesman into the hole he had dug for himself. Would the Member for Bedwellty, inquired Carlisle, be so good as to 'get up at the Dispatch Box and name the schools where children are drawing lots for books and equipment so that I can inquire, as I should do, into his allegations'?

From his study of rugby Kinnock has drawn the moral that 'Counter attack . . . is the only sensible form of defence',[16] and this was the tactic he tried. Would Carlisle deny, he demanded, 'that children are using books on rotas [*uproar and shouts of 'Which schools?'*], that sharing is extensive and that the use of worksheets is universal? Does he deny that?' Kinnock repeated that there was a 'books from bingo system' in operation, and his attempts to brazen it out reached an heroic climax as he accused Carlisle of 'dodging answers by making references to my speeches instead of dealing with his own responsibilities'. Carlisle replied:

> of course . . . books are from time to time shared, and I suspect that that has happened over many hundreds of years. What I am equally aware of is that, having specifically asked the hon. Gentleman to cite the schools at which he said, on Saturday, 'children draw lots to use books and equipment', he specifically failed to do so. The House must draw its own conclusions. . . .

He then produced figures to support his claim that the Conservatives were now spending more on books, materials and equipment than Labour did in its last year in office and accused Kinnock of 'hypocrisy and humbug'.[17] According to Alexander:

> [Kinnock's] Tribunite friends watched with slight smiles. And less Tribunite characters like Mr Barnett and Mr Sheldon, former Treasury Ministers [whom Kinnock had attacked in 1977 for treating the City of London like a 'winnable Tory marginal'] chuckled quite hugely throughout the incident which was brief but memorable. . . . By the way, anyone who knows of a school where they do raffle textbooks should send the information as soon as possible to the Labour Party, marking their envelope 'The Save Neil Kinnock Fund'.[18]

The embarrassment was made worse by the fact that the Chamber was packed with MPs waiting for Prime Minister's Questions, which were to be taken next.

The incident revealed how little support Kinnock had among MPs. It is almost certain that if the franchise for the election of party leader had remained solely in the hands of the PLP, Kinnock would not have won in 1983. It was not that he was generally a poor Commons performer (even the best must have their off-days). He had simply neglected Parliament in favour of political activity outside and had failed, as a result, to build up a base of support in Westminster. He did not hang around the place like some whose homes are far away in their constituencies and who have nowhere else to go. Kinnock was usually on the road; on the rare occasions when he was not, he liked to be at home with his family. He had never had much affection for Parliament, and some aspects of his treatment by the PLP since joining the front bench can only have deepened his distaste. 'You see a lot of dirty things as an MP,' Kinnock once said. 'The House of Commons is like a factory. That's where I happen to work. I have some close friends there, and some not close friends. Just because you work with people in the same party, it doesn't mean to say you like them.'[19]

Kinnock had been notably unimpressed by the PLP in 1976, when he had canvassed it on behalf of Michael Foot in the leadership election. Ever since then the one change in Labour's constitution which he had fought for unswervingly had been the ending of the PLP's exclusive right to elect the party leader. And in the autumn of 1980, four years after Kinnock had first written to *Tribune* advocating change, the issue was back on the agenda of the Labour Party conference at Blackpool.

It would be ridiculous to suggest that Kinnock's motive in pushing for an electoral college was purely a matter of self-interest. Because the reform was the most obviously dramatic, its importance tended to be exaggerated by the media, but it was arguably far less radical than either mandatory reselection or control of the manifesto. (In 1977, for example, an NEC working party had reported that the labour or socialist parties of Denmark, France, West Germany, Israel, Italy, Holland, Norway and Sweden all chose their leaders on a franchise wider than the British; only the Australian Labor Party had a system comparable with Britain's.)[20] Equally, it

138

would be naive to pretend that by 1980 Kinnock was unaware of how enormously he stood to benefit by the change.

The motion, in two parts, was considered by the conference on the afternoon of Wednesday, 1 October. First the conference was asked to approve the idea of an electoral college 'in principle' – 'an irresponsible device', according to Austin Mitchell.[21] This was the crucial vote, and it was expected to be close. When Lena Jegar, the chairman of the conference, rose to announce the result of 'Card Vote Number 8 on Motion 2a' no one could be sure of the outcome. The result she was handed and read out was: in favour of an electoral college, 3,609,000; against, 3,511,000 – a majority of 98,000, little more than 1 per cent. The conference broke into prolonged applause. Callaghan, who had opposed the motion, looked grim. The most remarkable platform demonstration was given by Neil Kinnock. 'To this day,' recalls one MP, watching from the floor of the hall as the delegates cheered, 'I can see Kinnock leaping around with his hands clasped above his head. He went crazy. He knew what it meant for him.'

Once the principle had been accepted, it remained to work out the percentages of the new college. The NEC put forward two alternatives. One was to give 50 per cent of the votes to the PLP, 25 per cent to the unions and 25 per cent to the constituency parties; the other distributed the votes evenly, giving one-third to each. To the dismay of the NEC, both were defeated. In confusion, the NEC met at 5.30 that afternoon and asked its officials to draw up a new set of proposals which it could place before the delegates the following day.

That night, the CLPD went to work, operating from the bar of the Imperial Hotel, where most of the NEC members were staying. They tried to persuade the hard left on the Executive to support a fresh proposal giving 40 per cent of the votes to the unions and 30 per cent each to the constituencies and the MPs. Tony Benn was lobbied after midnight in his hotel room by his former political adviser, Frances Morrell. 'I suppose you are right,' he is reported to have told her, 'but isn't it late now?'[22] By 2 a.m. the CLPD's leaders had convinced Jo Richardson and Tony Saunois, the Young Socialist representative on the NEC. Dennis Skinner had refused on principle to stay at the Imperial, putting up instead at a nearby boarding house. But apparently he had no ideological objections using the Imperial's lavatory, for there, at 7 a.m. the following morning, he was discovered by Jon Lansman. Skinner wanted to give the unions 90 per cent, but Lansman, who agreed with him, nevertheless managed to persuade him to accept the CLPD idea. When the NEC met at 8 a.m., the hard left pushed through the 40–30–30 proposal. 'I think,' lamented the right-wing Shirley Williams, 'someone was missing from our side.'[23]

And so, in conditions close to farce, the Labour Party staggered towards an electoral college. The 40–30–30 proposal was the one the party would eventually accept. But on Thursday afternoon, despite the recommendation of the NEC, it was defeated. Instead the party decided to postpone the decision until a special one-day conference in January. In the meantime the left could console itself with the knowledge that, whatever the proportions, an electoral college was now inevitable. In future, becoming leader would depend as much upon popularity among ordinary party members as upon support among MPs – and that week, despite the rows over the manifesto and the education cuts, Neil Kinnock retained second place in the NEC elections, neatly tucked in behind Tony Benn, with 432,000 votes.

Chapter Fourteen

FOOT, WEMBLEY AND THE RISE OF THE SDP

In 1976 a senior colleague had claimed that Jim Callaghan's greatest strength was his natural rapport with ordinary party members: 'those dreary committee rooms, the bad teas, the duplicating machines that get ink everywhere, the old ladies writing notices with exasperating slowness. Jim *likes* all that.'[1] By 1980, whatever else it was, the party's image was not one of inky old ladies. Callaghan stared bleakly at the delegates as if at strangers. 'However much you may wish me dead,' he insisted after the decision to introduce an electoral college, 'I am alive and I am kicking.'[2] But compared with the self-confident, avuncular Prime Minister of a few years before, he looked crumpled, beaten, isolated. The 1980 Blackpool conference was his last as leader. Two weeks later, at a meeting of the Shadow Cabinet, he announced his intention to resign. As he rose to go, Michael Foot took the dispirited leader gently by the arm. 'There is nothing but friendship around this table for you,' he reportedly told Callaghan.[3]

Aside from his personal feelings, Callaghan had a clear political motive for resigning when he did. He wanted Denis Healey to succeed him and knew that the longer he waited, the more likely it was that an electoral college would be in operation: Healey's only hope was to win under the existing system and then to use the incumbency to beat off any challenges from the left. The manoeuvre caught out the hard left. 'Jim Callaghan had no business to resign as leader,' said one. 'It was positively indecent of Callaghan to retire just after the party had chosen a new method of election.'[4] Tony Benn wanted to stand but was persuaded not to do so: he would only have lost, his supporters told him, and by contesting the election he would confer upon it a legitimacy they did not want it to have. For a time it looked as though Peter Shore would be Healey's main opponent, a prospect the hard left viewed with horror: although radical in his opinions on economics and the EEC, Shore had a deep distaste for the party's far left. Initially it was thought that Shore would be backed by Foot. Chris Mullin and Stuart Holland, the MP for Vauxhall, hastily drew up a list of twenty left-wing MPs who would support Foot but would not vote for Shore. They tried to send it to Foot in the form of a telegram, but it was Sunday and no telegrams could be sent that day. Holland went round to Foot's house in Hampstead and pushed the list through his letterbox. Two days later Foot declared his candidacy.

Kinnock now claims that his enthusiasm for Foot's candidature has been exaggerated and that he expressed reservations about it to Jill Craigie. Yet if he had any doubts about Foot, at the age of sixty-seven, seeking to lead a fast-disintegrating party, he does not appear to have done much about them. On the contrary, he played an important part in convincing Foot that he should stand. Together with two other MPs, Peter Snape and Jim Marshall, he compiled figures which suggested that Foot would get at least 40 per cent of the votes in the election and that he might even win. According to one account, he and Clive Jenkins, leader of the managerial union ASTMS, actually, 'rang everybody they could think of: trade unionists, constituency parties, friends and colleagues of Foot from his earliest days in the Labour Party. They had the same message for all: if they wanted Michael to stand, they should phone or telegraph him immediately. Letters, calls and telegrams began to arrive . . . at first in a trickle and then in a flood.'[5]

On 4 November the result of the first ballot was announced:

HEALEY	112
FOOT	83
SILKIN	38
SHORE	32

Shore and John Silkin were eliminated. Healey had not done as well as he had expected, and on 10 November Foot, picking up almost all of Silkin's votes and around half of Shore's, won the run-off against him by 139 votes to 129. When the result was announced in a Commons committee room by the PLP's chairman, Fred Willey, it was met by a restrained pattering of hands on desk tops and a low rumble of 'Hear hear.' Neil Kinnock 'felt this response was inadequate: his substantial fist crashed down on the table and he let out a blood-curdling Indian war whoop.' At a subsequent victory celebration Foot tried to say a few words. 'Comrades,' he began, 'this is a historic and unique occasion – ' 'Yes,' interrupted Kinnock, 'we bloody won.'[6]

A combination of factors had brought Foot victory. There was, to begin with, a sizeable personal vote for a man whom most people liked and who represented an honourable and comforting link with the days of Bevan and the orthodox, parliamentary left. To this was added the support of the traditional left-wing constituency within the PLP centred on the Tribune Group. Then there was a substantial faction of MPs in the centre of the party who were unable to stomach the abrasive Healey. And finally there was a ragbag of MPs whose various motives eventually tilted the balance of the election in favour of Foot: those who hoped he would unite the party, those under pressure from left-wing constituency parties, even some ultra-right-wingers keen to see the party saddled with a disastrous leader, an outcome which would help them in their aim of bringing about a political realignment in Britain.

The most immediate consequence of Foot's election was that it forced the social democrats to come to a decision about their position in the party. A number of senior right-wing

MPs had had their doubts about even Denis Healey's willingness to stand up to the left. They had no doubts about Foot, an 'amiable and eccentric man of letters', who in their opinion 'had no hope of stopping the inexorable advance of the left within the party, even had he wished to do so'.[7] David Owen, former Foreign Secretary, announced that he would not stand for election to a Shadow Cabinet presided over by Foot. Shirley Williams, former Education Secretary, who had lost her seat in the general election, told her local party in Stevenage that she would not be its candidate again. William Rodgers, former Transport Minister, pondered his position.

A couple of weeks after Foot's installation as leader, on 29 November, the three of them lunched with Roy Jenkins at his home in the country. In his Dimbleby Lecture a year before, Jenkins had suggested to Labour politicians that they should not 'slog through an unending war of attrition, stubbornly and conventionally defending as much of the old citadel as you can hold' but should 'break out and mount a battle of movement on new and higher ground'. At first his ideas had been scorned by Labour's right. 'I am not interested in a third party,' declared Shirley Williams. 'I do not believe it has any future.'[8] Then came the 1980 Blackpool conference, which not only voted for a new electoral system for the leadership but also supported unilateral nuclear disarmament and withdrawal from the EEC. The right was now receptive to Jenkins's notion of a new centre party, and on 18 January, at a supposedly secret meeting which was nevertheless heavily publicized, what had become known as the 'Gang of Four' began drafting its declaration of independence. They fixed their next meeting for Sunday, 25 January, the day after the special conference that Labour was convening at Wembley to determine the new system for electing the party leader: it promised to be an ideal launching pad for what Jenkins had described as an 'experimental aeroplane'. Other members of the Labour Party looked on in disgust. Kinnock attacked the four as 'political lounge lizards'.[9] He told the Bedwellty General Management Committee that the social democrats'

11 In 1970 Neil and Glenys presented his parents, Mary and Gordon, with a grandson, Stephen. In 1971 Kinnock suffered the greatest tragedy of his life, when his parents died within a few days of one another. (Kinnock family)

12 Election victory: in 1970, at the age of only 28, Neil Kinnock was elected as MP for Bedwellty, one of the safest Labour seats in the country. (Kinnock family)

13 Kinnock's father, both his grandfathers and five of his uncles were miners: Kinnock has one of the most impeccable working-class backgrounds of any modern Labour politician. (Frank Herrmann)

14 November 1977: Kinnock and Dennis Skinner sit alone in the Chamber of the House of Commons, having refused to listen to the Queen's Speech. The following year these two rising stars of Labour's left were elected on to the Party's National Executive together. Shortly afterwards Kinnock and the hard left began to part company. (PA photo)

15 In 1979 Kinnock was given what the *Guardian* called 'an astonishing leg up' and was appointed Labour's education spokesman. Here, he addresses a demonstration against Conservative cuts in public spending. (Tony Gay)

16 Anti-nuclear campaigner: Kinnock addresses a CND rally in Hyde Park. 'All Labour MPs are paid political activists,' says Kinnock. (PA photo)

17 'Brooding': Kinnock's children play behind him, but their father is distracted. This photograph was taken the day before Kinnock had to face a stormy meeting of his local party in December 1981 – the most unpleasant period of his political life. (*Sunday Times* photo)

18 Kinnock addresses the 1982 Labour Party conference. Two days earlier he had survived an attempt by the hard left to remove him from the National Executive; his colleague, Joan Lestor, had not. Kinnock received a standing ovation for this speech on education – a significant indication of his popularity in the party. (PA photo)

19 A touching moment: Kinnock on the platform, shortly after his election as leader at the Labour Party Conference in October 1983. Friends all agree that Glenys is the most important influence in his life. (Andrew Wiard, *Report*)

20 The dream ticket: Kinnock winks as he and Roy Hattersley acknowledge the applause moments after their election as leader and deputy leader
of the Labour Party. (PA photo)

behaviour was a 'demonstration of vanity' and a 'desertion of responsibility. He had been frustrated in not getting his own way but would never leave the party. . . . If they want to leave, let them.'[10]

Kinnock had set out his own political position in an article entitled 'Which Way should Labour Go?', published in the *Political Quarterly*. It showed how prominent the strain of pragmatism in his thinking had become. He argued that Labour faced a basic choice between 'two brands of socialism':

> Socialism by prescription and socialism by plod. The former is all say and no do, all plans and no power. . . . That leaves plodding. It is as dour an idea as can be found. . . . Such a course is offensive to monorail militants because it is gradualist.

(The phrase about 'plodding' had clearly been in his mind for some time. Back in July, speaking to his GMC about the political situation, he had said 'that he wished he could suggest some dramatic and inspiring solution but that frankly and realistically we can only use the traditional routes of slog, plod, agitation and education'.) He reiterated his commitment to pulling out of the EEC and giving up nuclear weapons, but he now accepted that 'socialism by plod' might well mean that Labour would have to reconsider its hostility to an incomes policy:

> Any incomes policy which follows previous examples and is all incomes for capital earners and higher salaried non-unionized people and all policy for unionized workers has not a hope of existence. But if progressive income tax and effective wealth taxes can be introduced, there is still a surviving possibility of inducing practical support for a policy of incomes control. It would have to include a statutory national minimum wage, it would have to permit cost bargaining . . . it would have to relate money incomes to social wage. But it would be feasible as part of a consistent and realizable policy for planning the means – and rewards – of production, distribution and exchange.

This went much further than most of the left of the Labour Party were willing to go, and Kinnock also had a revealing observation to make about the party's constitutional changes. The social democrats might regard them as revolutionary; he was sanguine that

145

the hopes invested in mandatory reselection and other changes concerning leadership election and manifesto drafting are, like the fears, somewhat exaggerated. Mass redundancy in the PLP is not even a remote possibility. A leader who – three weeks before a general election – threatens to resign rather than fight on a manifesto which is unacceptable to him is not going to have his bluff called by any NEC which wants to win that election. An electoral college for the leader . . . will not elect anyone who is incapable of securing parliamentary support, except in the unlikely event of enmity towards the MPs being so great and ignorance of the political issues being so crushing that the Labour Party would have in any case to cease to exist.[11]

It was a clear illustration, on the eve of the Wembley Conference, of the difference in approach between Kinnock and the adherents of the outside left. They demanded changes in order to transform the party; he supported them, at least in part, because he was satisfied that their hopes were exaggerated.

The right was beaten at Wembley before the conference even began. It had made a last-minute attempt to rally support for a proposal giving every member of the party a vote in the election of the leader and his deputy. 'I am amazed,' said David Owen, making his last appearance at a Labour conference, 'that you have to come to the Labour Party and defend the issue of one member, one vote.' To vest the power to elect a leader or possibly a Prime Minister in the unions, with their block votes, would be 'an outrage . . . a disgrace'.[12] But Owen's cause was hopeless, and not only because the unions, with an overwhelming majority of the votes, were not about to let themselves be cut out of the new system. The case for one member, one vote lacked credibility when it was advanced by people who had happily acquiesced in the old arrangement for years. 'They did not object to the block vote when it worked in their favour,' one delegate pointed out. 'There is something very peculiar about so-called democrats who only agree with democracy when they win.'[13] One member, one vote fell at the first hurdle, supported by only 431,000 votes; the option of an electoral college to be held at a party conference won 6,283,000.

That decided, it remained to agree the allocation of proportions within the college. What followed was probably the outside left's finest hour – an achievement later considered sufficiently dramatic to be turned into a one-hour play by the BBC. The conference debated seven formulae, three of which had a chance of being accepted. There was the NEC's proposal, which was to give one-third of the votes each to the PLP, the Constituency Labour Parties (CLPs) and the unions. There was a formula favoured by the right, supported by Michael Foot and advanced by David Basnett of the municipal workers' union, to give 50 per cent of the votes to the PLP and 25 per cent each to the CLPs and the unions. And there was the option that the outside left had begun pushing for at Blackpool: 30 per cent each for the PLP and the CLPs and 40 per cent for the unions. This was regarded as the least likely of the three to be accepted, and if it fell, its sponsor, the moderate shopworkers' union USDAW, proposed to transfer its votes to support 50–25–25.

The CLPD and the Rank-and-File Mobilizing Committee (RFMC), a coalition of far-left groups, including Militant, recognized the danger. What was likely to happen was that in the first vote 30–30–40 would get the least number of votes of the three and would be eliminated, and 50–25–25 would go on to win with the support of USDAW's 430,000 votes. To prevent this the outside left aimed to ensure that the final run off was between 50–25–25 and 30–30–40, a plan which entailed ditching the NEC's chosen formula before the final ballot. Delegates, exhaustively lobbied by the CLPD and others, began switching their votes to 30–30–40. Some mystery surrounds Clive Jenkins's role in this process. Shortly before 1 p.m. he went to the rostrum to announce that his delegation had decided to swing ASTMS's 150,000 votes behind the USDAW amendment. Then, when the conference adjourned for lunch, he entertained a number of other union bosses to lunch. The right believes that this was a conspiracy to keep them occupied while the CLPD did its mischief. 'It is now quite clear to me,' alleges Roy Grantham of the moderate clerical union APEX, 'that as we gathered, the object was to prevent us talking while the outside left set about organizing and swung support behind USDAW. . . . The Labour Party is still paying for the unnecessary and stupid conduct of Clive at that time.' Jenkins denies this: 'It is quite untrue there was any kind of plot,' he says.

What is not in dispute, however, is that while the union leaders drank, the CLPD briefed delegates on tactics, and when the conference resumed and the first ballot was held, the result revealed the effectiveness of its campaign. Out of seven possible options, 50–25–25 was the most popular, with 2.4 million votes, but tied in second place were the NEC and USDAW proposals, with just over 1.8 million votes each. The conference immediately went on to a second ballot between these proposals; the other four were eliminated. When the results of this were announced a few minutes later, 50–25–25 was found to have stayed top with 2.7 million votes. But by a tiny majority, 50,000 votes, the USDAW motion had squeezed the NEC's formula into third place. It was now the contest that the hard left had always wanted – a straight fight betwen 50–25–25 and 30–30–40, between left and right.

Neil Kinnock, who had supported the NEC's scheme, watched the proceedings from the platform with a growing sense of alarm. According to Jon Lansman, while the final ballot was being held he and Eric Heffer complained to the reporters covering the conference that the CLPD 'have lost the whole thing for us'.[14] But in fact the hard left had judged things to perfection. The engineers, the most right-wing of the big unions, who had advocated an electoral college giving 75 per cent of the vote to the PLP, chose to abstain. This empty gesture, designed to demonstrate their opposition to what was happening, cost the right its victory. By 3.4 million votes to 2.9 million Labour found itself with an electoral college which gave the greatest say to the unions – the result which at the outset had been the one least preferable to most of the delegates. The outside left was jubilant. As Lansman later put it, they had 'won against . . . the National Executive

Committee, the Transport and General Workers' Union, the Parliamentary Party and Michael Foot. We won against all the establishment figures.'[15]

The person most badly damaged by the outcome at Wembley was Michael Foot. He had not spoken in the debate but had relied upon the leaders of the big unions to deliver him 50–25–25. His faith had been misplaced and his position undermined as a result. 'Michael Foot,' wrote Austin Mitchell, 'had courageously faced the first test of his leadership by giving no lead at all.'[16] 'I cannot pretend to you that absolutely all the results this afternoon were the ones that I wanted,' he said in his speech a few minutes after 50–25–25 had been defeated. 'I agreed with the case put by David Basnett. . . . I wish Conference had reached that conclusion.' Having said which, he then urged everyone in the party to accept the result and devoted the main part of his speech to an inspiring attack upon the Conservative Government, reminding delegates of the 'multitudes . . . living through this winter of fear, overcast by the storm clouds of mass unemployment' who 'look to us to settle our internal debates and to mobilize all our strength against the enemy. . . . Let us all, right, left and centre, never forget the real enemy.'[17] He was given an enthusiastic reception.

Foot's first conference speech as leader set the pattern for all the rest. Right and left would brutally attack one another all week, pause to listen to Foot orating about unemployment, disarmament and the need for unity, give him an ovation, and then immediately resume fighting. His leadership speeches were not the keynote of a conference: they were occasional commercial breaks for socialism. The Labour Party, working out the tensions and frustrations of a decade, was probably unleadable between 1980 and 1983; Foot was the unhappy individual called upon to try. 'He got the job at the worst possible time,' says Alan Fox, a close friend of Foot as well as of Kinnock. 'Someone had to be crucified. The party needed a martyr.' One by one Foot's assets seemed to turn into liabilities. His kindness looked like weakness; his tolerance, indecision; his culture, bookishness; his originality, eccentricity; his sense of history, the obsessions of an old man living in the past. Few leaders have been treated as badly by their colleagues. Kinnock, at considerable cost, was one of a handful who remained both publicly and privately loyal.

Wembley, according to the opinion polls, had a cataclysmic effect on Labour's support in the country. Before the conference Gallup recorded 46.5 per cent of the electorate as supporting Labour; after it the figure fell to 35.5 per cent. For the first time since the general election, the party was less popular than the Conservatives.[18]

Those who stood, in the short term, to gain most by the outcome of Wembley were the right-wingers preparing to defect. 'I want them all to stay in our ranks to help us,' Foot had said in his closing speech. 'I do not agree with those who say it does not matter if they go. I want them all to stay.' But the following day, after a meeting at David Owen's home in east London, the Gang of Four issued 'The Limehouse Declaration':

> The calamitous outcome of the Labour Party Wembley Conference demands a new start in British politics. A handful of trade union leaders can now dictate the choice of a future Prime Minister. The Conference disaster is the culmination of a long process by which the Labour Party has moved steadily away from its roots in the people of this country and its commitment to parliamentary government.

The four stopped short of leaving the party but announced the setting up of a 'Council for Social Democracy' and made it clear that a decisive break was not far off.

> We recognize [they concluded] that for those people who have given much of their lives to the Labour Party, the choice that lies ahead will be deeply painful. But we believe that the need for a realignment of British politics must now be faced.[19]

Kinnock was contemptuous. 'They want a kindly capitalism,' he complained on 5 February, 'a gentle market economy, an air-conditioned jungle.'[20] Four days later, on 9 February, Shirley Williams resigned from the NEC, telling the party's

General Secretary, Ron Hayward, that she believed 'the party I loved and worked for over so many years no longer exists.'[21] On 26 March 1981 the Social Democratic Party was launched by a fanfare of television publicity which the SDP later reckoned would have cost it £20 million to buy.

An optimist in the Labour Party might now reasonably have expected the worst of the internal dissension to be over. The left had won on mandatory reselection and the electoral college. In Michael Foot they had a leader who supported unilateral nuclear disarmament, withdrawal from the EEC and the other main elements of left-wing policy. With Denis Healey installed as his deputy, there was no challenge to Foot's leadership from the right. The right-wing Campaign for Labour Victory wrote in its newspaper: 'Michael Foot will remain leader . . . for however long he personally chooses.'[22]

But instead of marking the end of Labour's civil war, the departure of the social democrats merely signalled the start of a more ferocious period of blood-letting. This was unlike anything the party had ever seen, for the old breakdown of loyalties into 'left' and 'right' was no longer adequate to describe the two sides. The traditional left was in pieces: hard, soft, outside, inside, RFMC, LCC, CLPD. . . . After Wembley these coalesced into two broad factions. Tony Benn was the undisputed leader of one. Neil Kinnock emerged as the most prominent member of the other.

Chapter Fifteen

ANTI-BENNITE

Tony Benn had run for the deputy leadership of the Labour Party in 1971 and for the leadership in 1976. He had wanted to run for the leadership again in 1980. In February, after the widening of the franchise, he began to consider having another try. 'I supported Foot as leader, and therefore there was no question of standing against him,' said Benn later, 'but I discussed the deputy leadership with a lot of trade union leaders, and on a weekly basis with a group of people.'[1] This group, largely composed of supporters of the CLPD and outside-left activists, strongly advised him to stand. One hundred and fifty Labour MPs, some of them traditionally regarded as left-wingers, had signed a statement condemning the decision of the Wembley Conference. 'We'd got the electoral college,' recalls Jon Lansman, 'but the right were threatening to overturn it. There was a great deal of hysteria and we were worried. One of the main reasons the CLPD wanted Benn to run was to put the machinery into practice immediately and divert people's attention from the more fundamental question of trying to remove it.' Benn decided to delay his announcement until after the formation of the SDP because 'I didn't want it to be argued that my candidature had in some way triggered off the defections.'[2]

On the night of 2 April Benn and his supporters learned of a petition circulating among members of the Tribune Group – which he had joined for the first time only in March – calling upon him not to stand. In order to pre-empt this, in the early hours of the morning, exactly one week after the formation of the SDP, Benn issued a statement to the press from his office in the Commons announcing his intention to challenge Denis Healey for the deputy leadership. The statement, which had been through six drafts, claimed that he was standing in order to ensure that 'all those elected to positions of responsibility will be more fully accountable to Parliament, the public and the labour movement for their stewardship.' The following day a number of left-wing MPs, including the Scottish Member, Robin Cook, pleaded with him to stand down: he would only divide the party, divert attention from the struggle against the Conservatives and, in the long run, destroy his popularity within the party. Few thought he stood any chance of winning. Even his supporters expected he would get only about 35 per cent of the vote.

Kinnock, like most of the other Tribune MPs, was furious with Benn.

> I was against the contest from the start [says Kinnock]. I thought we needed a contest like we needed bubonic plague. . . . My immediate reaction was: no one should be running. It was about seven days after the bloody SDP was born. I was thoroughly against putting them in the equivalent of an oxygen tent. One reason put forward was that we had to 'test the machinery'. That's like Christmas morning when a kid's given a watch and starts taking it apart to see how it works.
>
> The weekend Benn decided to run I was in my constituency and a union branch secretary asked me, 'What the bloody hell's going on?' It was then I thought, this is going to spread like wildfire. In South Wales people talk about politics a lot, and that was all people were saying: 'What the bloody hell's going on?' If you get bashed by your opponents, you try to resist it and the only cure is to fight back more effectively. But when the wounds are self-inflicted, what can you do?

Kinnock admits that he has 'never exactly been a soul mate of Tony Benn', and it would be hard to think of two figures on the left of the Labour Party who have less in common. Benn began life in an upper-middle-class home; the son of a Labour Cabinet Minister, he was educated at Westminster public school and at New College, Oxford. He was elected an MP for Bristol in 1950, at a time when Kinnock was still banging the drum for Nye Bevan and dreaming of life as a private detective. He started out on the right of the party and only gradually moved leftwards: in 1969, for example, he supported *In Place of Strife,* the issue which sufficiently disgusted Kinnock to make him think of leaving the party. ('I do not come out of that episode very well,' Benn subsequently admitted, 'my judgement was totally wrong.')[3] Kinnock was from childhood instinctively on the left; Benn was radicalized by sitting in Cabinet: he later confessed that in the closing stages of the 1964–70 Government he 'experienced a sort of crisis within my own mind' between 'the week-day Minister and the socialist who's trying to think it out in weekend speeches . . . It was after the 1970 defeat that the outcome of that inner conflict began to take shape for me, in a clear socialist perception.'[4] From 1970 onwards Benn emerged as one of the party's main champions of left-wing policy. Contrary to the normal pattern, the older Benn got, the more radical he became. 'He immatures with age,' complained Harold Wilson.[5]

In the 1960s, as Minister of Technology, Benn had been Labour's leading scientific visionary, exponent of a technocratic, chromium-plated Britain. In the 1970s he turned his attention from the future to the past – to the history of the English working classes and the tradition of dissent. From the skin of Anthony Wedgwood Benn emerged Tony Benn, mug of tea in one hand, sandwich in the other. It was a spectacle which caused considerable grinding of teeth among other MPs. Many thought his performance a ludicrous caricature, like one of those German spies reportedly parachuted into Norfolk in 1940 wearing spats and a monocle in the mistaken belief that this was how the British behaved. 'Those of us who worked our passage from working-class backgrounds are frankly sick to the back teeth of posturing public schoolboys,' says one of the Tribunite MPs who refused to back Benn for the deputy leadership. 'Benn suffers from the Lady Chatterley syndrome: he's spent so much of his life divorced from the working classes, he sees them like gamekeeper figures –

virile and romantic. That lies at the bottom of a lot of the gut reaction against Benn.'

It may be that the greatest mistake of Benn's career was his decision not to resign when Wilson demoted him in 1975. 'If he had done that,' says one left-winger, an adviser of his at the time, 'he would certainly have ended up leader.' Kinnock agrees: 'There's no doubt that if Benn had been in 1980 where he was in 1975, there wouldn't have been any other serious candidate for the leadership.' But Benn stayed in office until Labour lost power in 1979 and in so doing undermined his credibility among many on the parliamentary left. He looked like someone who, while pushing collective responsibility to the limits, nevertheless always wanted office as long as it was available. People like Kinnock, who had refused jobs, or like Eric Heffer and Joan Lestor, who had resigned, resented his occasionally 'holier than thou' tone. This was especially infuriating to those close to Michael Foot. 'For the first time since Lansbury,' says Jill Craigie, 'the party had a genuinely left-wing leader. Michael wouldn't join the 1964–70 Government because of the Vietnam war: but Tony was there. Michael was on the CND marches in the early sixties: Tony wasn't there. Yet Tony treated Michael like a political crook.' This had a profound impact on Kinnock. 'More than anything else,' says Glenys Kinnock, 'he was affected by the way it was affecting Michael. He cared very much when he thought people were betraying Michael. He couldn't understand it.' Foot read out a long statement to Benn at a Shadow Cabinet meeting, urging him, if he was dissatisfied with the way the party was being run, to stand against him for the leadership rather than against Healey for the job of deputy. Benn declined the invitation.

For three weeks after Benn's announcement Kinnock kept quiet. Then, on 24 April, in a speech in Hull, he broke his silence. Although his remarks were supposedly aimed at both left and right, no one was in any doubt as to their principal target. In 1980 Benn had told the party conference that a future Labour Government would introduce 'three major pieces of legislation within the first month of the election': an industry Bill 'to extend common ownership . . . within a matter of days'; withdrawal from the EEC 'within a matter of weeks'; and the creation of 'a thousand peers' to bring about the abolition of the House of Lords.[6] Kinnock had been angered by these sweeping commitments but had held his tongue. Now he denounced those people who 'think that unity can be won or electoral support gained by giving the impression that major policies can be simultaneously fulfilled in a few weeks of government with instant prescriptions'; they were, he said, 'offering a fantasy that insults adult intelligence, invites derision and guarantees disappointment'; they were 'pushing and dragging the labour movement into narrow bigotry':

> We know in the Labour Party that we live together or we die separately, and if that is expediency, then breathing is opportunism. What we demand is that the arrogant, the obsessive, those whose political activity consists of attacking or defending the past, those who give their energies to inventing a fictitious future, recognize that too, or leave now to become the insignificant ravers in the impotent fragments that they would be without the status and the opportunity that the Labour Party gives to them.[7]

Kinnock's Hull speech found a sympathetic audience on Labour's soft left. A group of Tribunite MPs, including Robin Cook, now approached him to ask whether he would consider running for the deputy leadership on their behalf: his support in the constituencies, second in size only to Benn's, gave his attacks on the outside left an authority which few others possessed. Kinnock considered the offer briefly, then refused. Eventually John Silkin emerged as the soft left's compromise candidate.

The fact was that Kinnock was by no means yet sure in his own mind what he was going to do. Only one option was definitely closed.

> I cannot vote for Denis Healey for a leading position in the party [he wrote]. He is on the right, I am on the left. We share hostility to Toryism, agree on some areas of policy, enjoy a friendly relationship. But there are issues of policy in which I have had a strong, abiding and active belief for many years – particularly unilateral disarmament – and

the plain fact is that the difference of view over such issues makes it impossible to endorse him in a contest for office.[8]

But if supporting Healey was out of the question, what should he do? Support Benn or Silkin? Or even abstain? He talked his decision over with Glenys. 'We had more disagreements at that time than at practically any other,' she recalls. 'I often said: "Oh, for goodness' sake, why don't you leave it and vote for Tony?" He could've made our lives much easier, there's no question of that.'

The agonizing lasted throughout the summer. Kinnock appears to have made up his mind and then changed it several times. In the end it was the activities of Benn's supporters rather than of Benn himself which, he claims, gradually forced him to a decision. At a Scottish miners' gala on 13 June Arthur Scargill, leader of the miners' union, accused those members of the Labour Party 'who have openly criticized Tony Benn and, by implication, supported the candidature of Denis Healey' of 'sabotaging not only the candidature of Tony Benn but the principles of socialism which are basic to our movement'.[9] Kinnock subsequently attacked this as ' "guilt by association" tactics'. 'Arthur,' he wrote in September, 'should really know by now that the most fundamental beliefs of many socialists arise from a deep loathing of bullying. He might be interested to know that it was the strutting demagogy of that statement in Scotland which finally convinced me not to vote for Tony Benn and the attitude which his candidature had come to represent.'[10]

Six days after Scargill's speech, on 19 June, Kinnock told the fifty members of Bedwellty's General Management Committee that he had finally made up his mind to vote for John Silkin in the first ballot. He gave as his reason the 'false promises' made by Benn:

Tony's statement on creating one thousand peers to abolish the House of Lords and pull out of the EEC within twenty-four hours of winning an election are the wrong statements to make. It is giving a false prospectus to the electorate because they cannot be carried out as easily as is suggested in Tony's speeches. . . . We must not look for some kind of

Messiah. We are in danger of spoiling our chances at an election because our policies are being misrepresented and distorted.[11]

When the Bedwellty GMC next met, on 17 July, Kinnock had evidence to substantiate his belief that the deputy leadership contest was damaging Labour's standing with the electorate. The previous day had seen a by-election for the traditionally safe Labour seat of Warrington. Roy Jenkins, fighting the SDP's first parliamentary campaign, had polled over 40 per cent of the vote. He had not won, but he had cut Labour's majority from over 10,000 to less than 2,000. 'It was a disaster for us,' Kinnock told the GMC delegates. 'The internal wrangling as represented in the press has damaged our chances. We did not get a mandate in the by-election that we are wanted to take over the running of the country.'[12]

Even so, although Kinnock had now decided to support Silkin in the first ballot, he had apparently not made a definite decision to abstain in the second. 'There was a period at the beginning of August,' he says, 'when I still thought I might end up voting for Benn. Things seemed to be cooling off. I thought, well, he's standing: it's a pity not to vote. That feeling lasted about four days.' What brought it to an end, he claims, was a demonstration against unemployment in Cardiff the following week, attended by several thousand Labour supporters, including members of the Bedwellty party. Denis Healey was among those on the platform, and when he got up to speak he was howled down. 'It was very ugly,' recalls Barry Moore. 'They almost destroyed the rally.' He and Gwyn Evans exhorted people to keep quiet, but tempers became inflamed and a fight broke out between Evans and a local NUPE official. Tony Wilkins, another NUPE organizer, remembers that Evans and his colleague had to be dragged apart. Undoubtedly some of those heckling were Benn supporters. According to Terry Burns, it was 'started by communist and Socialist Worker people, and then it spread spontaneously among the miners and steelworkers who were sitting around them. People just thought they'd give Healey a good belting.'

Kinnock was disgusted, both at the intolerance and at the results it produced in the following day's papers: they ignored the reason for the rally and reported only the shouting down of Healey. 'Well,' says Kinnock, 'when the issue of unemployment could be totally flattened by the deputy leadership I thought, sod it. That put the tin hat on it.' By the time Kinnock and his family went away on holiday, he had reached a decision not to vote for Benn. 'We talked about it a lot,' recalls Glenys, 'but his mind was made up by then. He told me things might get a bit rough when we got back and it became known. In the end it was a thousand times worse than we'd expected.'

On his arrival home in London Kinnock wrote a 3,000-word article for *Tribune* setting out the reasons why he would not be voting for Benn. It was vitriolic, and *Tribune*'s editor, Dick Clements, admits to having had 'second and third thoughts' about whether or not to publish it. His decision to go ahead involved him in a heated argument with Chris Mullin, now a staff writer on the paper who had become one of Benn's closest allies.

Entitled 'Personality, Policies and Democratic Socialism', the article appeared on 18 September, only nine days before the votes were due to be cast at the party's annual conference. If Kinnock had any lingering doubts about his decision, he did not reveal them. He argued that the deputy leadership election had proved to be

> six months óf bitter and totally unnecessary division. . . . It never has been 'the only means of voting for someone who believes in Labour's policies' or anything so abjectly simple. By emphatically pressing the view that it is only possible to support radical Labour policies by supporting Tony Benn, Tony's associates have turned the contest into a gamble with policies, [yet any] disagreement with those claims has been slandered as 'opportunism', 'careerism' and evidence of every kind of departure from socialist conviction and purpose. That is the truly dangerous product of these months of contest.

He accused the Bennites of peddling the 'betrayal theory of politics', which he dismissed as 'nonsense':

> The New Testament is not the story of Judas, and the history of the

Labour Party obviously does not consist wholly, mainly or irretrievably of MacDonalds and Jenkinses or sell-out trade union officials or corrupt councillors.

After forty years in the Labour Party, thirty years in Parliament – nearly all of them on the front bench in Government and Opposition – and after over twenty years on the National Executive Committee Tony Benn obviously understands that.

However, he appears to have made no effort of which I know to disown the tactics of some of his most eminent supporters and he has spent some time in the last few years expressing views to listeners that there can be no confident hope that Labour Party policies will be implemented unless some system of regulation of leadership exists which will guarantee adherence to policy.

Kinnock accused Benn once more of making promises no Labour Government could hope to keep. He quoted the opening sentence of Benn's election manifesto for the deputy leadership, pledging 'as a first priority, to restore full employment during the lifetime of the next Labour Government'. 'I want that more than anything else,' wrote Kinnock. 'But we shall inherit a ruined industrial economy.'

A solemn promise to provide jobs for all seeking and needing them within such a short time scale is a reckless simplicity. That is why both the NEC and the TUC have refused to make such a promise.

Persistent refusal to acknowledge that fact and to convey it in reasoned explanation to reasoning audiences severely diminishes any claim that Tony has to occupy a leadership position. Whatever bruises and ill-feeling may be generated by clashes within the party they are nothing by comparison with an unsupportable promise to the millions faced with unemployment and all its effects. . . . it is not morally, economically or politically excusable to offer the most serious of all pledges of full employment when we and the jobless know that Labour could create 4 million jobs and still after five years not get full employment.

I believe that Tony has fostered antagonism within the party, he has undermined the credibility of credible policies by over-simplification, he has not disowned those who insist upon support for his candidature as the test of loyalty to Labour policy.

I believe that, through an inaccurate analysis of the position and power of the labour movement and by a tactically mistaken decision to contest the deputy leadership in 1981, Tony has significantly harmed the current standing and electoral opportunities of the Labour Party.

Kinnock denied that he was making a personal attack on Benn. If people accused him of that, 'the fault is entirely theirs for making the person of Tony Benn and support for him the definition of political conviction.' He concluded by admitting that many might accuse him of 'giving the media a field day'.

> I might [he wrote]. But it is too late to worry about that. There have been many field days. There will, I regret to say, be many more. Those who want to give the hostile media less ammunition should look to their own tactics, expressions and pronouncements.[13]

It was a virulent attack, not forgiven quickly – indeed, not forgiven at all in some quarters. For by the time it appeared the Benn campaign team knew that the result was likely to be desperately close. For several months, despite an illness that put him temporarily out of action, Benn had fought his way, with great skill and vigour, around the summer circuit of trade union conferences, steadily piling up support. The campaign had been too noisy and brash for the taste of some, including Vladimir Derer, who refused to have any part in it. 'The Bennite left ran for the deputy leadership like it was the presidency of the United Kingdom or something,' he says. 'They treated union meetings like election primaries. It came over on television simply as a naked power struggle.'

Nevertheless, the election of Benn, written off as hopeless in April, was now a strong possibility. 'At the start I don't believe Tony thought he could win,' says Jon Lansman, who acted as a full-time organizer for Benn. 'But by the beginning of the summer it was clear we could win, and certainly by the time Tony became ill we knew we were in with a chance. The press were still enormously sceptical. I think the first journalist persuaded of the seriousness of the challenge was Robert Taylor, the labour correspondent of the *Observer*. Nowadays, only the labour correspondents really understand how the Labour Party operates. The political writers haven't a clue.'

There was great excitement on the left. 'That election was not a small matter,' insists another of Benn's closest supporters. 'In those last few weeks, you really could feel the ground of British politics begin to move beneath your feet. As Fleet

Street woke up to the fact that Benn might win, reporters started ringing me up and asking me out for lunch who wouldn't normally be seen dead in my company.' Given this atmosphere, it was not surprising that Kinnock's intervention, in the closing stages of the contest, was seen as a calculated act of treachery, the last throw of an ambitious man suddenly fearful of seeing his main rival on the left get ahead of him.

There was a great deal of anger in the Brighton air that autumn as Labour assembled for its annual conference. Kinnock rode into town like a gunfighter expecting a shoot-out. For the first time Glenys stayed at home in London with the children. 'He wouldn't let me go,' she says. 'He knew what it was going to be like.' Kinnock had a foretaste of what was to come even before the election took place, when he was heckled outside the conference hall. 'Why don't you stand, Neil?' shouted one delegate. 'Then everyone can abstain.'[14]

On Sunday, 27 September, as the votes were about to be cast, the rumour in the seafront bars and hotels was that Benn had won. The right-wing Solidarity group held a rally for Healey in the morning, at which the Dunkirk spirit was much in evidence. In the afternoon, in the bar of the Grand Hotel, Kinnock met a friendly television producer who had with him the BBC's latest estimate of voting intentions. Together they went out to the back of the hotel, and over the dustbins Kinnock scanned the figures, which showed that if the Transport and General Workers' Union and NUPE both went for Benn on the second ballot, Healey would lose. Kinnock returned gloomily to the bar. Half an hour later the producer was back. He had just bumped into a NUPE official – the union was backing Healey after all.

Shortly before 8.30 that evening the chief teller read out the result, calculated to the nearest one-thousandth of 1 per cent:

BENN	36.627
HEALEY	45.369
SILKIN	18.004

Silkin was eliminated, and in the second ballot, in which Kinnock and a number of other Tribunites abstained, Healey narrowly scraped home with 50.426 per cent to Benn's 49.574. Benn had captured more than four-fifths of the constituency votes, almost two-fifths of the unions but only one-third of the PLP. The margin of Benn's defeat was exactly matched by the votes of the MPs who had abstained. If the twenty or so Tribunites said to have deserted Benn had voted for him, he would have won by 2 per cent. Ironically, if the electoral college had been divided in the way that Kinnock and the NEC had proposed at Wembley, 33–33–33, Benn would have won even without the support of the abstaining MPs.

At a party in the Queen's Hotel that night, arranged by his supporters on the Greater London Council, Benn ran through the list of organizations which had supported him: 'The Rank-and-File Mobilizing Committee, the Institute for Workers' Control, the Campaign for Labour Party Democracy, the Labour Co-ordinating Committee and many others. Comrades, thank you all very much for the tremendous work that has been put in. This is only the beginning, not in any sense the end of our campaign.'[15] While Benn was speaking, in the lobby of his hotel, a few hundred yards away, Kinnock was being surrounded by a hostile group of Benn's supporters. There was some brandishing of fists and pushing, and as he turned to leave, someone spat at him. It was not unexpected. Kinnock, as his wife says, both gets very angry himself and makes other people angry in return. He operates close to that border where political passion can sometimes turn to physical violence, and his week in Brighton in 1981 was punctuated by scuffles and shouting matches.

The day after the vote he was invited to discuss the result on the BBC television programme *Panorama*. 'I went to fetch him at about 7.30,' recalls a member of the programme's staff, 'only to find him in the middle of a furious row at a fringe meeting.' During transmission Kinnock got into yet another argument, this time with a man who was emerging as

163

a particular enemy of his, Arthur Scargill. 'The left-wing MPs,' taunted Scargill, 'or those who claim to be left-wing, actually betrayed not merely their supporters but the fight that's taken place over many years.' He accused Kinnock of dishonesty and 'sabotage', of ensuring the victory of a candidate 'who supports the Common Market, who supports nuclear arms, who supports . . . the continuation of the present system under which we live'. Kinnock, incensed, rounded on the miners' leader:

> Arthur thinks he's got a licence to call me dishonest. He hasn't. I've been fighting for those policies longer than the candidate that he supported and, indeed, in the party longer than Arthur himself and I won't take it from anyone that when I make a decision about what is best in my view, democratic view, for the party and pursue that course that I'm being dishonest. The fact is, Arthur, that when Tony – with the greatest respect to him – was occupying a seat in that Cabinet which he now claims to despise, I was voting against it and campaigning to try and divert that Government back to what I believe is the socialist path and I won't take claims of dishonesty from you or anybody else. One other thing I've got to tell you, as I've told you before in print. The fact is that it wasn't Tony Benn that lost the election yesterday. . . . If anybody lost him that deputy leadership election yesterday it was you by the attitudes you espouse and the people like you who espouse them. We're not having them in the Labour Party, mate. We want to beat the Tories.[16]

(Kinnock is scathing about Scargill to this day, especially regarding his performance as President of the NUM. 'He's destroying the coal industry single-handed,' said Kinnock during his campaign for the leadership of the party in 1983. 'He's the labour movement's nearest equivalent to a First World War general.')

The results of the NEC elections, announced on the day after his *Panorama* appearance, provided Kinnock with the first tangible evidence of the price he would have to pay for his opposition to Tony Benn. While Benn's vote jumped to 530,000, Kinnock's slipped to 371,000 – a drop of 61,000 votes since the previous year. From second place on the Executive he fell to fifth. There was speculation that he would lose his seat altogether the following year.

His roughest time at the conference came on Wednesday

night, at the *Tribune* rally. He was repeatedly heckled and taunted with being a 'Judas' ('Oh, so Benn's Christ now, is he?' shouted an unidentified voice). Six years before Kinnock had made his name at the rally and raised a record collection; now someone contributed thirty pieces of silver. In 1978 the MP Margaret Beckett had been among those who had helped him celebrate his election to the NEC; now she made what the *Observer* called

> a speech dripping with venom, a lengthy attack on Kinnock which avoided mentioning his name. The gist of it was that there are times when everyone must jump into line for the common cause, and that in the first serious test of his loyalty to the left, Kinnock had failed. The subject of this tirade sat white and numbed, as if watching his torturer plunge the poker into the coals.[17]

After she sat down Mrs Beckett was attacked in her turn by Joan Lestor, one of the Tribunite abstainers, who pointed out that such criticism came ill from the woman who had replaced her as a junior Minister in the last Labour Government – especially as Miss Lestor had resigned in protest at cuts in public expenditure. It was a rancorous evening from start to finish. Kinnock had known what to expect but had decided to fulfil his regular engagement anyway. 'When you're picked,' he explains, 'you play.'

The ugliest week of his political career was rounded off on Friday lunchtime in the lavatory of the Grand Hotel. He was alone, washing his hands, when a young man walked in. Kinnock paid him no attention. Suddenly the youth swung round and lashed out at him with his foot, a high kick which caught Kinnock a painful blow on the elbow. The shadow education spokesman seized his attacker and pulled him in close. 'Then I beat the shit out of him.' When Kinnock rejoined his companions in the bar he told them what had happened. One went back in to check, but the youth had gone. 'Apparently there was blood and vomit all over the floor,' says Kinnock. A few hours later he boarded a train out of Brighton.

Few could have imagined that two years later, literally to

the day, Kinnock would be returning to the same town in triumph, endorsed by an overwhelming majority as Labour's next leader. In 1981 he appeared to have done irreparable damage to the main source of his political strength: his popularity among the rank and file. Robin Cook for one, shocked by the bitterness of Kinnock's reception, no longer regarded him as a 'viable candidate for the leadership'. The Bennites kept a special place of hatred in their hearts for him. Although there is no evidence to support it, the belief was widespread that Kinnock had personally organized the Tribunite abstentions. He dismisses the suggestion as 'complete rubbish'. But he was the most prominent of the abstainers, and the forcefulness with which he advanced his case in *Tribune* may have swayed some who might otherwise have voted for Benn. The outside left wanted revenge. Nationally, they began to plot his removal from the NEC. Locally, like the other abstainers, he faced the prospect of a reselection conference the following spring. 'I think they must expect some discomfort from the rank and file in their own constituencies in the coming months,' predicted Jeremy Corbyn, a hard-line Benn supporter, on television that week. 'I'm sure that people in this hall will do their best to discuss the matter with them at the appropriate time.'[18]

Chapter Sixteen

MILITANT, TATCHELL AND RESELECTION

Bedwellty, like more than four hundred other Constituency Labour Parties, had supported Tony Benn. 'He was practically a god round here,' says one local activist. When he had fallen ill in June the General Management Committee had sent him a get well card. In September they had decided by a margin of three to one to support him for the deputy leadership. Kinnock found himself in a minority in his own back yard: even his close friend Barry Moore supported Benn. It was inevitable that his behaviour would bring criticism, and on 9 October, a week after his return from Brighton, he was closely questioned by the General Management Committee. Kinnock reiterated his views: 'He could not give Tony Benn his vote because his decision to stand had caused great difficulty within the party' – the events of the last six months had 'jeopardized the prospect of ever winning another election'. He went on:

> The threat to our existence is greater than it has ever been in our history. If we do not conquer the threat of the SDP taking votes from us, we will be cast into the political wilderness for years. The party is far more important than the career of individual MPs. . . . Tony Benn has actually said he would only accept a Shadow Cabinet post if certain conditions are met. This is not socialism. Neil said he would be voting for Tony in the elections to the Shadow Cabinet: but do not con yourself into thinking that he will support the leader. . . .

A number of delegates were dissatisfied with Kinnock's answer. 'I don't support individuals, but the policies they stand for,' said one. 'It was a sad loss to the movement that Tony had not won the election.'[1]

There was a faction within the constituency which had been growing increasingly suspicious of its MP ever since the beginning of 1980, when he had refused to guarantee full restoration of the cuts in public expenditure. Kinnock's failure to vote for Benn seemed to them a confirmation of their fears. 'I was totally outraged at the way he orchestrated the anti-Benn campaign,' claims Ray Davies. 'From that point on I saw him as more of a threat to the left than Margaret Thatcher.' Terry Burns says it was 'the thing that galled me most. . . . I felt it was a stab in the back.'

Burns and Davies had both known Kinnock in the period before he became an MP. In 1967, as a young apprentice, Burns had attended Kinnock's WEA classes, and Kinnock had encouraged him to try for higher education. Burns had been successful. He had become a college lecturer and, in his words, 'discovered the classic texts of Marxism'. In the early 1970s he became a member of the Militant tendency and he and Kinnock 'drifted apart'. Burns 'moved to Cardiff, which was more fruitful ground for Militant than Bedwellty, which was centre-right'. He worked there full-time for Militant for a year, before returning to Bedwellty in 1977. At that time Kinnock and his supporters had tight control over the constituency. 'The GMC was like a bloody fan club,' says Burns. 'There was no criticism. Whatever Neil did was right.' In 1978 Burns was elected to the GMC. So were his wife Ros and his brother Tony, a shop steward; they, too, were Militant members: 'We were the people who used to ask the awkward questions.'

Militant was never very strong in Bedwellty. 'It's difficult to build up support when you've got a charismatic candidate like Kinnock,' says Burns. There were perhaps three or four Militant members on the GMC. But there were other GMC delegates, such as Ray Davies who works for the British Steel Corporation, who sympathized with them. The hard left in Bedwellty was in a minority. But it was a minority which was sufficiently substantial and vocal to cause Kinnock some concern. His abstention in the deputy leadership election cost him its support. Then, in rapid succession, came a series of issues which set the two sides on a collision course.

The first concerned the Militant tendency itself. In 1975 the party's then General Secretary, Reg Underhill, had prepared a detailed report on the organization. Having interviewed former members and analysed its internal publications (in particular *British Perspectives and Tasks,* on which, said Underhill, Militant 'cut the teeth of their new supporters'),[2] he concluded that it was a party-within-a-party, an 'entryist' Trotskyite organization with its own structure, full-time organizers and finances. At the time the NEC had refused to act on the Underhill report. But at the 1981 party conference the right made significant gains in the NEC elections, and as Labour's image among the electorate deteriorated, Michael Foot came under pressure to take action against the extreme left. Several Militant supporters, including Dave Nellist in Coventry and Pat Wall in Bradford, were selected as Labour parliamentary candidates. At the beginning of November a full inquiry into Militant was demanded by the Manifesto Group of MPs. There was also a call for the NEC to refuse to allow Tariq Ali, formerly a prominent member of the International Marxist Group, to become a member of the Hornsey Labour Party.

The hard left in Bedwellty was watching these events with mounting concern. On 13 November it submitted a resolution to the monthly GMC meeting calling upon the National Executive 'to firmly reject any form of "witchhunt" against the Labour left and in particular the supporters of "Militant" who have been singled out for special attention. . . . We call upon the NEC to confirm the right of all party members to hold any views, provided those views are not hostile to socialism and do not reject the authority of the National Conference.' The motion was passed overwhelmingly by twenty-seven votes to three.[3]

In December the crisis in the Labour Party suddenly

deepened. A young man called Peter Tatchell had been selected as Labour's prospective parliamentary candidate for the south London constituency of Bermondsey. Tatchell was not a supporter of Militant, but he exemplified the new breed of activist which, traditionalists in the party thought, was destroying Labour's electoral chances. Describing his speech on the night he was selected to fight the seat, Tatchell later said:

> I emphasized the importance of extra-parliamentary struggles to carry out a left-wing programme which included withdrawal from the EEC and NATO, troops out of Ireland, extended public ownership under workers' control, a thirty-five hour week and £80 national minimum wage, opposition to nuclear power, abolition of the House of Lords and private medicine, democratic control of the police, positive action for women and ethnic minorities, repeal of racist immigration laws, unilateral nuclear disarmament and its replacement by a system of territorial defence with a citizens' army, and a new international economic order to secure development and justice for the exploited poor countries of the world.[4]

Whether this was all to be achieved within the lifetime of a Parliament was not made clear, but whatever else it was, it was not Kinnock's 'socialism by plod'.

It was that phrase 'extra-parliamentary' which was to dominate the controversy that followed Tatchell's adoption. On 26 November James Wellbeloved, a former Labour MP who had defected to the SDP, raised in the House of Commons an article by Tatchell published the previous May. Writing in the outside-left monthly magazine *London Labour Briefing*, Tatchell had claimed:

> Debates and parliamentary divisions are fruitless cosmetic exercises given the Tories' present Commons majority. And if we recognize this, we are either forced to accept Tory edicts as a *fait accompli* or we must look to new more militant forms of extra-parliamentary opposition which involve mass popular participation and challenge the Government's right to rule. Is it not perfectly legitimate to confront and defy the Government when its actions so tangibly threaten the essence of our Welfare State, the living standards and trade union rights of working-class people, and the equality of women and ethnic minorities?

Tatchell went on to advocate 'a "Siege of Parliament" to demand jobs – a march on the House of Commons led by 250

Labour MPs and 1,000 Labour mayors and councillors', who would hold a 'sit-down occupation of the Westminster area'. Along with this there should be a GLC-sponsored 'Tent City [for] the unemployed and homeless in the grounds of County Hall'.[5]

Having read out choice extracts to MPs, Wellbeloved challenged Michael Foot and Roy Hattersley, the party's Shadow Home Secretary, to 'denounce Mr Peter Tatchell and all those who support him'. Foot and Hattersley stayed silent, but a week later, on 3 December, Wellbeloved raised the subject again during Questions to the Prime Minister. Did the Prime Minister not agree, taunted Wellbeloved, that such an 'irresponsible demand should be condemned by all those who hold precious parliamentary democracy and should not be condoned by craven silence'? This time Foot was stung into replying: 'Since the matter has been raised, can I say, Mr Speaker, that the individual concerned is not an endorsed member . . . of the Labour Party, and as far as I am concerned, never will be.'[6]

It was a dreadful blunder, a self-inflicted wound from which Foot, in a sense, never fully recovered ('as if Ramsay Mac-Donald had written the Zinoviev Letter to himself', as one left-winger puts it). Foot's humiliation began a few hours later, when he had to issue a statement correcting the word 'member' to 'candidate'. The truth was that under the constitution of the Labour Party no one had the right to refuse the party's endorsement to a candidate unless there had been some irregularity in the initial selection procedure, which in Tatchell's case there had not been. Nevertheless, in order to avoid public ridicule of the leader of the party, Foot's loyalists now had to pretend that there had.

Back in November Kinnock's original advice to Foot had been that Tatchell should be left alone: he was bound to do so badly in a by-election that he would seriously discredit the outside left and its policies. Now he was in a dilemma. He was appalled by Foot's action but could not bring himself to desert him. On 16 December the Labour Party's headquarters in

Walworth Road was besieged by the media as the National Executive met to consider what it should do. The committee was divided evenly and, as over the issue of who should draft the manifesto, it was Kinnock's vote which was later seen as having been decisive. While soft left-wingers like Judith Hart and Joan Lestor voted against Foot, Kinnock voted with him; by fifteen votes to fourteen the NEC decided to withhold its endorsement from Peter Tatchell. The committee also decided, by nineteen votes to ten, to set up a fresh inquiry into the Militant tendency: again Kinnock voted with the majority.

Emerging from the meeting a few minutes later, Tony Benn told waiting reporters that he was now 'speaking as deputy leader, because of course Denis Healey's majority has now defected to the SDP'. He called on party members 'not to be discouraged' by the NEC's decisions 'but to go on campaigning for peace and justice'. Michael Foot said Benn was 'talking through his hat'. John Golding, one of the party's more aggressive right-wingers, called Benn a 'loony'.[7] To complete the party's disarray, that night Hornsey Labour Party voted to grant Tariq Ali membership – despite the presence of an NEC representative with a letter instructing them not to. 'For Labour's National Executive,' wrote Peter Kellner, the *New Statesman*'s political editor, 'the Tatchell–Ali dilemma has acquired the importance El Alamein had for the Eighth Army – the battleground, insignificant in itself, where a decisive contest was fought between two armies.'[8]

Kinnock's decision to support Foot over Tatchell met with widespread dismay on the left.

> If Kinnock and people like him justify their action on the basis of personal friendship with Foot [wrote Tatchell], what price are socialist principles when 'old pals' can supersede them? I was the victim, the sacrifice required, to ensure that Foot's face could be saved. Kinnock again implied as much when he said on television that as a good socialist I would understand why he had to vote in the way he did. I did not understand it then and I still do not understand it now.

The logic of Tatchell's argument is inescapable, and he had other bitter, personal comments to make:

Kinnock, especially, did lasting damage to his standing among the left of the party, not only by his vote on my endorsement, but also by his insensitive and reactionary remarks before and after the NEC meeting. Since he had become shadow spokesperson on education Kinnock had noticeably lurched to the right, not an unfamiliar characteristic of many Labour MPs when the carrot of high office is dangled in front of their noses. Kinnock was quoted in the *Express* as saying: 'I'm not in favour of witchhunts but I do not mistake bloody witches for fairies.' It took no great insight to recognize the blatantly anti-gay tenor of those remarks. . . . It was sad to see a 'socialist' pandering so crudely to anti-gay prejudice. Perhaps he felt he had to play to the macho, rugby-playing gallery, protesting his masculinity. . . . [9]

Kinnock was scheduled to meet the Bedwellty General Management Committee in two days' time, and he could be in no doubt now that he seriously risked alienating even his staunchest supporters. Immediately after the NEC vote he received from Barry Moore a highly critical letter rushed to his house via Special Delivery. 'I said to myself: "Sod this, I've got to get things down on paper," ' Moore later recalled. 'I wrote to Neil asking where the hell we go from here, and what Michael Foot was playing at. Neil's Tatchell vote will be remembered against him even longer than not backing Benn. It was a major blunder.' [10]

Kinnock was shaken. He had built his career on his instinctive rapport with ordinary party members. He thought he understood them. He relied upon them. He once wrote warmly of 'the most practised pathology unit known to politics, my rod and staff who usually comfort me – the Activists'. [11] Now they were the ones who were attacking him. 'When he seemed to be falling out with his constituency,' says Glenys, 'that worried him a lot.' The day after the NEC meeting a reporter visited Kinnock at his home in Ealing and left a vivid portrait of him on the eve of his confrontation in Bedwellty. He looked 'pale and distracted', 'on the verge of exhausted misery', 'close to tears' as he 'snapped at the family's frisky Persian cat'; he was 'up one minute, down the next'. A photograph taken at the time shows him huddled up on a park bench, his chin sunk on his chest, with the caption: 'Brooding'.

He was fatalistic about the next day's meeting with his local party:

> I hope to persuade them by argument to the view I took. If I don't, well, that's how it goes. There's no point in getting all bitter about it. . . . My grandfathers and father used to take their whole existence in their hands when they told the bosses where to get off – but they did it, and I can't do any less. . . . If losing my seat on the NEC is the penalty I face, then so be it. If the price of popularity is the auction of your integrity, it's not worth a damn. Periodically, I've seriously considered quitting Parliament. Week after week you put in seventy to eighty hours work and have nothing tangible to show for it. What I decide to do after the next election will be dictated by the necessary attitude the party has to adopt. . . . We must get away from this belief that anyone with ambition in the party must support Tatchell or invite Tariq Ali to dinner.[12]

Kinnock's spirits, ebbing all year, had reached rock bottom. 'I'm fed up with the disputes in my own party,' he said to one writer. 'I'm depressed that it's so hard to get across alternative policies. . . . I'm tired because I'm doing too much. I'm buggering myself at the moment. I don't get a hell of a lot of enjoyment out of it. . . .'[13] 'Before Christmas,' he told the *Morning Star* in 1982, 'I was on the point of despair.'[14]

That Friday he travelled down to Pontllanfraith. In the evening sixty-three members of the GMC met Kinnock to discuss the state of the party. Various resolutions and letters before the delegates condemned the recent actions of the NEC. Kinnock belligerently tabled three motions of his own:

1. This CLP endorses the NEC rejection of Tariq Ali's membership of the Labour Party.
2. This CLP endorses the NEC rejection of Peter Tatchell as Prospective Parliamentary Candidate for Bermondsey.
3. This CLP endorses the NEC action in instigating an inquiry into the Militant tendency.

The official minutes discreetly describe what followed as a 'long and full debate'.[15] It was, by all accounts, a shouting match. The resolution on Tariq Ali was 'carried overwhelmingly on a show of hands', but the other two were much more closely fought. Defending his decision to support Foot over Tatchell, Kinnock quoted his father. It was easy enough to stand by people when they were right, Gordon once told him;

the true test of loyalty was to stick with someone when you knew he or she was wrong. It is not an argument which withstands much analysis. As for Militant, there is general agreement that Kinnock completely lost his temper. 'I know what they're like,' Terry Burns alleges Kinnock shouted. 'They once stuck a dead rat and a used sanitary towel through my door.' Ray Davies also remembers Kinnock claiming that Militant members 'stuck dead rats through his letterbox'. Ros Burns burst into tears. 'My brother Tony asked him point-blank if he was suggesting we'd done it,' says Terry Burns. 'Kinnock denied it. There was absolute uproar. He'd gone way over the top. He's capable of that. He doesn't like being heckled. The result was a great deal of verbal abuse between the two of us.' When the vote was eventually taken, Kinnock's motion on Tatchell was narrowly carried by twenty-six votes to twenty-one. On the question of Militant, perhaps as a result of his outburst about dead rats, he lost by twenty-two votes to eighteen.

If Kinnock harboured any hopes that this might mark the end of his constituency problems, he was quickly disappointed. Ominously, the same meeting also laid down the timetable for its reselection procedure. On 5 January nomination forms would be sent out to anyone who wished to challenge him; nominations would close on 19 February; a shortlist would be drawn up on 5 March; and the selection conference itself would take place on 19 March. That night, infuriated by Kinnock's attack on Militant, his opponents met to discuss putting up a candidate against him.

There was never much doubt that Kinnock would retain the seat. The left's aim was simply to force him to go through the reselection procedure and at the same time to attract enough votes to give him a nasty jolt. The most credible challenger would have been Ron Davies. He was thirty-five years old and had been a member of the local party for seventeen of them. He was the education officer for the Mid-Glamorgan County Council and an active member of the hard left. But

Davies was ambitious. He had his eyes on the safe Labour seat of neighbouring Caerphilly and he was not eager to waste his time on a kamikaze mission against Kinnock in Bedwellty. Despite several days of persuasion, he refused to stand, although he did promise to give his help and support to whomever Terry Burns and the rest eventually picked. (Rather than let Kinnock hear about this at second hand, Davies rang Kinnock to tell him what he proposed to do: 'The conversation,' he recalls, 'was abruptly terminated.') After Davies turned them down, Burns thought he might have to do the deed himself. 'I decided,' he says, 'that if no one else would stand, I'd do it. Then Ray Davies announced that he'd like to take Kinnock on, and I was happy to support him.'

As was the case with Lance Rogers twelve years before, there was a sense in which Ray Davies was the best possible challenger from Kinnock's point of view. A likeable and charismatic figure, a singer with the Caerphilly Male Voice Choir, Davies nevertheless had a reputation as a maverick. During the steel strike of 1980 he achieved notoriety in the press as the Justice of the Peace who had been arrested twice on the picket lines and thrown off the Bench as a result. As a local councillor he had proved so rebellious that he was currently suspended from the ruling Labour Group – the third time this had happened over the past couple of years. In Davies's mind Kinnock was an enormous danger to the left, an ambitious opportunist who had to be stopped. 'As early as 1980 I began to feel he should be challenged by someone,' says Davies. 'It seemed the most important thing in my life to get someone to stand against Neil. But I couldn't persuade anyone. They all said he was impregnable and that no one would even get a nomination. So I made the decision to do it myself, and after that GMC meeting on Militant I got the support of the hard left.'

Davies told his wife and son of his decision over the Christmas holidays. There was a violent family argument. It was a 'shocking thing to do', said his son. Mrs Davies was more forthright. 'My wife's an ardent Neil supporter. She said that if I went ahead and did it, my bags would be packed and I'd be out the door. She made her decision and she stuck to it. She booted me out. She thought a lot of Neil Kinnock.'

Kinnock made a point of trying to keep out of the controversy. 'He never appeared on any platform with me,' claims Davies. 'He never took any part. He left all the work to his boys.' Kinnock's supporters were organized by Barry Moore, and once they realized they had a fight on their hands they lobbied hard. Davies is convinced that he was the victim of a series of dirty tricks. In order to campaign for nominations he asked for a list of affiliated organizations. 'I had complete trust and faith I'd get it. But I had to wait fourteen days, and by the time it came half of them had already made their nominations. I was angry and bitter about that. . . . The Kinnock machine was trying to scoop up as many nominations as possible.'

He also alleges that the Annual General Meeting of his own branch of the constituency party, Bedwas and Trethomas, was packed by thirty-four people 'most of whom had not attended party meetings for the past few years'. The turnout, he claims, was the result of a 'secret meeting' convened by Barry Moore with the right-wing branch secretary, Cissie Powell, who, along with her friends, ferried parties of elderly members to the meeting in cars. Davies's appeal for the branch's nomination was heard in total silence. 'I made a reasonable speech, but I never even got a clap.' When Mrs Powell read out a letter from Kinnock asking for their support, she received a 'standing ovation'. Not only did Davies fail to get the nomination, but he was also thrown out of his job as information officer, a post he had held for seven years. 'The Kinnock people wanted it to look as though I couldn't even win support in my own area,' complains Davies. 'One ward which I did win, Machen, was challenged by Moore and Co., went to the NEC in London and was declared null. It was dirty.'

On their side, the Kinnock camp allege malpractice by the hard left. According to Gwyn Evans, 'The Davies people went round to branches and often told blatant lies, along the lines of "Neil welcomes reselection". I'm still very bitter about the whole thing.' Kinnock accused Davies in the local press of personalizing the issue. News of the in-fighting was leaked by Davies's supporters to the radical Welsh magazine *Rebecca*, which claimed:

> The knives are out in Bedwellty, where steelworker Ray Davies has dared to challenge Neil Kinnock, would-be leader of the Labour Party. The MP's henchmen – horrified at the sacrilege – have stopped at nothing to block Davies's path. Kinnock himself is taking care to get no blood on his hands, but his disciples have forged some unholy alliances.

The magazine suggested there had been 'plots' and 'skullduggery':

> Kinnock could advise his boys to lay off. . . . After all, he is a member of the Campaign for Labour Party Democracy.[16]

After two months of ill-tempered campaigning, on 5 March 1982 the GMC met to draw up a shortlist. Kinnock had won thirty-seven nominations, Davies six, of which only one, Cefn Fforest, was a constituency branch; the others were from affiliated organizations, including Rhymney Valley Trades Council, an NUM lodge and branches of the ISTC and ASTMS. The GMC agreed a shortlist of two, Kinnock and Davies, and also decided to turn down a request from Granada Television, which wanted to film the proceedings. The reselection conference was to take place in a fortnight's time. 'I have to concede,' Davies was quoted as saying, 'that Mr Kinnock is the favourite.'[17]

On the night of Friday, 19 March, seventy-four delegates assembled in the council offices in Pontllanfraith to listen to the two candidates. Each was to be given fifteen minutes to put his case and then to answer ten minutes of questions. Hubert Morgan, the General Secretary of the Welsh Labour Party, was on hand to ensure that the rules were enforced. Kinnock came alone, without Glenys, and was clearly nervous. Barry Moore was sympathetic: 'It was like Tottenham Hotspur coming to play Blackwood Town. Neil had nothing to gain. All he could do was lose face, so there was a certain trepidation.'

Ray Davies, on the other hand, was feeling in tremendous form. His young daughter had been seriously ill in hospital for several weeks, and for a time there were fears that she might not recover. His wife was sleeping by her bedside every night. On the evening of the selection conference Davies went to the hospital.

> Time was getting on and I thought I might even miss the meeting. Then the surgeon came out and told us she was going to be all right. I left straight away and went up to the conference, and it was as though a great weight had been lifted off my shoulders. I couldn't believe it: I wasn't nervous. I just couldn't wait to get there. I arrived five minutes late. I walked into the back room where Hubert and Neil were waiting. I'd never been more calm and relaxed in my life, and I'd never seen Neil more upset and fidgety.

A coin was tossed. Kinnock lost and went on first.

He made a poor speech. 'It was the worst I've ever heard him speak,' recalls one of the delegates. 'He was a nervous wreck. Nothing came together. Even his supporters had difficulty in sustaining more than polite applause.' He began by thanking 'those people who had supported him when he was in a minority in the past over such items as devolution and public expenditure cuts'. He said that he felt reselection was 'good, because it gave the constituency a chance to review its MP' and 'to restate political ideals and beliefs'. He spoke about the need to protect 'the old, young and infirm' and attacked the arms race and capitalism, while repeating his familiar refrain: 'We will not achieve power and carry out our socialist ideals unless we present an acceptable and convincing argument to the electorate.'[18] During questions he was asked about coalition government (he would never accept it, said Kinnock) and devolution (equally unacceptable). He was caught slightly off-balance by a technical question about why he was not supporting a Ten Minute Rule Bill relating to unilateralism. According to Tony Wilkins, a Davies supporter, this question was supplied to them by a 'sympathetic London journalist'.

179

After Kinnock had finished he made his way to the back room where Davies was waiting. 'Go on, it's your turn,' he told him. Davies was startled by Kinnock's appearance as he passed him. 'He looked utterly and completely drained,' he says. 'Sweat was pouring off him.'

Davies devoted the bulk of his speech to a lengthy account of the betrayals of party policy by previous Labour Governments and the inevitability of further betrayal given the nature of the Parliamentary Labour Party:

> For every Dick Taverne or Woodrow Wyatt, George Brown, David Owen, William Rodgers, Shirley Williams, Reg Prentice we have always had a goodly band of PLP members who are not committed to the socialism you and I believe in. And the real truth is, comrades, that because of its very character and nature, the Parliamentary Labour Party and its leadership has mutilated some fine and great policies over the past years.[19]

As the votes were counted, Kinnock and Davies sat together in a cold and musty room at the back of the hall. 'His attitude towards me was one of extreme politeness,' recalls Davies. 'I tried to talk about politics while we were waiting, but he kept turning the conversation back to small talk – how were Audrey and the family? How was my work going on the council? I got the impression they were fifteen minutes he could have done without.'

His performance notwithstanding, the result was an overwhelming victory for Kinnock, by sixty-two votes to twelve. Davies made a good-humoured speech of congratulation to the winner. 'Despite the closeness of the vote. . . ,' he began. Kinnock 'thanked the conference for endorsing him and said that we must fight together to win the next election to implement our policies'.[20]

To his credit, Kinnock refused to bear any grudges against the people who had opposed him. Both Ron and Ray Davies were eventually selected to fight other constituencies in the general election: Ron in Caerphilly, which he won by a majority of over 11,000, and Ray in Cardiff Central, where he was decisively beaten into third place by the Conservatives and the SDP/Liberal Alliance. In both cases, Kinnock campaigned for them. He spent a day in Cardiff with Ray; Barry Moore also helped Ray out with his organization. In Caerphilly Kinnock spoke at Ron Davies's eve-of-poll rally. He even continued to greet Terry Burns with a friendly nod and a 'Hiya, kid' whenever he saw him. 'For all that I think he was wrong at that time,' said Burns grudgingly shortly after Kinnock's election as leader, 'I still believe that as leader he'll be a million times better than anything we've had in my lifetime.'

After the reselection battle Kinnock had no further trouble in his constituency. In June he and Barry Moore pushed through the GMC a motion disaffiliating Bedwellty from the Campaign for Labour Party Democracy; at the same time Kinnock decided not to renew his own subscription. In September the GMC voted by thirty-five votes to six to support the NEC's proposal to set up a register of groups operating within the Labour Party, the first stage of the long-awaited purge of Militant. In October an attempt by Terry Burns and Ron Davies to persuade the GMC to send a delegate to the hard-left 'Steering Committee Against the Witchhunt' was beaten decisively, thirty-one to seven. A few months after that boundary changes took away much of the hard left's numerical strength on the GMC and redistributed it to neighbouring constituencies. A chapter in Kinnock's political life came to a close. In 1983 Bedwellty officially disappeared, to be replaced by a new constituency, Islwyn.

Chapter Seventeen
HIT-LISTED

The impact of Labour's internal chaos was reflected in the opinion polls. In December 1981, with the SDP at the peak of its fortunes, Gallup found that Labour was supported by only 23.5 per cent of the electorate. There was a slight rally in the spring of 1982, but then came the Falklands crisis, and by July the party's share of the vote stood at 27.5 per cent. Privately, Kinnock told people that he now knew how it must have felt to be a Liberal MP in the 1920s. Publicly, he blamed Labour's troubles on the narrow-mindedness of sections of the left.

> As a socialist [he told the *Morning Star* in May], I accuse those who only want to win an election under certain terms and conditions of irresponsible unreality. They are making intolerable demands and when you do not acquiesce in them they accuse you of deviation or worse. . . . To get a leadership committed to the policies and to ruin them seems to me to be a Pyrrhic victory.

He went on:

> They say, 'Better no Labour Government than one like the last one.' That self-indulgence infuriates me. . . . They are willing to condemn millions of people to unemployment, bad housing, deficiencies in education, bad health provision and so on. . . . they surrender the right to call themselves socialists since they are willing to fight to the last drop of someone else's blood.

Kinnock was bitter about Benn, but he took care not to attack him in person.

> There is personal antipathy toward Tony Benn, but I do not share it.

There are far too few socialists to go around picking and choosing between them on the basis of personal animosity.[1]

Kinnock directed his attacks instead at the 'Bennites', the people around him, and they, for their part, returned his hostility in more than equal measure.

A new umbrella group, known as Labour Liaison '82, was set up by the outside left. Jon Lansman and Vladimir Derer were on its steering committee, Arthur Scargill among its supporters. The decision was taken early on that Benn should not again challenge Healey for the deputy leadership. Instead the aim of the group, which drew support from a number of hard-left organizations, was to tighten the hard left's grip on the NEC. A slate of candidates was drawn up. In the constituency section Labour Liaison's target was to remove the two soft left-wingers who failed to vote for Benn, Neil Kinnock and Joan Lestor, and to replace them by Norman Atkinson and Audrey Wise, two MPs unlikely to deviate from the hard left's line. This slate of approved candidates was given extensive circulation in the constituencies and trade unions.

Their manoeuvrings were well reported in the press. On 19 May, for example, *The Times* carried a detailed account of a meeting at the House of Commons of ten MPs who supported Labour Liaison '82, among them Tony Benn, Les Huckfield, Stuart Holland, Joan Maynard, Michael Meacher, Dennis Skinner and Reg Race. The meeting lasted four hours and was attended by representatives from the CLPD and a Trotskyite organization, the Socialist Campaign for Labour Victory. All the group's candidates for the NEC were reportedly asked to sign a 'purity oath' promising to support such things as withdrawal from the EEC, unilateral nuclear disarmament, and a campaign of opposition to 'witchhunts directed against groups, individuals or candidates'.[2]

Kinnock and Joan Lestor, watching these activities, tried to affect a kind of gallows humour. At the beginning of the summer they wrote a joint letter to the *Guardian* expressing concern at the fact that the paper had published an editorial which had attacked Benn while applauding their behaviour: such support might well 'in these neurotic times be used as a nail in the political coffin that Mr Reg Race and other funeral contractors are apparently trying to make for us'.[3]

Kinnock pinned his hopes of survival on his traditional links with the constituencies. Back in 1980 he had told his local party that 'he was breaking with normal parliamentary conventions and taking labour movement engagements even when the three-line whips are on.'[4] Now, with his NEC seat in jeopardy, Kinnock was busier than ever before. Between November 1981 and October 1982 he did not ask a single oral question in Parliament, put down only twenty-eight written questions and voted in just seventy-nine out of a total of 332 divisions.[5] Excluding those who died during the session or who represented Northern Irish seats, this gave Kinnock the tenth-worst attendance record in the entire House of Commons – an astonishing performance for a Shadow Cabinet spokesman.

Leaving his colleagues behind in Westminster, Kinnock went off on what he called 'mini-tours', driving an average of 500 miles and making ten speeches a week. He would visit schools and colleges during the day and address Constituency Labour Parties and trade union branches in the evenings. He developed an intimate knowledge of the workings of British Rail. 'I use sleepers a lot,' he once explained, when asked to describe a day in his life, 'so I could start the morning stranded in some siding.' He usually had only one Saturday in three free to spend with his family. 'At least two nights a week will mean meetings in or near London. . . . If I can get home by eleven o'clock, Glenys will stay up and we'll have a cup of tea and a chat, but unfortunately it's often later. I like to get a really good kip, about eight hours, once a fortnight, but otherwise I can manage on four or five. There's no alternative.' He paid tribute to his wife: 'I couldn't do what I do without Glenys,' he said.[6]

While Kinnock toured the country over the summer trying to shore up his support, the hard left actively sought to undermine it. He did not expect to be invited to address the *Tribune* rally that autumn – as a member of the paper's board, he had voted against the appointment of its new editor, Chris Mullin, a prominent Bennite. He confessed to being 'amazed' when he was invited, in the third week of September. Never one to duck a challenge, he immediately accepted.

He had no illusions about the vulnerability of his position on the Executive. There were plenty of people who wanted to see him lose: at the party conference that autumn Gwyn Evans bumped into one delegate who told him that his mandate from his constituency was to come to Blackpool and vote for anyone, as long as it was not Kinnock. But although the threat was undoubtedly a serious one, beneath the surface opinion in the party as a whole was beginning to shift in Kinnock's direction. On 27 September, the first day of the conference, Jim Mortimer made his debut as the new General Secretary with a strong attack on Militant. 'Militant is not just a newspaper,' he said. 'The Militant tendency is an organized faction [with] its own long-term programme, principles and policy quite distinct from those of the Labour Party.' By more than 5 million votes to less than 2 million, delegates voted to set up a register of groups operating within the party. The way was now clear for a purge – not, Mortimer hastened to add, of Militant's 'wider circle of sympathizers' but of the 'inner, organizing group'.[7]

The setting up of the register was the first blow to the hard left. The second came the following day. Centre and right-wing unions, co-ordinated by a caucus of general secretaries meeting regularly at the St Ermin's Hotel in London, had organized a counter-coup to recapture control of the NEC. They had done well in 1981; now they made further and decisive gains in the sections where the unions controlled the votes. Off the Executive came Eric Clarke of the mineworkers' union, Les Huckfield, Joan Maynard and Doug Hoyle. The hard left still retained control of the constituency section and managed to achieve one of their aims: Joan Lestor, beaten by Audrey Wise, was thrown off the Executive. But the major prize, Kinnock's seat, eluded them. He hung on to fifth place, albeit by his fingertips, with 335,000 votes, a drop of 36,000 on the year before.

Kinnock was exultant. On Wednesday night he ran the gauntlet once again at the *Tribune* Rally. But this time he jeered back. He was glad, he said, that he had not voted for Benn. If the left did not like the fact that the party was now beginning to swing rightwards and the election looked like being won by the Tories, well, they only had themselves to blame. He rounded on the CLPD, from which he had just resigned. Organization, he said, could never replace policies: 'It cannot because it produces hit lists.' This was met by loud heckling. 'I know what I'm talking about,' Kinnock shouted back, 'because I was on just about everybody's hit list, and I got elected.'

The other Tribunite speakers attacked Kinnock. Joan Maynard – variously known on the right as 'Stalin's Granny' and 'the Member for Leipzig East' – told Kinnock, to loud cheers, 'the divisions in the Labour Party are between the socialists and the non-socialists.' Dennis Skinner mocked Kinnock's quotation from the Marxist scholar Eric Hobsbawm: 'This 'Obsbum, 'oo's 'e?' Tony Benn, who spoke last, deplored Kinnock's use of the phrase 'hit list': 'I greatly regret the use of the language of the Mafia to describe the democratic process.'

The hard left might not have forgiven him, but elsewhere in the party Kinnock was still enormously popular. In the education debate the following afternoon he made a superb speech, at least as good as his first in 1979. He mocked the two Conservative education Ministers, Rhodes Boyson ('a man who thinks that flowers grow by night') and the new Secretary of State, Sir Keith Joseph ('the thinking man's Rhodes Boyson'), who the previous week had told Kinnock, 'it would be more healthy for the universities if they did not depend so much on Governments and taxpayers':

> I look across this hall today [said Kinnock] and I see people who are rightly proud of their contribution and their work, who are intelligent

people. But they were never offered higher education or the means of fulfilling their talent. Not because they were awkward or because they turned down a choice – they never had it. I look around this room too and I see people like myself who were offered that – no better, no brighter than our brothers and sisters in this hall and elsewhere in this community, but freer in that we did have the opportunity of higher education. I say freer because I had choices, securities, that my mother and father – as intelligent in every atom of their being as I will ever be – were never offered. Why? Because they did not have a healthy system, as Joseph calls it. [*Applause*] They did not have it. It was not by sacrifice that they gave me a higher education – though, by God, they did sacrifice – but they could have sacrificed to tenfold and still not have been able to afford it. That is the mockery of sacrifice.

What they could manage, they did, but I went into higher education and hundreds in this hall went there and millions in our country went there and will go there. We got it because the community provided, because the taxpayer and the Government were the source of a healthy education system. [*Applause*]

He concluded:

We are not just outraged by the sabotage of talent, the unfairness of it all: this cuts policy is an assault on our liberty, the source of our freedom. We will fight against it as people fighting for their liberty fight.[8]

It was a powerfully delivered speech. Kinnock sat down to loud applause, which gradually swelled until most of the delegates were on their feet in a standing ovation.

As the clapping went on, the significance of this spontaneous demonstration sank in. It became obvious at that moment, watching Kinnock smiling on the platform, acknowledging the applause, that he was still a force within the Labour Party. And if he was a force now, having endured everything the hard left could throw at him, it was apparent that his support must be much more broadly based than most people had suspected.

Proof of that came in the results of the Shadow Cabinet elections a few weeks later. For the past two years Kinnock had been steadily improving his position. He had done well in 1981, when his opposition to the hard left had brought him votes from the centre and right of the Parliamentary Party. In 1982 he did even better. He won 131 votes and leapt from seventh place to second, outstripping two men who had each long been spoken of as possible leaders of the party – Roy Hattersley and Peter Shore. Now Kinnock had beaten them in the arena in which he was supposed to be weakest, the PLP. This had important implications for, unlike them, Kinnock had just proved he also had a following in the country – an essential asset, given Labour's new electoral college.

Kinnock was too shrewd a politician not to realize the potential that his NEC and Shadow Cabinet votes had demonstrated. Over the years plenty of people had spoken of him as a possible future leader. There had been Chris Mullin in 1973 and Michael Foot in 1975. In 1979 Russell Kerr, the former chairman of the Tribune Group, had told Kinnock in the car going home from the Commons one night that he thought Kinnock could be leader in ten years' time. 'With suitably becoming modesty,' says Kerr, 'he replied that he thought it would take a little longer than I was suggesting.' In 1980 Kinnock had told a friend in Wales he would probably run when Foot resigned. 'It was a possibility that we used to joke about,' says Glenys. Suddenly, at the end of 1982, the idea ceased to be either a joke or a distant prospect.

It took a while for most people to assimilate the fact. Only a few months before, Kinnock had seemed to be battling for his political life. But he had survived, and in that survival were the seeds of his leadership victory in 1983. Inevitably, this appears more clearly in retrospect than it did at the time, but November 1982 was the moment when a wise man would have put a large bet on Kinnock as Michael Foot's successor. Kinnock knew it, and he seized his chance.

Part Four
CANDIDATE

Chapter Eighteen
DECISION TO RUN

By the time of the Shadow Cabinet elections, Neil Kinnock had been education spokesman for three and a half years. He wanted a change, and Michael Foot wanted to promote him. Accordingly, a week before the Shadow Cabinet poll political correspondents were given a briefing by a member of Foot's private office. They were told that union leaders had been urging Foot to give Kinnock the job of employment spokesman. 'They believe that Mr Kinnock has the personality to elevate unemployment to a burning issue of debate, which it has not been up to now,' reported one newspaper. 'Labour's present employment spokesman, Mr Eric Varley, has been accused of being too low-key in his approach to the issue.'[1] When the results of the election were announced three days later, on 18 November, Eric Varley's vote was found to have dropped, while Kinnock's had substantially increased. On Saturday, 20 November, Foot telephoned Varley and told him he had decided to take his job away from him and give it to Kinnock. Varley, a former Secretary of State for Energy and for Industry, currently the party's Treasurer, was too important to appear to be demoted, so Foot did a little job creation and offered him a new title: 'Co-ordinator' of the Industry and Employment portfolios.

Varley, normally a calm and mild-mannered fellow, was incensed, not only at this attempt to kick him upstairs but also at the way in which Foot had leaked his intentions beforehand

and at the prospect of being replaced by the upstart Kinnock. 'It was the first time I'd ever seen Eric really foaming,' recalls one of his colleagues. Over the next few days Varley had four 'very acrimonious' meetings with Foot. Varley told him that if the Employment portfolio was taken off him, he would retire to the back benches. 'He just dug his heels in,' says one associate, 'and refused to move.' He was supported by other right-wingers, notably his close friend, Gerald Kaufman.

The longer the row dragged on, the more embarrassingly public it became. When Varley tried to make an attack on the Secretary of State for Employment, Norman Tebbit, in the Commons the following Monday, Tebbit offered his sympathy to an opponent suffering from 'job insecurity'. 'Mr Varley gritted his teeth,' said the *Guardian*, 'and did not reply.' Indecisive as ever, Foot finally left it up to Kinnock to decide whether or not he wanted to press the issue further. If he did, Foot promised he would back him, even if a number of shadow Ministers resigned. Kinnock was placed in an impossible position. 'It became clear,' he recalls, 'that if Michael installed me at Employment, some of the Shadow Cabinet would have been disruptive. If it hadn't been for the fact that there looked like being an election in 1983, then my instinct would've been to say to hell with it. But in the end I preferred peace in the party to Kinnock as employment spokesman.' After six days of frantic intrigue, on Wednesday, 24 November, Foot capitulated and Kinnock and Varley both stayed where they were.

Kinnock was as angry with Varley as Varley was with Foot. There was no job he had wanted more. Unemployment was the subject he cared most about, an issue which lent itself well to his populist, campaigning style. He longed to take on Norman Tebbit (whose distinctive political personality Kinnock has described as 'like a boil on a verruca').[2] He also felt he deserved the promotion, that his showing in the Shadow Cabinet elections had proved the extent of his support. He felt bitter about his colleagues' behaviour, and according to Kinnock's friends, it was at this point that for the first time he began to talk seriously about standing for the leadership. 'I was in London,' remembers Gwyn Evans, 'and met him in the House of Commons at the time of the row over whether or not he should take Varley's job. I said to him: "Varley doesn't seem to be keen on moving." He looked at me, and I've never seen him so angry. "I'll tell you this," he said, "I'm going to be standing for election as leader. People have been asking me about it for years, and I've never said anything. Well now – sod them. I'm going to stand." '

'It influenced me to run for the leadership,' claims Kinnock, 'because the demonstration of vanity so irritated me. I thought, the only way to deal with this is to lead the party on the basis that vanity is not to be tolerated.'

Kinnock calculated his chances and swiftly reached a conclusion: if he stood, he would probably win. He talked the possibility over with Barry Moore and Gwyn Evans in Moore's house in Blackwood just before Christmas. 'He said that if he got through to the second ballot, there was no way the electoral college would fail to elect him,' recalls Evans. 'All he had to do was stay out of trouble. A lot depended on Benn being knocked out on the first ballot.' Could he beat Benn? Kinnock was fairly confident he could, at least in the Parliamentary Labour Party (where Benn had just failed, by seven votes, to win election to the Shadow Cabinet) and in the unions.

But there was an even more enticing prospect: if Labour did as badly in the general election as the polls were predicting, Benn, whose Bristol constituency would become marginal as a result of boundary changes, would be out of Parliament. In that event, he would not even be eligible to stand for election. Pacing Moore's living-room, Kinnock talked about the right's attempts, organized by John Golding, to ensure that Benn did not win selection for a safer seat, Bristol South. According to Evans, he said that if Benn failed to get elected, 'there wouldn't be any stopping him.' Three months later Benn lost the nomination in Bristol South to Labour's right-wing Chief Whip, Michael Cocks.

*

If Kinnock harboured any resentment against Foot for the way he had handled his proposed promotion, he did not show it. The Labour leader had no more loyal supporter in the Shadow Cabinet than Kinnock. In September, when there had been rumours of a plot to remove Foot and replace him with Peter Shore, Kinnock had quickly come to his defence. 'The guessing and the kite-flying has got to stop,' he said in a statement widely reported in the press. 'If it continues, it will cripple us politically. . . . There is no justification for anyone who diverts attention from the pursuit and presentation of policies by a formal or informal campaign to replace Michael Foot as leader of the Labour Party.'[3]

Foot appreciated Kinnock's loyalty and was aware how much it had cost him, especially over Tatchell and Militant. 'Right from 1979 onwards,' says Foot, 'and especially after I became leader, he gave me great support. He showed considerable courage, especially in the period immediately after the contest for the deputy leadership.' The relationship between the two men was closer than ever. Foot and his wife often saw Neil and Glenys socially, and they discerned a change in him. Jill Craigie, when she first got to know him, had thought Kinnock, for all his charm, 'a little glib'. But during the batterings of 1981 and 1982 she watched him develop and believed he 'matured enormously. He gave things much deeper thought.' By the end of 1982, she had become, and remains, Kinnock's most effusive admirer:

> We live in an age when it's fashionable to cut people down to size and considered rather vulgar to praise them. I don't praise people very much myself. I'm not naive. But I think that boy's got it, I really do. It has been my good fortune in life to have met several outstanding people – Vaughan Williams, Henry Moore, Graham Sutherland, Aneurin Bevan. I have no hesitation in saying that Neil has a touch of genius, like them. I'm convinced of it. One day he will be the biggest radical Prime Minister since Lloyd George.

His greatest strength, she believes, is the way he manages to blend 'simplicity with a great underlying sophistication'.

Michael Foot's respect for Kinnock had also grown. 'I'd thought way back, ten years ago, that he'd be a future leader,' says Foot. 'He'd got all the qualifications for it. What I didn't expect was that he'd be a candidate so soon.' Certainly, in 1979 he thought his young protégé had a long way to go before he would have acquired the necessary maturity and experience. But by 1982 Foot had changed his mind. 'From about the summer onwards,' he says, 'I thought he was the best man for the job.' He made up his mind that when he relinquished the leadership he would try to do so in circumstances as propitious for Kinnock as possible.

This was another great potential advantage for Kinnock. But it rested on the assumption that Foot would be able to pick the moment of his departure, and there was a time, soon after the Shadow Cabinet elections, when it looked as though that decision might be taken out of his hands. In December Militant and Tatchell, the two ghosts he had sought to lay a year ago, rose once more to haunt him.

Foot's long-awaited action on Militant amounted to a proposal to expel the five members of the tendency's 'Editorial Board' (in effect, its leadership). The left attacked him for organizing a witchhunt. The right attacked him for not going far enough: what was the point, they argued, of expelling five and not dealing with the half-dozen avowed supporters of Militant who had been selected as parliamentary candidates? To add to the impression of chaos, on 10 December Militant applied to the High Court for an injunction, claiming that the expulsions were illegal under Labour's constitution. The application was eventually turned down, but the row did further harm to Labour's image in the eyes of the public. Either Militant supporters were a 'pestilential nuisance', as Foot had called them, in which case they ought to be eradicated, or they were unimportant, in which case there was no need for the party to go to the trouble of expelling anyone, let alone a mere five out of a strength of several thousand. Foot had succeeded only in drawing attention to a problem and then conspicuously failing to do much about it.

From Foot's point of view, the Tatchell affair was even

more damaging. This was the man who, he had said, would 'never', as far as he was concerned, be an official Labour candidate. It was a statement from which he could not escape: 'Houdini did easier tricks,' said the *Daily Mirror.*[4] In 1982 the London Labour Party had snubbed Foot, voting by more than two to one to support Tatchell. On 9 January 1983, having been forced by the NEC to go through a second selection conference, Tatchell was once again chosen by the local party as its candidate. Foot had no alternative but to endorse him. He was photographed with him outside the Houses of Parliament, wearing the frozen smile of a man who has just had a cigar explode in his face. What followed was aptly summed up by Tatchell himself as 'the dirtiest and most notorious by-election'.[5]

The events of the Bermondsey by-election anticipated much of what was to happen to Labour on a national scale during the general election four months later. There were the party's unnecessary blunders, such as that at the beginning of the campaign, when Labour's Walworth Road headquarters insisted on pulping 25,000 leaflets printed on Militant's Cambridge Heath press (because, argued Labour's officials, it would embarrass the party at a time when it was trying to expel Militant members.) The effect was simply to draw attention to something which might otherwise have passed unnoticed. The seizure of the leaflets leaked out to the press and dominated the beginning of the election.

There was also the unremitting hostility of the media. Tatchell's character was assassinated, just as Foot's was to be. The smears were different, but the effect was the same. Tatchell was an Australian homosexual draft-dodger, 'Red Pete', a naive puppet of sinister hidden forces. . . . Opinion polls showing the Alliance gaining on Labour were given greater and greater prominence, and no distinction was drawn between the findings of scientific surveys and of notoriously inaccurate telephone polls. The Alliance campaign was transformed as a result. Every increase in its support was presented as a judgement on Tatchell, feeding the belief that he was unsuitable to be an MP, encouraging more people to switch allegiance, leading to more polls, more headlines, more desertion from Labour. It was the same in the general election.

Polling day was fixed for 24 February. On the 22nd an opinion poll put Tatchell neck and neck with Simon Hughes, the Alliance candidate. On the 23rd the NEC met and agreed, by nineteen votes to nine, the expulsion of the five members of the Militant Editorial Board. Pictures of Labour Party members denouncing one another dominated the news bulletins on the eve of the poll. It was the final tactical blunder. The following day Tatchell lost what had once been a safe Labour seat by a majority of 10,000 votes. Labour's vote dropped by 38 per cent. It was the largest by-election swing in living memory, the ninth in a sequence of bad by-election results for Labour since the formation of the SDP. A Marplan poll in the *Guardian* put the Conservatives 21 per cent ahead of Labour.

The response of many in the Parliamentary Labour Party was to turn on Michael Foot. A group of MPs, largely on the left of the party, began telling journalists that, in their view, Foot should resign immediately. Jack Straw, Jeff Rooker, Robert Kilroy-Silk, Phillip Whitehead, Joe Ashton and many more believed the party faced disaster at a general election with Foot as leader. Dale Campbell-Savours reportedly interviewed 117 MPs 'mostly on the left', and found 'ninety-six saying unequivocally that Michael Foot should go, including some of the most surprising people on the left actually wanting Healey as leader'.[6]

The plot came to nothing. Labour's new electoral college would have meant a protracted and uncertain leadership campaign, and few of the MPs had the courage even to tell Foot their views, let alone speak out on the record in public. 'I had screwed up the nerve to go,' wrote Austin Mitchell, 'first with another marginal seat Member, then, when he dropped out, on my own. At that point my book, *The Case for Labour*, was published. Michael, ever the most intellectually interested and considerate of the Shadow Cabinet, was the only Member to come to the launch. I gave up my contemplated brutality.'[7]

Foot's friends rallied round him, and once again Neil Kinnock was prominent among them. 'My loyalty for this man and what he stands for,' he said of Foot in a speech on 4 March, 'was not won by favours or sentiment. . . . I am proud to stand by such a man. I want him to be the leader of our country, for I trust him with my children's lives. I trust him with the future of our people and I trust him with world responsibility.'[8] Thanks to the support of his friends in the PLP and the unions, Foot won a stay of execution. Four weeks later, on 24 March, the Alliance fielded a poor candidate in the Darlington by-election, and Labour held on to the seat with a 1.3 per cent swing in its favour. This had been the crucial test for Foot. If Labour had lost, he might well have been forced to step down. Having won, it was certain that he would lead the party into the general election.

If Foot had gone, perhaps to be replaced by Denis Healey, Kinnock's hopes for the leadership would have suffered a setback, probably temporary but possibly longer-term. Instead his luck held; Foot stayed; and he increasingly began to look the heir apparent. On 25 April he was invited to Scarborough to address the annual conference of the professional and clerical union, APEX. The predominantly right-wing audience gave Kinnock a standing ovation, a significant indication of the breadth of his support among the unions. At the same time the hard left called off its attacks upon him. In the face of the looming general election a new spirit of unity belatedly began to spread through the party. Even Tony Benn made a strong pledge of support for Denis Healey 'in his capacity as deputy leader'.[9] Of all the potential leadership candidates Kinnock, acceptable to the left on policy, tolerable to the right on presentation and style, stood to gain most from this new mood.

Unfortunately for the party as a whole, the outbreak of peace came much too late to stave off electoral defeat. The

Conservative Prime Minister, Margaret Thatcher, had no intention of allowing Labour the luxury of recovery. Six weeks after the Darlington by-election she asked the Queen to dissolve Parliament: a general election was to be held on 9 June.

Chapter Nineteen
THE DO-IT-YOURSELF ELECTION

In 1979 the Conservatives had promised in their manifesto to 'rebuild' Britain's economy. In 1983, after four years of Tory government, Britain's situation was more desperate than ever. There had been a fall in manufacturing output of 19 per cent and in investment of 35 per cent. In 1982 alone more than 12,000 companies, the highest ever total, had gone into liquidation. Unemployment stood at more than 3 million, another new record. Despite the subsidy provided by North Sea oil, Britain's economy remained among the most depressed in the industrialized world. For the first time since the industrial revolution the country was importing more manufactured goods than it was exporting.

Victory in the Falklands war had provided a colourful diversion from this domestic gloom and had dramatically improved the Government's popularity. But there was plenty of evidence that it was the Government's own negligence that had precipitated the war in the first place, and the triumph was bought at a heavy cost: over a thousand British servicemen were killed or wounded and over £2,000 million added to the defence estimates.

Yet, despite its record, the Government started the election 13 per cent ahead of the Opposition in the opinion polls, a measure of the damage Labour had inflicted upon itself. 'The election was lost not in the three weeks of the campaign,' said Denis Healey afterwards, 'but in the three years which preceded it. . . . In that period the party itself acquired a highly unfavourable public image, based on disunity, extremism, crankiness and general unfitness to govern.'[1] Even if Labour had fought a brilliant campaign, it would almost certainly have proved impossible to make up the ground lost since 1980. As it was, the party's shambolic campaign served only to reinforce the impression of its 'general unfitness to govern'.

In 1974 the party's use of television had been as sophisticated as the Conservatives'. The actor Stanley Baker, Michael Deeley (a film producer, subsequently responsible for *Blade Runner* and *The Deerhunter*) and Barry Spikings (the former head of film production for EMI) helped Labour to draw up a 'battle plan' for the projection of Harold Wilson. Throughout the election Deeley travelled ahead of the party leader, checking that the television cameras covering the night's main speech were in the best positions to convey a flattering impression of Wilson; often, to the anger of local party officials, Deeley would insist that they were positioned in the centre of the hall, rather than at the sides. 'The TV cameras were treated like VIP guests,' wrote Marcia Falkender, Wilson's powerful political secretary, 'and everything on stage or platform was considered from the point of view of how it would appear to them, rather than to the audience as a whole.'[2] A freshly laundered suit was waiting for Wilson before every major appearance. George Blackler, a film industry expert, was recruited as Wilson's private make-up man. In the carpentry department of Pinewood Studios a portable backdrop was made to go behind the podium: 'the visual impact of the 1970 platform presentation of Edward Heath had impressed us enormously because of the clarity of the images used, and the forceful simplicity of the message,' wrote Lady Falkender. 'We had learned an important lesson from this.'[3]

Nine years later, like Wilson and Falkender themselves, such slickness was in disgrace in the Labour Party. The relaxing, beige-coloured backdrop of 1974 was replaced in 1983 by a garish blood-red screen. Wilson and Callaghan had tailored their speeches to the requirements of television, speaking in a simple, low-key style pitched at the millions of voters at home in their living-rooms. Michael Foot shouted his way through unscripted tirades, never clearly beginning or ending a point. Poorly lit against a lurid background, he looked like a master of ceremonies trying to whip up a crowd at a public execution.

In 1979 Labour's manifesto had been brief and bland. In 1983 it ran to 15,000 words. It promised a £10 billion expansion programme, with increased spending on housing, transport and social services. Unemployment was to be reduced to below 1 million 'within five years of taking office'. Britain would pull out of the EEC 'well within the lifetime of the Parliament'. All nuclear bases and weapons would be removed from 'British soil' and 'British waters'. There was a host of other promises, from the breaking up of all 'major concentrations of press ownership' to the abolition of fox hunting. Forty pages long, divided into seventy-seven separate sections, the manifesto was a triumph of policy over presentation. One right-wing Shadow Cabinet Minister called it 'the longest suicide note in history'. Conservative Central Office immediately put in a bulk order for 5,000 copies.

Incompetence at Walworth Road compounded the problems. There appeared to be no co-ordinated strategy for putting across Labour's message: on 18 May, for example, when the Conservatives launched their manifesto, no one from the Labour Party was lined up to comment upon it. 'Most of the leaders seem to be on permanent tour,' complained Jim Innes, a Scottish journalist working in Labour's press office, who wrote up his experiences in the form of a diary. 'Their schedules are worked out by the national agent's department, whose motto is: never mind the media, the mileage is the message.'[4]

The body nominally in charge of Labour's election strategy was the Campaign Committee.

Average attendance at this decision-making committee is between thirty and forty [wrote Jim Innes]. In Harold Wilson's time average attendance was about six. There are not enough seats in the general secretary's office, so our leaders are perched on tables or lined up along the walls. One chap was in there for the first two days and nobody recognised him. On the third day someone asked who he was and he told them he was Foot's Special Branch detective. Given the make-up of the committee he was probably quite right to go in.[5]

Lacking central direction, Labour's campaign repeatedly blundered. Denis Healey was sent to a factory in Huddersfield which was later discovered to be supplying parts for Argentine warships. The *Daily Mirror* carried an advertisement with the baffling slogan:

ARE YOU GOING TO VOTE BREAD OUT OF THE
MOUTHS OF THE OLD?
Or will you put it to work for Britain?

(The second line was part of the copy from a different advertisement; the two had accidentally become mixed, but no one had bothered to check the text before it was printed.) The party's official eve-of-poll leaflet bordered on the surreal:

ARE YOU
GOING TO
VOTE FOR
NO
TOMORROW?

One regional office of the Labour Party received 80,000 of these leaflets from Walworth Road. Party workers were so appalled that they refused to distribute them, handing them over to a couple of local unemployed men who had set up a paper-recycling business. 'Our biggest contribution to the 1983 election,' says one full-time official, 'was to save a tree.'

Neil Kinnock was playing a prominent role in the party's national campaign for the first time. He was shocked by the lack of professionalism. When he wanted to hold a press conference on education he had to persuade a sympathetic teacher to lend him a school hall. 'There was no sense of being part of an organized army,' he recalls. 'You had to do the whole thing on your own.'

This do-it-yourself approach to electioneering produced one success. Francis Beckett, a National Union of Journalists official working in the press office at Walworth Road, obtained a set of confidential minutes of a recent meeting of the National Economic Development Council (NEDC). According to these, the Council had decided in March not to publish a review of Britain's economic prospects because, the president of the Confederation of British Industry was recorded as saying, it was 'so gloomy, that people reading it would want to get the first boat out of the country'.

Beckett wanted to exploit the minutes even though, according to Innes, writing in his diary on 20 May, 'the hierarchy aren't interested.' Frustrated, Beckett by-passed them. 'Francis goes to Kinnock,' wrote Innes. 'Kinnock buys it and they plan a weekend release.'[6]

It was one of the few occasions in the course of the election on which Labour gained the initiative. Kinnock handed out photocopies of the NEDC documents to the press and accused the Conservatives of suppressing the extent of Britain's economic problems. 'At best it was an attempt to find time for cosmetic surgery,' he alleged. 'At worst it was an attempt to hide the real truth about the so-called recovery from the people of Britain.' 'Kinnock wins the weekend,' claimed Innes triumphantly. The following day the *Daily Telegraph* warned its readers not to 'underestimate Labour's capacity for recovery'.[7]

The excitement soon fizzled out. Lacking a strategy or even a coherent theme for its campaign, Labour was quickly overtaken by events. On 25 May James Callaghan severely damaged the party by attacking its policy on nuclear weapons. His speech focused attention on one of the weakest sections of Labour's manifesto, a compromise between left and right which committed the party to 'a non-nuclear defence policy' while seeking simultaneously to secure 'nuclear disarmament agreements with other countries'.[8]

Was this unilateralism or multilateralism? 'Defence, defence and more defence' read one canvass return at the end of that week, describing public reaction on the doorstep. A MORI opinion poll gave the Conservatives a 22 per cent lead.

Locked into an exhausting tour of the country, Kinnock grew increasingly tired and unhappy. Most of the halls in which he spoke had not been provided with microphones. He began to lose his voice. He was travelling hundreds of miles, visiting five or six constituencies each day. Transport arrangements were chaotic. Frequently he would find himself in the evening doubling back to where he had begun in the morning. Hours were wasted sitting in cars and trains. 'I kept going by doing more,' recalls Kinnock. 'I got myself into a state of battle-happiness where I could get by on four hours sleep instead of five. The sheer size of the incompetence should have led me to peg out in the first week. There was not a single area in which we properly used our resources. It was insane – there's no other word for it.'* 'He tells me he's travelling all over the country,' wrote Innes, following a phone call from Kinnock, 'beginning to feel tired already, and suspects he may completely run out of steam in the last week.'[9]

It was an accurate prediction. As the Conservative lead showed no sign of diminishing and as exhaustion took over, Kinnock's contribution to the campaign became increasingly testy. On 1 June, without consulting Walworth Road, Kinnock issued a statement calling for a public inquiry into the sinking of the Argentine cruiser, the *General Belgrano*: 'Since the Prime Minister and her Government have drawn credit for their conduct of the Falklands conflict, they should

---

* The formidably efficient Glenys Kinnock, who buys all her husband's clothes, raises their children, runs their house and still manages to work part-time as a remedial teacher is equally scathing about Labour's incompetence. When she and Kinnock went to America on an official visit six months after his election as leader, the flight to Washington, which landed in Boston, took ten hours. 'Who booked this flight?' demanded someone during the interminable journey. 'Walworth Road?' 'If it had been left to Walworth Road,' replied Glenys, 'we'd be going via Hong Kong.'

be eager to demonstrate that their orders were not given before all prospect of negotiated peace on acceptable terms was absolutely exhausted.' Michael Heseltine, the Defence Secretary, quickly denounced Kinnock's attack as a 'disgraceful misrepresentation', calling it 'contemptible that Kinnock plays the dictators' game'. Michael Foot was dismayed when he heard of Kinnock's statement: it was his view that the issue of the *Belgrano* should be left out of the campaign.

Three days later, in Harlow, Kinnock struck out again. This time his target was 'Thatcher totalitarianism'. He alleged that the Prime Minister had begun 'the long process of removing all opposition in the great institutions of Britain, from the Bank of England to British Rail, from Church to BBC, from Arts Council to the Commission for Racial Equality, from the Manpower Services Commission to regional health authorities'. The Prime Minister's appointment of 'fellow travellers to positions of social and civic power' was a 'clear effort to create a state in the image of Margaret Thatcher, a genteel junta of yes-men'.[10]

Kinnock's most celebrated loss of temper came on the Monday before polling day. He was appearing on a local television programme, *The South Decides*, when a member of the studio audience shouted out, 'At least Mrs Thatcher has got guts.' Kinnock whirled round in an instant: 'And it is a pity that people had to leave theirs on the ground at Goose Green in order to prove it.' Like Denis Healey, who the previous week had accused Mrs Thatcher of 'glorying in slaughter', Kinnock had been unable any longer to contain his frustration at seeing the Prime Minister riding high on the credit for the British victory in the South Atlantic. Unlike Healey, Kinnock decided not to apologize for his remark. 'There was a public meeting in Markham [a village in Kinnock's constituency] the night that blew up,' recalls Gwyn Evans. 'We got into a huddle. Glenys asked me what I thought. I said there was no way he should withdraw it. We all agreed.'

The issue was a particularly sensitive one in Wales. In two

days' time it would be the first anniversary of the disaster at Bluff Cove in which thirty-three Welsh Guardsmen had been killed. Kinnock met the issue head-on. He held a press conference in Cardiff the morning after the broadcast and read out the text of a letter he intended to send to all the families bereaved in the Falklands war, stating that his remark had been unrehearsed and that he had not meant to cause offence. A few hours later, campaigning in the seaside town of Barry, he spoke on the telephone to two families who had lost their sons. Both told him they understood he had meant no offence. Kinnock, emotional even in normal circumstances, emerged from the conversations in tears. Later, in a speech in the town centre, he hit back at Heseltine, who had dubbed him the 'self-appointed king of the gutter of politics'. 'If I was in the gutter,' said Kinnock, 'which I ain't, he'd still be looking up at me from the sewer.'

The effect of the controversy upon the election result was almost certainly negligible. Labour's support had already reached rock bottom: its campaign, as the *Guardian* put it on 7 June, had 'been dead in the water for a fortnight'. The *Daily Mirror* had already wistfully put away the front page it had been planning to print in the event of a sensational Labour victory: the banner headline 'GOTCHA!' over a picture of Mrs Thatcher leaving 10 Downing Street.

Kinnock, like Healey, had begun the campaign well but finished badly, made careless by fatigue and then ambushed in front of the television cameras. Healey subsequently argued that the 'travel and speaking programmes' of the party's senior figures should be 'far more restricted, allowing more time for food, rest and thought'; less time should be spent in trains, cars or aeroplanes, and above all much more control should be exercised over the occasions on which the leadership appeared before the news cameras.[11] Kinnock knows how to exploit television as well as any politician in Britain. The bungling of the 1983 campaign made a deep impression upon him. He is determined not to allow the mistakes to be repeated.

On the eve of the poll, with the Conservatives poised to gain a massive majority and with Labour struggling to fend off the Alliance and retain second place, Kinnock wound up his campaign tour in South Wales. He spoke at a series of last-minute local rallies and at one of them, in Bridgend, summoned up his most powerful rhetoric of the campaign. The hoarseness of his delivery intensified the effect of his words as, like an Old Testament prophet, he intoned his warning of the future:

If Margaret Thatcher is re-elected as Prime Minister on Thursday, I warn you.

I warn you that you will have pain – when healing and relief depend upon payment.

I warn you that you will have ignorance – when talents are untended and wits are wasted, when learning is a privilege and not a right.

I warn you that you will have poverty – when pensions slip and benefits are whittled away by a Government that won't pay in an economy that can't pay.

I warn you that you will be cold – when fuel charges are used as a tax system that the rich don't notice and the poor can't afford.

I warn you that you must not expect work – when many cannot spend, more will not be able to earn. When they don't earn, they don't spend. When they don't spend, work dies.

I warn you not to go into the streets alone after dark or into the streets in large crowds of protest in the light.

I warn you that you will be quiet – when the curfew of fear and the gibbet of unemployment make you obedient.

I warn you that you will have defence of a sort – with a risk and at a price that passes all understanding.

I warn you that you will be homebound – when fares and transport Bills kill leisure and lock you up.

I warn you that you will borrow less – when credit, loans, mortgages and easy payments are refused to people on your melting income.

If Margaret Thatcher wins on Thursday, I warn you not to be ordinary. I warn you not to be young. I warn you not to fall ill. I warn you not to get old.

On Thursday, 9 June, more than 30 million people went to the polls and recorded a devastating verdict upon the Labour Party. The Government was returned with a majority over all other parties of 144. The final result was:

CONSERVATIVES	397
LABOUR	209
LIBERAL	17
SDP	6
PLAID CYMRU	2
SNP	2
OTHERS	17

For Labour the situation was even worse than it looked. Although the party ended up with nine times as many seats as the Alliance, it was only slightly ahead in terms of the popular vote: 8.5 million to the Alliance's 7.8 million. At 27.6 per cent the party's share of the vote was lower than it had been in 1931, lower than in any election since 1918. One could reach back even further, to 1900 and the formation of the Labour Representation Committee, and still not find a time at which the average vote for Labour candidates had been as low.

The election was fought in 650 constituencies. The Conservatives lost five deposits; the Liberals, five; the Social Democrats, six. Labour lost 119. South of a line drawn from the Wash to the Severn Estuary, excluding London, Labour now had only three seats: Bristol South, Thurrock and Ipswich. Out of the remaining 151 southern constituencies, Labour held on to second place in only eighteen; the Alliance was the runner-up in all the rest.

Even in Wales and the north of England, areas in which it was traditionally strong, Labour suffered a 10 per cent drop in its support. 'Labour was forced back into its recession-racked city redoubts,' wrote the *Economist*. 'An aspiring Labour Member of Parliament must now find a decaying city centre with high unemployment, an ageing population and an air of despair. It is not much of a basis for a party of the future.'[12] Peter Kellner, writing in the *New Statesman*, believed that the party faced 'something that looks appallingly like terminal collapse in its support in much of the rest of Britain'.[13] Less than 40 per cent of trade unionists and less than half the unemployed voted Labour.[14]

Candidate

'The Labour Party,' Tony Benn had argued in 1980, 'must align itself with the women's movement, the black movement, the environmental movement, the peace movement, the rural radical movement, the religious movements that object to monetarism and militarism': by doing so, it would be possible to recreate 'that winning coalition of 1945'.[15] Ken Livingstone echoed the same idea in 1981. What was happening in the party, he believed, was 'very similar in a sense to the sort of alliance that backed George McGovern in 1972 against Richard Nixon'.[16] It was a philosophy which proved to be as flawed when tested in Britain in 1983 as it had been when first applied in America eleven years earlier. Minorities, however righteous and vocal, were not strong enough, even when welded together, to make up a majority.

Labour failed to achieve a sufficiently broad base of support, and Tony Benn was one of the casualties. His old constituency had disappeared following boundary changes. He fought a new seat, Bristol East, which, if it had been in existence in 1979, would probably have given him a majority of around 4,000.[17] Many of the electorate were skilled, home-owning working-class – exactly the sort of voters who deserted Labour in 1983. Benn lost the seat to his Conservative challenger by 1,800 votes. There was no personal animosity in the result: Benn was simply swept away by the same uniform swing which gave the Conservatives their enormous majority.

The news that Benn was out of Parliament came through in the early hours of Friday morning. It was met with cheers by Conservative workers at their headquarters in Smith Square and by groans of disappointment in Walworth Road. Most people expected a leadership election in the party within the next few months. Now, on the eve of battle, the hard left suddenly had to face the fact that its most articulate champion would be ineligible to stand. Michael Meacher was arriving at a television studio in Manchester when he heard that Benn had lost. 'I was badly shaken,' he recalls. 'I hadn't thought it likely he would lose.' Jon Lansman, one of Benn's most effective lieutenants, was watching television at the count in Woolwich, where Audrey Wise, another hard-left MP, was also facing defeat. 'I was bitterly disappointed,' remembers Lansman. In April, anticipating a leadership contest, he had prepared a report for Benn on the state of the electoral college. Having analysed the figures, he appreciated the implications of Benn's defeat at once. 'My immediate thought was: Kinnock's got it sewn up. All the work, all the effort, all the reforms – now it was Kinnock who would get the benefit.'

Chapter Twenty
THE MAN WHO CAME TO DINNER

Michael Foot conceded the election shortly after 2 a.m. on Friday morning. He called it a 'tragedy for the nation', adding, 'We have got to sit down and rebuild the Labour Party.' With a police escort he set off from Ebbw Vale back down the motorway to London at a speed of more than 100 miles per hour. He arrived to thank party workers shortly after dawn only to find Walworth Road half-empty: almost everyone had gone home.

By the time they got back to their own house in Hampstead, Foot and his wife, in Jill Craigie's words, were 'shattered': 'We just looked at one another without saying anything.' Foot is a tough and resilient man, far removed from the frail pensioner of newspaper caricatures. But he had been badly hurt. According to his wife, 'He felt he had let people down. He didn't show it, but I knew. There's no one more sensitive than him.' Leaders of the Labour Party have seldom enjoyed a good press, but few have been treated with the contempt accorded to Foot. 'What was so hurtful,' she says, 'is the fact that it was the posh papers that turned on him.'

'Mr Foot does not know anything about anything,' the *Economist* had claimed, in a profile typical of many published during the campaign. 'He knows no economics, no sociology, nothing about international relations. . . .' The journal dwelt on Foot's 'snow-white hair, thick spectacles, old man's hands and walk that reminds onlookers uncannily of Charlie Chaplin'.[1] Foot could console himself with the fact that the *Economist*, at least, was traditionally unsympathetic to Labour, but Anthony Howard, one of the country's most experienced political commentators, was a life-long Labour supporter. 'It is probably only fair that I should make a confession,' he had written in the *Observer* on 15 May. 'When I heard the news of the PLP's first leadership ballot on 4 November 1980, I distinctly recall a thrill of excitement. . . . Like the 139 Labour MPs who ended up voting for Mr Foot, I was, however, a victim of sheer self-indulgence. . . . if ever there was a "Yesterday's Man", it is Mr Foot.'

The image of a leader hopelessly out of his depth had been inadvertently reinforced by Jim Mortimer, the party's General Secretary. On 26 May he told an incredulous press conference that the party's campaign committee had agreed that 'Michael Foot is leader of the Labour Party and speaks for the Party.' It was an extraordinary remark to make in the middle of an election, and the assembled journalists looked at one another in amazement.

It was obvious that once the campaign was over, Foot would quickly have to stand down as leader. The PLP was due to meet on the Wednesday after the election. Amid rumours that he would face a motion of no confidence, Foot decided to regain the initiative. On Saturday, 11 June, he attended a Northumberland miners' gala in the small town of Bedlington. Reporters clamoured for a statement about a possible resignation the following week. 'I think the dates are a bit premature,' Foot joked in his speech to the miners. 'I have to disappoint my friends from the National Union of Journalists.' In fact, he had already made up his mind to go.

Foot wanted Kinnock to succeed him, and he was worried that if he delayed, there was a danger of others 'jumping in' ahead of him. At least one potential successor, Roy Hattersley, had already begun trying on the crown in private. During the election he had talked to several journalists about the forthcoming struggle for the leadership, telling them that

213

he would be a candidate and insisting that he would win. Foot and his inner circle of advisers had been furious at Hattersley's indiscretion in the middle of the campaign. Foot was keen to thwart the ambitions of the ebullient MP for Birmingham Sparkbrook. He talked over the timing of his resignation with Dick Clements on the train up to Northumberland. When they got back to London on Saturday night, Foot asked Clements if he wanted to come in for supper. Clements, exhausted after the election campaign, declined. As he prepared to drive away from Foot's door, he noticed Clive Jenkins coming round the corner.

Wherever Jenkins goes, a plot of some sort is generally not far behind. That night he dined *à trois* with the Foots and discussed the leadership. Their concern was to prevent the right from mobilizing effectively, while at the same time giving Neil Kinnock the best possible start in the campaign. Foot had already spoken to his protégé. 'I rang Neil at home,' says Foot, 'and said: "Are you ready to stand for the leadership?" He said, "Yes." ' What followed was a highly successful pre-emptive strike by Foot and Jenkins, throwing Kinnock's rivals into a state of confusion from which they never fully recovered.

The next day Clive Jenkins was due to meet the executive of his union, the ASTMS. High on the agenda was the question of whom the union should support for the leadership of the Labour Party. Guided by Jenkins, they decided to nominate Foot to serve for another year in office. Jenkins then went through the ritual of telephoning Foot to tell him of their decision. Foot thanked him but declined the offer, as Jenkins knew he would. Jenkins went back to his executive and told them that Foot would not be standing; they then nominated Kinnock, and Jenkins went off to telephone him with the good news.

It was Sunday morning. Kinnock, who had won the new Islwyn constituency by 14,000 votes, was at Broadcasting House for an interview on the Radio Four news programme, *The World This Weekend.* Jenkins's call was put through to him. They could not have chosen a more public forum for their conversation. Overheard by Adam Raphael, the political editor of the *Observer*, who was also appearing on the programme, Jenkins asked Kinnock if he was prepared to accept the ASTMS nomination. Kinnock said he was. Jenkins then publicly announced that Foot would not be contesting the leadership and that, as a result, his union would be supporting Kinnock, a 'young and sophisticated politician' capable of leading his party and the country into the 1990s. 'He has dash, sparkle, imagination, a persuasive quality and youth,' added Jenkins. Less than three days after Michael Foot had conceded the general election the fight for the Labour leadership had begun.

Foot was later reported in the press to be 'furious' and 'hopping mad' with Jenkins for effectively announcing his resignation for him. The opposite was the case. Foot was well pleased; indeed, the two men were seen together the following week at a cinema in Notting Hill, enjoying *The Ploughman's Lunch*, a film about the cynicism and corruptibility of the British media. The effect of their complicated manoeuvre was to deny the right the time to mount a 'Stop Kinnock' campaign, perhaps by foisting a compromise candidate on the party. Instead, by receiving the first nomination, Kinnock was presented from the start as the man everyone else would have to beat. By the end of the afternoon Kinnock already had the support of the national delegation of his own union, the Transport and General Workers, as well as the personal endorsements of Bill Keys, General Secretary of the printers' union SOGAT '82 and Alan Tuffin of the construction workers. By nightfall Kinnock, at 11–8, was odds-on favourite with the bookmakers.

News of Foot's resignation came as a complete surprise to the other potential candidates. Peter Shore, Labour's Shadow Chancellor, was giving a live television interview on *Weekend World* when Brian Walden broke the news to him. Walden asked him whether he intended to stand; Shore said he did. Roy Hattersley, the Shadow Home Secretary, was watching the interview at home. Walden's question was the first intimation he had that the contest was already under way. He chose a pre-arranged appearance on Channel Four's *Face the Press* at 5.30 that afternoon as the platform from which to announce his own candidacy. With the three main candidates all declaring themselves on radio and television that Sunday, the election began where it was to remain for the next three and a half months: squarely in the public eye.

Behind the scenes the right-wing unions were thrown into confusion. Terry Duffy, President of the engineers, publicly came out for Shore, while his General Secretary, Gavin Laird, simultaneously declared for Hattersley. Duffy was forced to change his mind when David Basnett, leader of the general and municipal workers, also endorsed Hattersley. 'I phoned the big unions,' recalls Duffy, 'but I couldn't get the rest of the guys to go with me. And if you've not got the big votes, then it's no use.' As a result of this private carve-up, Peter Shore's chances of becoming leader were effectively finished by the end of the first afternoon. In his statement Basnett, who controlled a block vote of 650,000, also ruled out a third attempt at the leadership by Denis Healey. 'I think we've really got to skip a generation,' said Basnett, 'and we've got to get young men in charge.' Healey, who would be sixty-six in a few weeks' time, took the hint and announced that he would not be standing.

Meanwhile the hard left were also coming to terms with the news. By coincidence a prominent group had already arranged to meet at Chris Mullin's flat in Brixton that afternoon for an election post-mortem. About eighteen people were crowded into Mullin's living-room, including Tony Benn, Stuart Holland, Jo Richardson, Frances Morrell, Ken Livingstone, Audrey Wise, Reg Race and Jon Lansman. Michael Meacher had not heard about Foot's resignation; he arrived around 3 o'clock to find the others discussing it.

The Bennites had always insisted that they were in politics to promote policies, not a particular personality. Benn's removal from the fight exposed the weakness of this assurance. Without his formidable personality the hard left's strength all but collapsed. In his report to Benn on the state of the electoral college, written earlier in the year, Lansman had assumed that there would be three main candidates for the leadership: Benn, Kinnock and Healey. Lansman, probably over-optimistically, had calculated that the breakdown of votes in the first ballot would be, roughly, Healey 40 per cent, Benn 35 per cent and Kinnock trailing in third place with 25 per cent. Lansman believed that Benn could just defeat Healey in the final ballot. Four months later, with Benn out of the running, who was there who could take his place and still win? Joan Maynard? Dennis Skinner? It was necessary only to run down the list of names to realize the truth. Lacking a candidate of Benn's stature, it was, in Lansman's words, 'all over'. 'Worrying about the leadership was irrelevant. Kinnock had it.'

Benn appeared less depressed at the prospect than most of his supporters. Tony Banks, who had just been elected for Newham North-West, was particularly upset. He even offered to resign his seat to enable Benn to get back into Parliament. The idea was quickly dismissed as impractical.

Of the potential candidates Michael Meacher was reckoned to be the strongest. Forty-three years old, the MP for Oldham for the past thirteen years, Meacher had been a junior Minister at the Departments of Trade, Industry and Social Security. At first, it was agreed that he should run for the leadership, while Jo Richardson, the MP for Barking, should stand as the hard left's candidate for deputy leader. This plan was abandoned the following week only when the inevitability of Kinnock's victory became clear. The group decided to concentrate on the deputy leadership, and after 'some pressure' had been applied Richardson stood down in favour of Meacher. At the same time, independently of the Bennites (whom he regarded with some suspicion), another hard left-winger, Eric Heffer, announced his candidacy for the leadership.

In all there were four candidates seeking to become leader

of the Labour Party: Hattersley, Heffer, Kinnock and Shore. As a fallback, and in the interests of party unity, Hattersley and Kinnock also agreed to stand for the deputy leadership along with Meacher and two relatively unknown outsiders, Gwyneth Dunwoody and Denzil Davies. It looked a large field, but in reality it was a contest in name only. Thanks to Michael Foot and the man who came to dinner, Clive Jenkins, Kinnock had got off to such a flying start that not once in the fifteen weeks of the leadership election did he look in danger of being overhauled.

Chapter Twenty-One
'SOMEONE UP THERE LIKES ME'

Kinnock had been surprised by the speed with which Foot announced his departure. He had expected him to stay on for at least a few more months, while the party sorted itself out in the wake of the election defeat. Now, with the leadership campaign under way and as the clear favourite, Kinnock contemplated his prospects with mixed emotions. One part of him was exultant. 'I can be leader of the Labour Party for the next ten years,' he said at one point during the campaign. 'I can retire at fifty-one and I'll still be younger than Hattersley is now.' However, like many extroverts Kinnock has darker moods, friends say, and at times during the campaign he expressed reservations about the suddenness with which he was being pitched into the leadership. It had all come too soon: the children were at an age when they needed more attention; he would miss seeing them grow up; he and Glenys were still young enough to travel and enjoy themselves; why should he burden himself with the additional work? He was also periodically seized by apprehensions about his lack of experience. He did not relish the prospect of taking on Margaret Thatcher at Question Time: it would be a difficult task, 'an exercise in damage limitation', he called it.

One of the first things Kinnock did on the Monday after Foot's resignation was to telephone Robin Cook, the Scottish MP, at his home in Edinburgh. They had known one another since Cook entered Parliament in 1974. Roughly the same age (Cook is four years younger than Kinnock), both were members of the Tribune Group, supporters of CND and opponents of devolution. They were not close personal friends – Cook spent much of his time in Westminster, while Kinnock was off on his visits around the country. But the fact that they had both opposed Benn's bid for the deputy leadership in 1981 had drawn them together. Cook, like Barry Moore, is one of those shrewd and calculating men who provide the organizational ballast upon which Kinnock depends. They had last spoken during the general election, when Cook had urged Kinnock to run and had offered his services to help canvass the PLP. Now that the contest had begun, Kinnock asked him to come down to London to act as his overall campaign manager.

Over the next few months Kinnock's small campaign team met regularly in a committee room in the House of Commons. It included Max Madden, the newly elected MP for Bradford West, formerly the Labour Party's director of publicity; Peter Hain, the defeated Labour candidate in Putney; and Charles Clarke, Kinnock's political assistant, who had made his name in the 1970s as the President of the National Union of Students. Moss Evans, General Secretary of the TGWU, and Clive Jenkins were also regular attenders. (Like Kinnock, both of these powerful trade unionists were from Wales – part of a syndicate of Welshmen in the Labour movement, known only half-jokingly, as the 'Taffia'.)

The sheer size of the electoral college was the biggest problem. Standing for both leadership and deputy leadership, Kinnock, like Hattersley, had signed 1,800 individual forms requesting nominations from constituencies, MPs and unions. To keep in touch with what was happening across this sprawling battleground, the Kinnock campaign installed a computer in an office at the House of Commons. 'We had a special programme prepared for us by a party member who is a lecturer in that technology,' said Robin Cook, 'identifying trade unions, constituencies and the members of the PLP so that we could instantly update our records and find out what stage we'd reached in gaining support.'[1]

The Kinnock team divided up responsibilities. 'The unions were left largely to look after themselves,' recalls one of the campaign team. Cook himself worked hard on the PLP, reckoned at the start to be the weakest area of support. It soon became apparent, however, that Kinnock would attract many more votes from MPs than was being predicted. The fact that he was so obviously the front runner was a decisive influence: few ambitious MPs were eager to be seen voting against the man who would probably be leader for the next decade. In July Cook briefed the lobby correspondents and was able confidently to predict that Kinnock would get more MPs' votes than Hattersley. Cook's figures proved to be accurate, although few at that stage believed him.

'It was the constituency parties which required the greatest amount of work,' recalls a member of the campaign team. 'Even making contact with half of them was a Herculean task and we set up a monitoring group to get nominations and to keep track of our support.' All the work Kinnock had put in during his eight successive campaigns for the NEC now began to pay off. Probably no other MP in the country, let alone candidate for the leadership, had visited as many local parties as Kinnock had since the mid-1970s. 'I put in the work beforehand,' he said at one point during the campaign, 'I make no excuse for that. All Labour MPs, not just members of the Shadow Cabinet, should have been campaigning across the country. Of course, I admit, for me it's all turned out to be bread upon the waters.'

As constituencies made up their minds, either at GMC level or by a ballot of the whole local membership, the results were fed in to Kinnock's computer. 'By the end of the first fortnight,' says a member of his team, 'it was obvious that Neil was going to sweep the CLPs and the unions. We knew we were going to win, and from then on it simply became a campaign to project Neil as the leader-elect of the Labour Party and to rebuild the morale of the party in the country.'

Few would-be leaders have enjoyed an easier campaign. 'More than two months before the selection conference itself,' wrote the *Sunday Times* in July 1983, 'the Labour leadership race seems all but over. What is more, Kinnock appears to have "emerged" in the best possible fashion – without seeming to have tried.'[2] There were contingency plans to step up activity, by making extra speeches and visits, in the event of an unexpected spurt in support for one of the other candidates. But as it turned out, Kinnock was able to stay above the fight. 'It was a question not of a battle to be won,' says Kinnock, 'but of a presentation to be made.' On 23 June a leading throat specialist advised Kinnock to stop making speeches for at least a month in order to avoid doing irreparable damage to his voice. It suited Kinnock, as it would any front-runner, to keep as quiet as possible, and he happily complied.

It seemed that only some unforeseen catastrophe could prevent Kinnock's election as leader at the party conference in October. On Wednesday, 13 July, that catastrophe almost occurred. It was shortly before two o'clock in the morning. Kinnock was at the wheel of the family's brand-new, bright red Ford Sierra. He was travelling home to London after an evening meeting in Barry in South Wales. Kinnock hates this 140-mile stretch of motorway. He helps the two-and-a-quarter hour journey to pass by playing cassette tapes – 'sometimes Beethoven, sometimes 1950s rock music, sometimes Welsh male voice choirs'.[3] On this occasion it was Brahms's First Symphony. It was a warm summer evening, the window was wound down, he was about thirty miles from home – then suddenly, just north of Newbury, the car swerved off the motorway, mounted a bank at the side of the road and took off, somersaulting a hundred yards before coming to rest on its roof. Hanging upside-down, Kinnock fumbled to unfasten his seat belt. Shaken and bleeding from a cut on his head but otherwise unhurt, he crawled out of the window. As he did so, he wondered guiltily what Glenys was going to say about it all.[4]

Passing motorists stopped to help. One of them had a

camera and took a picture of Kinnock standing calmly, his sweater draped casually across his shoulders, in front of the smashed car. He was interviewed by the police. He told them he had not been speeding. A breathalyser test proved he had not been drinking either. The cause of the crash remained a mystery. 'I'm lucky to be alive,' he told reporters. 'My escape was miraculous. It's a word which is somewhat over-used, but I know what it means. Someone up there likes me.'

Kinnock stayed at the scene long enough to see his wrecked car towed away. It only had 3,000 miles on the clock. As it was winched on to the back of a recovery truck, Kinnock warned the driver, 'Be careful not to scratch the paintwork.' He travelled the rest of the way home in a taxi. 'My face was caked with dried blood,' he recalled, 'and my hair was matted with it. Unfortunately, Glenys was waiting for me. I tried to hide, but she rushed downstairs and showered me with kisses. The morning after, I was given a sermon which lasted long enough to qualify for the *Guinness Book of Records*. I've promised to take it much steadier.'[5] Throughout the remainder of the campaign Alex Kitson of the TGWU saw to it that Kinnock was provided with a car and chauffeur, at the union's expense.

The following day every Fleet Street paper and television news bulletin carried details of the accident. The Kinnocks keep framed as a souvenir a cartoon which appeared in one Welsh paper: a pair of hitch-hikers stand at the end of the Severn Bridge, one holding a sign saying 'London', the other a placard which reads, 'No, thank you, Mr Kinnock.' The phrase 'someone up there likes me' went round the country. It not only summed up a remarkable escape, from a crash which would normally have left its victim dead or badly injured; it also, as several commentators pointed out, seemed to sum up Kinnock's entire career.

He had been born lucky. Many people had always thought it. His accident appeared to confirm it. It had a particular poignancy for those who knew Michael Foot. In 1963 Foot and his wife had been involved in a near-fatal car crash on the outskirts of Ross-on-Wye. Foot had been in hospital for months with what his biographers call 'appalling injuries'.[6] The accident left him reliant upon a stick and with the splayed walk which reporters took so much delight in describing during the election. 'Yet a similar thing happens to Neil,' said a mutual friend of the two men, 'and he leaps out and starts joking and posing for photographs. Poor Michael. He couldn't have been leader of the party at a worse time. Now everyone wants unity, and there's Neil to reap the benefit. For every piece of bad luck Michael had, Neil's having good. It's like a mirror-image.'

Foot's weaknesses served to accentuate Kinnock's strengths. Foot was old; Kinnock projected an image of youthful vigour. Foot was ill at ease on television; Kinnock was a natural performer. Foot appeared weak, Kinnock strong. After two decades of leadership by a generation of politicians whose formative years had been in the immediate aftermath of the war, Kinnock held out the promise of a new and more exciting style. He was the candidate who perfectly suited the party's mood following the election defeat, and one by one, throughout the hottest summer Britain had seen for years, the union block votes dropped into his lap. On 15 June the health service workers, COHSE, with a block vote of 230,000, voted at their annual conference to support him, as did ASLEF, the train drivers' union, with 28,000 votes. On 27 June ACTT, the television union, endorsed Kinnock, followed six days later by the Union of Communication Workers. The fourth of July saw the TGWU, in conference on the Isle of Man, deliver over its 1.2 million votes – 8 per cent of the electoral college. Later the same week the National Union of Railwaymen joined the stampede to Kinnock. Even centre-right unions, such as the steel and shop workers, decided to support him.

Kinnock, not surprisingly, was at his most ebullient. On 21 July he spent the day travelling around the suburbs of Manchester. He visited an overspill estate called Hattersley and, for the benefit of the cameras, posed beneath a sign outside the Hattersley Centre. 'Point to it,' pleaded the photographers. 'Only one finger,' shouted someone in the crowd. 'That's right,' grinned Kinnock. A woman gave him a bright yellow carnation. Kinnock held it in his teeth and performed a brief flamenco. In August he took part in a march of actors and actresses to protest at government cuts in arts spending. At Speakers Corner he addressed the crowd from the back of a lorry and confessed to being the actor among the leadership candidates.[7] He was interviewed by David Frost on breakfast television a few days later and was asked, in view of his previous record, whether the Royal Family would be safe in 'Kinnock's Britain'. 'Yes,' replied Kinnock immediately, 'and I hope every other family as well': a reply which in its shortness, directness, and lightness of touch in a potentially difficult situation, is close to being the consummate television answer.

One of the few occasions on which he appeared to be under any serious pressure was when the four leadership candidates met for a debate at the Central Hall, Westminster. The meeting, organized by the Fabian Society, was televised on 31 July. A member of the audience pointed out that Kinnock had no experience of office. Was he not rather like the man who wanted to lead an orchestra but, when asked whether he could play the violin, replied, 'I don't know, I've never tried'? 'I don't know, I've never tried,' said Kinnock. There was a moment's silence. 'I think what the questioner was trying to get at – ' began the chairman, Phillip Whitehead. 'Oh, the subtlety of the question had not escaped me,' snapped Kinnock. His loss of temper momentarily betrayed the anxiety he felt about his inexperience, and for the first time that summer he looked rattled.

Otherwise his campaign was practically flawless, and the ease with which he conducted it won him some unexpected allies. 'I think I shall vote for Kinnock,' said John Golding towards the end of July. 'He inspires confidence. I think he'll make it all the way to Downing Street.' Even the left's most hated bogeyman, the pugnacious leader of the electricians'

union, Frank Chapple, was warming to him. On Saturday, 3
September, Kinnock went up on stage to make a short
presentation at a London charity concert. As he reached the
microphone all the lights went out. 'Thank you, Frank
Chapple,' shouted Kinnock from the darkness, to a roar of
laughter. Chapple was actually in Blackpool that evening, for
the annual Trades Union Congress, over which he was to
preside as Chairman the following week. He had just finished
briefing industrial correspondents in his hotel suite. He violently attacked Roy Hattersley's record in standing up to the
hard left. He was a 'compromiser', growled Chapple, 'a
disaster, an embarrassment to those who want to fight for
moderation in the party. I would never vote for him in any
circumstances.' The reporters were surprised by his comments on Kinnock. 'It is possible that Kinnock can put the
party right,' he said. 'He's got balls.'[8]

Two days later, on Monday morning, Kinnock travelled up by
train to Blackpool 'to shake a few hands' among the assembled union leaders. He looked the epitome of a front-
runner, confident and relaxed, acknowledging waves from
well-wishers on the platform at Euston. He hunted for a
smoking compartment. Like many senior Labour politicians,
Kinnock smokes a pipe – although there can be few others
who sit back with their eyes half-closed, blowing smoke rings.
'Urgent work', which had to be completed by the time the
train reached Blackpool, lay spread on the table in front of
him.

The journey lasted four hours, the train travelling through
towns which had turned against Labour on an unprecedented
scale three months before. Rugby, for example, once a
marginal, now had a Conservative MP with a majority of over
14,000; Labour had been beaten into third place. Nuneaton, a
Labour stronghold for fifty years, was now a Conservative
seat with a majority of 5,000; Labour was left clinging on to
second place by fewer than 1,400 votes. After leaving London
Kinnock travelled for more than two hours that morning

before reaching a constituency with a Labour MP: Crewe, 160 miles from Euston, where Gwyneth Dunwoody had managed to scrape home by 290 votes. Yet he remained optimistic. 'I think Labour can win again for two reasons,' said Kinnock. 'First, Thatcherism is essentially self-destructive. The tragic thing is it destroys everything else as well. I'm not complacent: it won't die by itself. But it can be defeated. Secondly, I think we can defeat the Alliance because of their utter lack of substance. The fact that the Alliance is jelloid will permit us the opportunity to attack and destroy them. The precondition for both of these things is that we have a coherent party, united in personality and in content.' He went on: 'We've had a great response in the party during this campaign. If I do win on 2 October, that response has got to be sustained. Unless our resolve to win is sustained, our task is impossible.'

Kinnock strolled back along the train to the buffet car, stopping on the way to talk about the state of the railways with the ticket collector. Denzil Davies, making a forlorn bid for the deputy leadership, was sitting by the side of the bar, nursing a drink and reading a detective story. 'Hiya, kid,' said Kinnock. They talked about the leadership contest. Davies was also going to show his face around Blackpool.

'Hell of a nice guy,' remarked Kinnock when he returned to his seat. 'If he was deputy leader, we'd have a lot of laughs. Pity he doesn't have a chance.' Turning back to the issue of the general election, he said, 'Our whole attitude has to change. It's no good just stomping around, preaching change. We're going to have to make some managerial adjustments. We have a research department in Walworth Road that's made up of political activists with academic qualifications. They'd welcome a change which would involve them as much in presentation as in simply writing policy. They've been under-used but not under-employed.'

The train approached Blackpool. Kinnock gathered up his 'important work' (untouched) and made his way to the door. At the end of the platform a crowd of about twenty journalists was waiting. Robin Cook came running up the platform and began urgently whispering in Kinnock's ear the moment he stepped out of the train. Kinnock put his arm round his shoulders to draw him close and nodded as they walked towards the barrier. Photographers' lights flashed; three television crews jostled for pictures. With a wistful look Denzil Davies walked by, ignored.

Kinnock gave an impromptu press conference: he was in Blackpool to meet some teachers in his capacity as education spokesman; no, he didn't think Len Murray, the TUC General Secretary, would be annoyed at his presence, despite the fact that Murray had specifically asked the leadership candidates to keep away from Blackpool. (This was apparently true: the two men had dinner together privately at Murray's hotel that night.)

Kinnock went out to his waiting car. The photographers pleaded with him to come back. He had walked straight past a sign reading 'WELCOME TO OUR NEXT PRIME MINISTER', erected by station workers. Kinnock retraced his steps and posed beneath it. Then, with Robin Cook still talking to him in quiet and urgent tones, he clambered into the back of the car and disappeared into Blackpool's midday traffic.

Chapter Twenty-Two
DREAM TICKET

While Kinnock's bandwagon rolled steadily towards the leadership, Roy Hattersley's campaign struggled, with diminishing hopes, against the inevitable. Throughout the summer they operated from a cramped, third-floor flat in Pimlico, in central London. Like Kinnock, Hattersley had a team of helpers presided over by a canny Scotsman – in his case it was John Smith, a former Secretary of State for Trade. A group of MPs, including Joe Ashton and Giles Radice, canvassed the PLP. Ann Taylor, the former MP for Bolton West, looked after the constituencies. Everyone, including David Hill, Hattersley's political adviser, lent a hand in contacting the trade unions.

Kinnock always insisted that he had never gone out of his way to seek the leadership. 'I've been fortunate in that I've never suffered from personal ambition,' he told the *Daily Express* towards the end of 1982.[1] He repeated the same line to the *Sun*: 'I've managed for forty years without personal ambition.'[2] Roy Hattersley, on the other hand, had always been disarmingly honest about his desire to reach the top. As far back as 1977 he had talked of himself as the next-leader-but-one: after Jim would come Denis and after Denis, Roy. At that time, speaking of possible rivals, he would mention the young Foreign Secretary, David Owen, or possibly Shirley Williams, or Peter Shore, or even Tony Benn. Kinnock, then still a relatively unknown backbencher, featured nowhere on the list. It did not seem an unrealistic ambition. Hattersley seemed to have all the qualifications. After nineteen years in the House of Commons, he had been Secretary of State for Prices, Minister of State at the Foreign Office and a junior Minister at the Departments of Defence and Employment. But, like virtually everyone else wrapped up in the intrigues of Westminster, he had failed to appreciate the scale of the discontent which was welling up in the party outside. By 1979 the red boxes, the official limousines, the membership of the Privy Council – all the traditional badges of office – had become marks of Cain. In 1981 the party had stripped MPs of the privilege of electing the party leader, and suddenly, as if from nowhere, Kinnock was ahead of him.

It was galling, to say the least, and Hattersley did not intend to give up without a fight. During the course of the contest he travelled over 6,500 miles in pursuit of votes in the electoral college, while his team printed over 10,000 leaflets for distribution throughout the party. The message of his manifesto, entitled 'A Duty to Win', was not dissimilar to Kinnock's: the party had to modernize, to listen to the voters, to put a stop to internal bickering. Audiences were sympathetic, but increasingly, by the time Hattersley reached them, they had already committed themselves to Kinnock. Unlike his main rival, he did not have a computer to keep track of the electoral college – not that it would have been much use: Walworth Road did not provide him with a list of constituency secretaries until the third week of the campaign. 'How can we blast this contest open?' asked one of his supporters, despairingly, in the first week of August. No one had an answer.

Robin Cook and John Smith met regularly to ensure that the campaign stayed as friendly as possible. There was only one occasion on which tempers became seriously frayed. At a PLP meeting on 21 July Hattersley got into an argument with Foot when the Labour leader failed to support a motion calling on the unions and constituency parties to consult their members as widely as possible. The right had pushed through a motion to that effect in the Shadow Cabinet, and it had expected Foot to convey its views to the meeting. 'You betrayed us,' Hattersley is reported to have told him. Foot, who had not forgiven Hattersley for his behaviour during the election, wheeled on the Shadow Home Secretary: 'If you say anything like that to me again, I'll have your head off your shoulders. I'll have the skin off your back.' The row leaked to the papers and was the excuse for an angry exchange of abuse. Joe Ashton alleged on television that Kinnock was 'terrified of any discussion or of widening the ballot'. Kinnock demanded an apology, and Robin Cook told the *Sunday Times* that he was 'infuriated' by Ashton's remarks: 'I am not aware of any pressure that Roy Hattersley put on Terry Duffy that he should consult his members before committing his block vote to Hattersley.'[3] 'It was a tense weekend,' says one of Kinnock's team.

With the leadership election apparently already settled, interest switched to the race for the deputy leadership. From the outset it had been assumed that Kinnock and Hattersley, in whatever order, would be leader and deputy – a unity of soft left and centre-right quickly dubbed the 'dream ticket'. The hard left called it the 'nightmare ticket' and campaigned hard for the election of Michael Meacher as deputy.

Alan Meale, a full time official with ASLEF, looked after Meacher's interests in the trade unions. Jon Lansman tended to the constituencies. Stuart Holland co-ordinated the campaign in the PLP supported, among others, by Jo Richardson, Margaret Beckett and Joan Maynard. 'Our organization was run on an absolute shoestring,' recalls Meacher. 'We hadn't a clue what was going on around the country.' The Meacher campaign also had a computer. 'The trouble is,' as Meacher puts it, 'a computer's only as good as the information you feed into it.'

At first the Meacher campaign was dismissed as a lost cause. Meacher, a kindly, but shy and scholarly man, was an unlikely champion for the hard left: a Menshevik, as someone once put it, fallen among Bolsheviks. He was virtually unknown in the wider world beyond the constituency activists. But his campaign team shrewdly 'talked up' his chances. The media began to take more interest: here at least was a contest, as opposed to the walkover for the leadership. Then on 14 August the findings of two political researchers, backed up by an impressive array of statistics, were published in the *Sunday Times*. Assuming Meacher did as well as Benn in the constituencies and the PLP, and provided he did slightly better among the unions, the figures suggested that he could win the deputy leadership by a landslide 11.6 per cent. The Meacher campaign took off.

Hattersley, still committed to the struggle for the leadership against Kinnock, could not respond, for the moment he was seen to do so, it would be tantamount to admitting that he knew he could not be leader. Instead it was Kinnock's campaign team, now beginning to think about the post-election period, who became worried. 'Meacher as deputy leader would have been a problem,' says one of Kinnock's key campaigners. 'He would have compounded Neil's great weakness: his lack of government experience. We were concerned about Hattersley's failure to act. We'd known for sure, since the first week of July, that we were going to win. We assumed Hattersley knew it too. The fact that he carried on trying suggested a disturbing lack of judgement on his part.'

Hattersley did not change his tactics and take the offensive against Meacher for another three weeks, when he finally gave up hope of beating Kinnock. 'If Neil Kinnock was elected leader and then Michael Meacher was elected deputy,' he told an interviewer in Glasgow on 30 August, 'there would be people who were actually saying and voting for the proposition that they do not want a compromise within the party. They do not want the balanced leadership, they do not want the broad church.'[4]

For a moment it looked as though he had left it too late. In the middle of September Moss Evans and Alex Kitson warned Kinnock that they were having difficulty in delivering the TGWU for Hattersley. On 19 September the thirty-eight man executive of the union narrowly voted in favour of backing Meacher for the deputy leadership. Meacher was travelling to Manchester for a meeting. He knew that the executive was meeting that afternoon, but the first news he had of the result came when he was met off the train by a union official eager to congratulate him. For Meacher it was the high point of the campaign: he now believed he would win. *The Times* appeared to agree: its front-page headline the following day stated flatly: 'TGWU gives victory to Meacher'.

Hattersley was shaken, and so too, more importantly, was Kinnock. The following day his supporters in the union moved swiftly to overturn the decision. A telex was dispatched to all regional offices from Transport House, the union's headquarters, advising them that the vote of the executive was not binding upon the actual delegation to the Labour Conference.

Three days later, on Saturday, 24 September, Meacher addressed a rally in Newcastle with Tony Benn. 'There were two thousand people there,' he recalled, 'and there was a tremendous atmosphere – like a *Tribune* rally. It was the best meeting of the campaign. At the end I came off the platform and there was a man backstage who said, "Neil Kinnock has just said you're as weak as hell", and asked me for my comments. I was thunderstruck, and my immediate thought was: it's a trap.'

It was Kinnock's only serious blunder of the campaign. He had given an interview to the journalist Jilly Cooper, apparently under the impression that she still worked for the *Sunday Times*. Half-way through the interview he discovered she now worked for the *Mail on Sunday*. 'I expressed a strongly critical view of the paper,' said Kinnock. 'Miss Cooper said, "I know. But they pay very well." '⁵ The *Mail*, violently anti-Labour, certainly got its money's worth, and Kinnock, who had studiously avoided making any public comment about the deputy leadership battle, was deeply embarrassed. According to Jilly Cooper, Kinnock described

Meacher to her as 'kind, scholarly, innocuous – and as weak as hell'. Hattersley, on the other hand, was 'a nice man – I can work with him.' Tony Benn 'couldn't knock the skin off a rice pudding'. Harold Wilson was 'a petty bourgeois, and will remain so in spirit, even if they make him a viscount'. The interview was given a double-page spread. 'Revealed for the first time,' claimed the *Mail*, 'the real Neil Kinnock, a likeable, caring family man, but deep down is he ruthless, devious, calculating and lazy?'[6] The story was picked up and reported extensively in the rest of the press.

Meacher arrived home from Newcastle on the sleeper at eight o'clock the next morning. At 9.30 Kinnock rang him at his home in Highgate to apologize. He told Meacher that he had been quoted out of context and that he was issuing a denial.

> I had the whole of Fleet Street on the phone [recalls Meacher]. A man from the *Sun* arrived on the doorstep. We told him to go away. He didn't, and stayed lurking in the front garden, accosting my family as they went in and out. In all, the *Sun* phoned five times. When eventually Molly [his wife] and I escaped for a walk, an *Express* photographer got out of the car at the end of the street. I was so furious, I simply turned on my heel and walked back inside. The photographer told my wife I was the first politician he'd ever come across who didn't want his picture taken.

In his statement the following day Kinnock suggested that his actual comment about Meacher was: 'In reality he is kind and scholarly – which means that others would think of him as innocuous and weak as hell.'[7] It was not a very convincing denial. For anyone who has listened to Kinnock talk about other politicians – and he can be very funny when he mimics their mannerisms – the statements attributed to him had a ring of authenticity. Unfortunately, comments he could get away with as a backbencher were potentially highly damaging in the mouth of a party leader. 'Neil was wrong to agree to that meeting without a tape-recorder,' said one of his staff afterwards. 'That interview is one of the reasons why the press don't find him as readily available as he used to be.'

Despite Kinnock's comments, Meacher's hopes for the

deputy leadership remained alive until the last moment. The TGWU and NUPE – in size respectively the first- and fourth-ranking unions affiliated to the Labour Party, between them controlling over 12 per cent of the electoral college – were not due to announce their voting intentions until a couple of hours before the start of the leadership ballot on 2 October. But by then Evans and Kitson had worked over their delegation very thoroughly. 'I didn't know I'd finally lost until I met Alex Kitson in the lobby of the Grand Hotel,' says Meacher. 'I said, "Hello, what's happened?" He said "Hattersley's got it." Then I heard NUPE had gone for Hattersley as well, and I frankly felt like jumping into the sea.'

The hard left had based its hopes on the belief that it could command broadly the same level of support as it had in 1981. But it had underestimated the extent to which the election defeat had transformed the mood within the Labour Party. Meacher lost count of the number of people who would have supported the hard left six months before, but who now came up to him to apologize and to say they were going to have to vote for Hattersley. 'People were simply terrified of losing another election,' Meacher reflected afterwards. 'None of us realized the tremendous swell of support for the "dream ticket".'

Chapter Twenty-Three

LEADER

Kinnock arrived in Brighton with Glenys the day before the election, on Saturday, 1 October. That morning his campaign computer had run through the latest state of the electoral college and arrived at a prediction: that Kinnock would achieve 67 per cent of the votes on the first ballot.

Yet although it promised to be a famous victory, there was nothing approaching the excitement in Brighton that there had been over the deputy leadership election two years before. The result had been certain for months and the campaign so extensively reported that most delegates seemed bored by it. After a brief interview with reporters on the seafront, the Kinnocks retreated to their hotel suite. In the evening they went out for a private celebration dinner with Barry Moore, Gwyn Evans and various constituency friends. Afterwards Kinnock chaired a Fabian seminar at the Bedford Hotel. The speaker was Kinnock's favourite Marxist, Eric Hobsbawm. The session was gloomily entitled 'The Forward March of Labour Reversed?'

The media's demand for pictures was insatiable and the day of the election began, for the benefit of the cameras, with the Kinnocks strolling hand in hand along the beach – an attempt at stage-management which was ruined when the couple strayed too close to the incoming tide. A wave rushed up the shore, Kinnock gallantly tried to pull Glenys out of the way and, in the attempt, fell over. There were shouts of laughter from the cameramen. Kinnock groaned at the prospect of the following day's newspapers. Glenys laughed. 'You see,' she told them, 'he can't walk on water.'

At 3.30 in the afternoon delegates began collecting their ballot papers from the foyer of the Brighton Centre. An hour later they filed in to take their seats in the main hall, a vast and featureless auditorium, gleaming like a brilliantly lit aircraft hangar under the glare of the television lights. The delegates were penned in eleven blocks of seats on the floor of the hall. Visitors and media packed the higher tiers of seats, while photographers clustered beneath Kinnock, sitting on the platform. Sam McCluskie of the seamen's union, the chairman of the conference, ordered them to move back: 'He'll get no more uglier as the night goes on.'

The conference began at 5 p.m., and the result, when it was announced, was even better than the Kinnock team had hoped. Of the trades unions' 40 per cent of the electoral college Kinnock took 29 per cent; of the constituencies' 30 per cent he captured a startling 27.5 per cent; but the greatest surprise was in the PLP: Kinnock took almost half of it, with 14.8 per cent of its 30 per cent share of the college. Overall he beat Hattersley by a margin of more than three to one. The other two candidates saw their votes squeezed almost to nothing. Poor Peter Shore, who might have won had the election been held a couple of years before, was humiliated. The final figures were:

KINNOCK	71.3 per cent
HATTERSLEY	19.3 per cent
HEFFER	6.3 per cent
SHORE	3.1 per cent

Yet despite the extraordinary sweep of Kinnock's support, the result was greeted only by restrained applause from the delegates. The atmosphere was embarrassingly flat. Kinnock nervously stroked his tie as Glenys left her seat in the hall and came up on the platform. ('I was surprised when they told me in the afternoon that they wanted me to go up there,' she said later. 'I thought I'd be watching from the floor with my mates.') Kinnock stood up to greet her, clasped her round the waist with one hand and waved a bunch of red roses at the delegates with the other. The clapping went on for less than half a minute.

The tellers left to count the votes for the deputy leadership. The conference resumed routine business. Ninety minutes later the scrutineers were back with the second result, and this time it was Hattersley's turn to look pleased. What had seemed a close race a fortnight ago had turned into a landslide victory. Meacher's challenge was obliterated as Hattersley took 35 of the unions' 40 per cent of the college and more than half of the PLP. The most significant result was in the constituency section, where he narrowly beat Meacher by 15 per cent to 14. Meacher had been hoping for 20 or 25 per cent from the CLPs and was shocked at the scale of his defeat. Although he had sensed that the tide was running against him, he had not expected to be swamped so completely. Added together, the overall result was:

HATTERSLEY	67.3 per cent
MEACHER	27.9 per cent
DAVIES	3.5 per cent
DUNWOODY	1.3 per cent

Hattersley punched the air in triumph and sprinted up on to the stage. Like a presidential candidate with his running mate, Kinnock seized Hattersley's arm and hoisted it aloft. The party had its dream ticket.

Now Kinnock spoke, without notes, and began by acknowledging the 'honour' that they had both been paid. 'We shall repay the honour,' he promised, 'and we shall serve the duty by leading this movement to victory at the next general election.' This drew applause, as did his tribute to Foot, who was sitting beside him: he 'has been, is and will be, an inspiration, a glowing inspiration, to all of us who believe that the purpose of socialism is the gaining of liberty for human kind'. For the first time, the audience began to warm up.

I want to thank Glenys and my family [Kinnock went on]. They tolerate me out of love; they raise my spirits. I look at our children, and I look at their future, and I look at the future of their generation, and it makes me determined that they must not know war. It makes me determined that they shall not live in a world of want. I look at those children of mine and other people's children, and I say that the new generation shall not inherit idleness, or ugliness, or the prejudice of racism or sexism.

Kinnock moved into his peroration, reworking what had been his basic campaign speech over the past week: that Labour has to rediscover its 'common sense and realism':

If anyone wants to know the reason why we must conduct ourselves in this fashion, just remember old times and old temptations and remember how each and every one of you felt on that dreadful morning of June 10 and think to yourselves 'June 9, 1983 – never again will we experience that.' Unity is the price of victory. Not unity for four weeks before the general election, not unity four weeks before the European Assembly elections, but unity here and now and from henceforth, not a cosmetic disguise but a living, working unity of people of a movement, of a belief and conviction, who want to win in order to save our country and our world.

Now, at last, the party rose in acclamation. Even Eric Heffer hauled himself to his feet. Journalists looked to see what Tony Benn's reaction was, but he had quietly left the platform some time before.

Kinnock's oratory was a triumph, both over the acoustics of the hall and over the ingrained resistance of Labour activists to being impressed by their leaders. Robin Day called it one of the finest speeches he had ever heard delivered from the platform at a Labour party conference. 'That was a wee one,' McCluskie told the applauding delegates. 'Wait till you hear him try.'

Once out of the conference hall, the Kinnocks were borne by a crush of reporters, cameramen and photographers along the corridors of the Brighton Centre, past Michael Foot – who took shelter in a doorway – to the television studios, then to a press conference and finally to a victory celebration at the Metropole Hotel.

Kinnock stood on the stage with Glenys and made a short speech of thanks. He wished, he said, that Michael Foot was with them. 'He's here,' shouted someone from the crowd. Kinnock beckoned him forward, and Foot shyly climbed up on to the platform. It was twenty years since he had first met the young Kinnock at a picnic near Tredegar. Glenys kissed Foot. The three linked arms. Everyone began to sing.

Later, when the press had gone, Glenys went outside and changed into a T-shirt that she had ordered from a department store for the occasion. 'Neil Kinnock,' it proclaimed, 'eats four shredded wheat.'

The following morning, he and Roy Hattersley had breakfast together to discuss how they should begin fulfilling their 'duty' to win the next election. Twelve hours after his accession to the leadership, the making of Neil Kinnock had resumed.

Chapter Twenty-Four
EPILOGUE

A few weeks later, installed in his new offices at the House of Commons as Leader of Her Majesty's Opposition, Neil Kinnock was asked whether he was enjoying being leader of the Labour Party. He gave an emphatic shake of his head. 'The day I'm going to start enjoying this job,' he said, 'is the day I see that furniture van turning into Downing Street.' Kinnock's mouth smiled; his eyes did not.

For all his charm, his jokes, his occasional wistful remarks about retiring early to devote himself to watching rugby, Kinnock's desire for the premiership is so strong as to be almost tangible. The remnants of the 'card' are still there, of the young MP with the broad grin and the instant quip, but they have been diminishing ever since 1979. He yearns for power. He does not conceal it. 'You fight,' as he says, 'to win.'

It is Kinnock's misfortune that while his ambition may more than equal that of any previous Opposition leader, his prospects of ever entering 10 Downing Street appear much worse. By the spring of 1984 he had managed, at least temporarily, to raise Labour's opinion-poll standing to its pre-1981 level. But however well Kinnock performs over the next few years, he must bear on his back the legacy of he 1983 election. It seems an almost insupportable burden. To be sure of forming a Government, Labour must secure a swing of over 10 per cent from the Conservatives. Kinnock will never be Prime Minister, even with a bare majority, unless Labour wins 117 seats from its opponents: a task so huge that Mrs Thatcher's own constituency of Finchley is among those it must look to win.

The painful truth for Labour is that the rise of a third political force has led to a disastrous split in the anti-Conservative vote. In the end Labour must either destroy the Alliance or come to some electoral agreement with it. The first course currently appears to be impossible, the second intolerable. Kinnock, of course, has other problems – the continuing splits within the party and his own inexperience chief among them. But they are tiny when set against the mountainous task confronting Labour of defeating both the Government and the Alliance.

And yet somehow one cannot feel that Kinnock has come so far to go no further. Labour's situation is not entirely hopeless. Mrs Thatcher and the Conservatives are not as popular as the electoral system contrives to make them appear. In 1983, with everything on their side, they won the support of only 42 per cent of the electorate, a smaller proportion than they achieved in 1979. By the late 1980s or early 1990s they are likely to be much more vulnerable. Assuming he can hold Labour together, Kinnock, the Alliance notwithstanding, will remain the only realistic alternative Prime Minister. Those complacent Conservatives who dismiss him as a lightweight and profess to be unable to imagine him as head of a Government would be wise to remember that Labour used to say exactly the same sort of thing about Margaret Thatcher.

A political upheaval in the Labour Party made Kinnock its leader. A political or economic upheaval in Britain could make him Prime Minister. He has ambition and he has time. And he has what Napoleon regarded as that most precious of all commodities. He has luck.

NOTES

PART ONE: CARD

1 Prologue: Blackwood, 31 January 1969.

1 Bedwellty CLP Minutes, 31 January 1969.

2 The Kinnock Inheritance

1 House of Commons Debate, 21 May 1973; Hansard, vol. 857, col. 62.
2 House of Commons Debate, 16 January 1974; Hansard, vol. 867, col. 800.
3 Hunter Davies and Frank Herrmann, *Great Britain: A Celebration* (London, 1982), p. 174.
4 House of Commons Debate, 30 June 1976; Hansard, vol. 914, vol. 546.
5 *Observer Magazine*, 2 October 1983.
6 *Guardian*, 31 July 1978.
7 Interview in *Marxism Today*, June 1983.
8 House of Commons Debate, 3 December 1970; Hansard, vol. 807, col. 1579.
9 *Guardian*, 31 July 1978.
10 Foreword to *In Place of Fear* (London, 1978), p. 7.
11 *Marxism Today*, June 1983.
12 *In Place of Fear*, p. 21.
13 *Observer Magazine*, 2 October 1983.
14 Letter from Neil Kinnock to Bill Harry, 21 July 1983.

3 University, Glenys and the WEA

1 House of Commons Debate, 4 February 1971; Hansard, vol. 810, cols. 2004–10.
2 House of Commons Debate, 30 October, 1974; Hansard, vol. 880, cols. 242–3.
3 *Guardian*, 31 July 1978.
4 *Observer*, 1 July 1979.

Notes

5 *Observer Magazine*, 2 October 1983.
6 *Guardian*, 3 October 1977.
7 *Guardian*, 22 June 1977.
8 Davies and Herrmann, *Great Britain: A Celebration*, p. 175.
9 *Observer*, 1 July 1979.

4 Battle for Bedwellty

1 House of Commons Debate, 12 March 1974; Hansard, vol. 870, cols. 51–4.
2 Davies and Herrmann, *Great Britain: A Celebration*, p. 175.

5 Young MP

1 House of Commons Debate, 13 July 1970; Hansard, vol. 803, cols. 1181–6.
2 House of Commons Debate, 28 November 1973; Hansard, vol. 865, cols. 509–13.
3 House of Commons Debate, 5 March 1973; Hansard, vol. 852, col. 99.

6 'Attack, Attack, Attack'

1 Labour Party Conference Report, 17 July 1971.
2 Speech in Manchester, 4 July 1948.
3 House of Commons Debate, 22 May 1972; Hansard, vol. 837, col. 1074.
4 *Observer Magazine*, 2 October 1983.
5 *Sunday Times*, 20 December 1981.
6 House of Commons Debate, 14 February 1972; Hansard, vol. 831, cols. 133–9.
7 House of Commons Debate, 12 March 1974; Hansard, vol. 870, cols. 51–4.

PART TWO: REBEL

7 Kinnock and the Outside Left

1 Joe Haines, *The Politics of Power* (London, 1977), p. 222.
2 'Labour's Future', *Political Quarterly*, vol. 43, no. 4, Oct.–Dec. 1972, p. 381.
3 Harold Wilson, *Final Term* (London, 1979), p. 30.
4 Tony Benn, *Parliament, People and Power: Agenda for a Free Society* (London, 1982), p. 110.
5 David Kogan and Maurice Kogan, *The Battle for the Labour Party* (London, 1983), p. 34.
6 Ibid., p. 46.
7 Barbara Castle, *Diaries 1974–76* (London, 1980), p. 564.
8 Kogan and Kogan, *The Battle for the Labour Party*, p. 32.

9 Ibid., p. 44.
10 Labour Party Conference Report, 1976, p. 134.
11 House of Commons Debate, 30 October 1974; Hansard, vol. 880, cols. 242–3.
12 Wilson, *Final Term*, pp. 60–1.
13 Labour Party Conference Report, 1974, pp. 218–19.
14 Ibid.

8 Life and Soul of The Party

1 *Guardian*, 20 June 1977.
2 *Guardian*, 17 October 1977.
3 House of Commons Debate, 26 February 1975; Hansard, vol. 887, cols. 610–12.
4 Anthony King, 'Politics, Economics and Trade Unions', in *Britain at the Polls, 1979* (Washington DC, 1981), p. 35.
5 Wilson, *Final Term*, pp. 114–15.
6 Ibid.
7 Ibid., p. 143.
8 Marcia Falkender, *Downing Street in Perspective* (London, 1983), p. 169.
9 Castle, *Diaries 1974–76*, p. 410.
10 Robert Jenkins, *Tony Benn: A Political Biography* (London, 1980), p. 227.
11 Ibid., p. 224.
12 'An Attack on Inflation', statement in the House of Commons, 11 July 1975, reprinted in Wilson, *Final Term*, pp. 269–72.
13 House of Commons Debate, 23 July 1975; Hansard, vol. 869, cols. 646–51.
14 Castle, *Diaries, 1974–76*, pp. 511–12.
15 Ibid.
16 Ibid.
17 Wilson, *Final Term*, p. 33.
18 Eric Hobsbawn and others, *The Forward March of Labour Halted?* (London, 1981), p. 90.
19 Wilson, *Final Term*, p. 200.
20 Ibid., p. 231.
21 Bedwellty GMC Minutes, 19 March 1976.
22 Labour Party Conference Report, 1976, p. 318.
23 House of Commons Debate, 17 March 1977; Hansard, vol. 928, col. 707.
24 Quoted in *Sunday Telegraph*, 21 March 1976.

9 Devolution

1 *Observer Magazine*, 24 February 1980.
2 House of Commons Debate, 3 February 1975; Hansard, vol. 885, cols. 1029–35.

Notes

3 *Guardian*, 8 November 1978.
4 House of Commons Debate, 26 January 1978; Hansard, vol. 942, col. 1810.
5 Simon Hoggart and David Leigh, *Michael Foot: A Portrait* (London, 1981), p. 139.
6 Labour Party Conference Report, 1976, p. 200.
7 *Financial Times*, 17 November 1976.
8 House of Commons Debate, 19 January 1977; Hansard, vol. 924, col. 147.
9 *Guardian*, 8 November 1978.
10 *The Times*, 17 November 1977.
11 Quoted in *Daily Telegraph*, 3 March 1978.
12 *Daily Telegraph*, 6 July 1978.
13 King, 'Politics, Economics and Trade Unions,' p. 84.
14 Letter from Neil Kinnock to Bill Harry, 21 July 1983.

10 The Party Man

1 *Guardian*, 21 June 1979.
2 Labour Party Conference Report, 1977, p. 176.
3 *Sunday Times Magazine*, 28 April 1978.
4 House of Commons Debate, 7 July 1975; Hansard, vol. 895, cols. 119–26.
5 *The Political Companion*, vols. 20–33.
6 *Guardian*, 21 November 1977.
7 House of Commons Debate, 26 June 1975; Hansard, vol. 894, cols. 779–82.
8 *Yorkshire Post*, 23 October 1978.
9 Labour Party Conference Report, 1978, p. 268.

11 The Winter of Discontent

1 Dick Leonard, 'The Labour Campaign', in *Britain at the Polls, 1979* (Washington DC, 1981), p. 97.
2 Labour Party Conference Report, 1978, p. 215.
3 King, 'Politics, Economics and Trade Unions', p. 82.
4 Bedwellty GMC Minutes, 26 January 1979.
5 House of Commons Debate, 5 February 1979; Hansard, vol. 926, col. 150.
6 *Guardian*, 29 March 1979.
7 *Daily Telegraph*, 29 March 1979.
8 Ivor Crewe, 'Why the Conservatives Won', in *Britain at the Polls, 1979* (Washington DC, 1981), p. 297.
9 Quoted in Kogan and Kogan, *The Battle for the Labour Party*, pp. 60–1.
10 Labour Party Conference Report, 1979, p. 187.
11 Benn, *Parliament, People and Power*, p. 65.

PART THREE: LOYALIST

12 Promotion

1 *Guardian*, 19 June 1979.
2 *Daily Mirror*, 20 June 1979.
3 *Financial Times*, 23 June 1979.
4 *Sunday Times*, 17 July 1983.
5 *Observer*, 26 September, 1982.
6 *Sunday Times*, 17 July 1983.
7 House of Commons Debate, 19 June 1979; Hansard, vol. 968, cols. 1228–37.
8 *The Times Educational Supplement*, 16 November 1979.
9 Labour Party Conference Report, 1979, p. 357.
10 *Guardian*, 5 October 1979.
11 *Financial Times*, 5 October 1979.
12 *Daily Mirror*, 5 October 1979.

13 Fratricide

1 Austin Mitchell, *Four Years in the Death of the Labour Party* (London, 1981), p. 41.
2 Labour Party Conference Report, 1979, p. 188.
3 Ibid., p. 275.
4 Labour Party Conference Report, 1980, pp. 147–8.
5 Labour Party Conference Report, 1979, p. 275.
6 Ibid., p. 188.
7 Ibid., p. 186.
8 Kogan and Kogan, *The Battle for the Labour Party*, p. 46.
9 Labour Party Conference Report 1979, pp. 229–30.
10 Quoted in Kogan and Kogan, *The Battle for the Labour Party*, p. 65.
11 *Tribune*, 2 September 1983.
12 Bedwellty GMC Minutes, 16 November 1979.
13 *Guardian*, 9 February 1980.
14 Bedwellty GMC Minutes, 22 February 1980.
15 *Daily Mail*, 11 June 1980.
16 Introduction to Frank Keating, *Up and Under* (London, 1983).
17 House of Commons Debate, 10 June 1980; Hansard, vol. 986, cols. 292–4.
18 *Daily Mail*, 11 June 1980.
19 Davies and Herrmann, *Great Britain: A Celebration*, p. 181.
20 Labour Party Conference Report, 1977.
21 Mitchell, *Four Years in the Death of the Labour Party*, p. 42.
22 Kogan and Kogan, *The Battle for the Labour Party*, p. 92.
23 Ibid., p. 93.

14 Foot, Wembley and the Rise of the SDP

1 Peter Kellner and Christopher Hitchens, *Callaghan: The Road to Number Ten* (London, 1976), p. 177.

2 Labour Party Conference Report, 1980, p. 193.
3 Hoggart and Leigh, *Michael Foot: A Portrait*, p. 4.
4 Kogan and Kogan, *The Battle for the Labour Party*, p. 98.
5 Hoggart and Leigh, *Michael Foot: A Portrait*, p. 6.
6 Ibid., p. 2.
7 Hugh Stephenson, *Claret and Chips* (London, 1982), p. 33.
8 Ibid., p. 24.
9 *Western Mail*, 22 January 1981.
10 Bedwellty GMC Minutes, 16 January 1981.
11 'Which Way Should Labour Go?', *Political Quarterly*, vol. 51., no. 4, Oct.–Dec. 1980, pp. 411–23.
12 Labour Party NEC Report, 1981, p. 128.
13 Ibid.
14 Quoted in Kogan and Kogan, *The Battle for the Labour Party*, p. 105.
15 Ibid.
16 Mitchell, *Four Years in the Death of the Labour Party*, p. 44.
17 Labour Party NEC Report, 1981, p. 151.
18 Quoted in Paul Whiteley, *The Labour Party in Crisis* (London, 1983), p. 210.
19 Quoted in Stephenson, *Claret and Chips*, pp. 185–6.
20 *Guardian*, 6 February 1981.
21 *Daily Telegraph*, 10 February 1981.
22 Quoted in Kogan and Kogan, *The Battle for the Labour Party*, p. 101.

15 Anti-Bennite

1 Quoted in Alan Freeman, *The Benn Heresy* (London, 1982), p. 153.
2 Ibid.
3 Benn, *Parliament, People and Power*, p. 13.
4 Ibid., p. 20.
5 Quoted in Falkender, *Downing Street in Perspective*, pp. 210–11.
6 Labour Party Conference Report, 1980, pp. 31–2.
7 *Guardian*, 25 April 1981.
8 *Tribune*, 18 September 1981.
9 Ibid.
10 Ibid.
11 Bedwellty GMC Minutes, 19 June 1981.
12 Bedwellty GMC Minutes, 17 July 1981.
13 *Tribune*, 18 September 1981.
14 Freeman, *The Benn Heresy*, p. 134.
15 *Panorama*, 28 September 1981.
16 Ibid.
17 *Observer*, 26 September 1982.
18 *Panorama*, 28 September 1981.

16 Militant, Tatchell and Reselection

1 Bedwellty GMC Minutes, 9 October 1981.
2 Labour Party Conference Report, 1982, p. 49.

3 Bedwellty GMC Minutes, 13 November 1981.
4 Peter Tatchell, *The Battle for Bermondsey* (London, 1983), p. 46.
5 Ibid., pp. 53–4.
6 Ibid., p. 11.
7 *Guardian*, 17 December 1981.
8 *New Statesman*, 1 January 1982.
9 Tatchell, *The Battle for Bermondsey*, pp. 77–8.
10 *Sunday Times*, 20 December 1981.
11 *Guardian*, 4 April 1977.
12 *Sunday Times*, 20 December 1981.
13 Davies and Herrmann, *Great Britain: A Celebration*, p. 180.
14 *Morning Star*, 7 May 1982.
15 Bedwellty GMC Minutes, 18 December 1982.
16 *Rebecca*, March 1982.
17 *News*, 26 February 1982.
18 Bedwellty GMC Minutes, 19 March 1982.
19 Extracted from Ray Davies's copy of his speech.
20 Bedwellty GMC Minutes, 19 March 1982.

17 Hit-Listed

1 *Morning Star*, 7 May 1982.
2 *The Times*, 19 May 1982.
3 *Guardian*, 28 May 1982.
4 Bedwellty GMC Minutes, 25 July 1982.
5 *Political Companion*, vols. 31, 32.
6 *Sunday Times Magazine*, 10 April 1983.
7 Labour Party Conference Report, 1982, pp. 40–2.
8 Ibid., pp. 214–16.

PART FOUR: CANDIDATE

18 Decision to Run

1 *Daily Mail*, 15 November 1982.
2 *Guardian*, 12 March 1983.
3 *Guardian*, 6 September 1982.
4 *Daily Mirror*, 11 January 1983.
5 Tatchell, *The Battle for Bermondsey*, p. 120.
6 Mitchell, *Four Years in the Death of the Labour Party*, p. 98.
7 Ibid.
8 *Guardian*, 5 March 1983.
9 Ibid.

19 The Do-It-Yourself Election

1 *Sunday Times*, 11 September 1983.

2 Falkender, *Downing Street in Perspective*, p. 56.
3 Ibid., p. 53.
4 Reprinted in the *Journalist*, July 1983.
5 Ibid.
6 Ibid.
7 Ibid.
8 Labour Party Manifesto, p. 36.
9 *Journalist*, July 1983.
10 *Sunday Times*, 5 June 1983.
11 *Sunday Times*, 11 September 1983.
12 *Economist*, 18 June 1983.
13 *New Statesman*, 17 June 1983.
14 BBC Exit Poll Survey.
15 Eric Hobsbawm and others, *The Forward March of Labour Halted?* (London, 1981), p. 89.
16 *Marxism Today*, November 1981.
17 Robert Waller, *The Almanac of British Politics* (London, 1983), p. 201.

20 The Man Who Came to Dinner
1 *Economist*, 28 May 1983.

21 'Someone Up There Likes Me'
1 *Newsnight*, 29 September 1983.
2 *Sunday Times*, 17 July 1983.
3 Davies and Herrmann, *Great Britain: A Celebration*, p. 172.
4 *Sunday Mirror*, 17 July 1983.
5 Ibid.
6 Hoggart and Leigh, *Michael Foot: A Portrait*, p. 147.
7 *Guardian*, 25 August 1983.
8 *Observer*, 4 September 1983.

22 Dream Ticket
1 *Daily Express*, 7 December 1982.
2 *Sun*, 17 December 1982.
3 *Sunday Times*, 24 July 1983.
4 Interview broadcast on Radio Clyde, quoted in *Daily Telegraph*, 31 August 1983.
5 *Daily Mail*, 26 September 1983.
6 *Mail on Sunday*, 25 September 1983.
7 *Daily Mail*, 26 September 1983.

INDEX

251

Index